Studies in

Chinese
Buddhism

Arthur F. Wright

STUDIES IN
Chinese
Buddhism

Edited by Robert M. Somers

YALE UNIVERSITY PRESS

New Haven and London

Publisher's Note

When Robert Somers died in 1983, his long labor of editing Arthur Wright's wide-ranging essays on China had yet to be distilled into final form. The publisher is particularly grateful to Sally Serafim for editing the present selection, to Stanley Weinstein for vetting the manuscript, and to Alexa Selph for compiling the index. The Press would also like to thank Conrad Schirokauer, Hiroko Somers, Jonathan Spence, and Maryś Wright for their advice and assistance at various stages in the undertaking.

Published with the assistance of the Frederick W. Hilles Publication Fund of Yale University.

Designed by Jill Breitbarth
Set in Sabon type by
Asco Trade Typesetting Ltd.

Printed in the United States of America by
Bookcrafters, Inc., Chelsea, Michigan.

Library of Congress Cataloging-in-Publication Data
Wright, Arthur F., 1913–1976.
    Studies in Chinese Buddhism/Arthur F. Wright; edited by Robert
M. Somers.
        p.   cm.
    Includes bibliographical references.
    ISBN 0-300-04717-7 (alk. paper): $22.50 (est.)
        1. Buddhism—China—History. I. Somers, Robert M., 1942–
1983.
    II. Title.
    BQ632.W75   1990
    294.3'0951—dc20   89-22604
                                                        CIP

The paper in this book meets the guidelines of permanence and durability of the Committee on Production Guidelines for Book Longevity of the Council on Library Resources.

10 9 8 7 6 5 4 3 2 1

For Duncan and Jonathan

CONTENTS

INTRODUCTION

Buddhism and Chinese Culture

The encounter between Buddhism and Chinese culture was a momentous experience with far-ranging effects not only on Chinese ways of thinking but also on Chinese social and cultural institutions. It is the story, initially, of a great universal religion which began its infiltration into Chinese life at a time when native ideologies had lost most of their force and authority, when, in the words of Etienne Balazs, "China...was not only partitioned, but also torn by social contradictions and unbridgeable differences of opinion, and full of a desperate longing for salvation." For the historian of ideas, Buddhism offers a fascinating case of the clash of doctrines and human sensibilities, for its fundamental view of the world—life-denying, attuned to the miseries of quotidian existence, and highly spiritualistic—was, in its ensemble, unlike anything the Chinese had ever seen before. Few aspects of Chinese life, from high politics to popular culture, were untouched by the increased influence and mass appeal of this sophisticated religious system and the church that articulated and disseminated its teachings.

The first essay in this volume, "Buddhism and Chinese Culture: Phases of Interaction" (1959), establishes the scope of the encounter between Buddhism and Chinese culture and suggests a broad periodization within which Arthur Wright assesses their evolving relationship. An opening quotation from the French Orientalist Sylvain Lévi suggests the ubiquitous presence of Buddhism in China, as it worked its way into all the domains of Chinese life—fundamental social doctrine, systems of belief, political institutions, and every sphere of culture, including architecture, sculpture, and painting. Arthur Wright then offers a historical outline within which he traces the developing relationship between Buddhism and its Chinese host culture. Here we see that the interaction proceeded through a series of linked stages, as an initial period of "preparation" was followed by the Chinese "domestication" of Buddhism, leading to a period of "acceptance and independent growth" which in turn gave way to a long era of "appropriation" in which Buddhist ideas became so securely embedded in Chinese thought and practice that their foreign origin and antagonistic premises were substantially obscured, with Buddhism becoming an integral part of Chinese philosophical syncretism.

But within this broad periodization, the introduction and development of Buddhist ideas in China was also a very human story, and it was perhaps at this level that Arthur Wright was most deeply fascinated. His first major scholarly project, "Fo-t'u-teng: A Biography" (1948, the published version of his doctoral dissertation), was a study of the career of the Buddhist missionary and thaumaturge Fo-t'u-teng, a career set in the violent and unstable context of fourth-century China, when much of the north China homeland was in the hands of Inner Asian invaders who had established the first in what was to become a kaleidoscopic series of conquest regimes. Himself a native of Kucha in Central Asia, Fo-t'u-teng gained service with the Hsien-pei rulers of north China and was used by his Hsien-pei masters for prognostication, political intelligence, medical knowledge, and even military strategy. Thus Fo-t'u-teng was a precursor of what became in later ages a common pattern, that in which missionaries joined their plans for religious propagation to secular service.

A slight but noteworthy companion piece to the life of Fo-t'u-teng is the "Biography of the Nun An-ling-shou" (1952), which documents a case of conflict between Chinese social ethics and Buddhist piety. A young woman born to an official family is determined to abjure her filial responsibilities to work as a nun, and so to benefit all sentient beings. Fo-t'u-teng, who ultimately ordained An-ling-shou, employed his verbal powers to persuade the young woman's father that her future life of religious devotion would bring glory to her ancestors and thus carry out, if indirectly, her filial duties. This story, though briefly told, embodies a fundamental conflict between the life of religious devotion and the life of secular duty and demonstrates one path to its resolution.

Fo-t'u-teng and An-ling-shou compel interest as people of their time and place, people whose lives illuminate the radically changed conditions and new choices available in China during the period between the unified dynasties of Han and Sui. But their names and the details of their lives are known to us not from their eminence in the standard histories, where Buddhist clerics in fact were systematically overlooked. Rather, it is their place in Buddhist hagiography, a distinctive and fascinating variety of Chinese biographical writing, which has kept alive the contours of their lives. "Biography and Hagiography: Hui-chiao's *Lives of Eminent Monks*" (1954) is a careful study of one of the foremost collections of clerical biography, compiled in the sixth century and the major source on the life of Fo-t'u-teng. The study and evaluation of such an early text raise numerous textual and philological issues and thus introduce the reader to the formidable technical demands of Buddhist historiography. But the importance of Hui-chiao's work, and of this study, is not solely the scholarly virtuosity Arthur Wright lavished on it. Rather, *Lives of Eminent Monks* is presented to us as a fine example of medieval prose literature, an invaluable source of information on the great figures in the formative period of Chinese Buddhism, and an excursion into a new and developing subgenre of biographical writing, one which employed, as Arthur Wright puts it, "new standards—alien in origin—for evaluating men's actions."

One telling measure of the widespread influence of Buddhism in Chinese society was the strength of the attacks launched against it. In some cases these attacks featured spectacular and sweeping proscriptions against Buddhism, most notably those carried out by Emperor Wu of the Chou dynasty in A.D. 574, a monarch who simultaneously sponsored imperial academies which countered the influence of the Buddhists through the advance of conventional secular values. One man trained in the highly charged ideological atmosphere of those imperial academies was Fu I, a scholar who prepared a comprehensive set of counterstatements to the arguments advanced in Buddhist apologetics and presented these to the T'ang emperor in 621 and 624. "Fu I and the Rejection of Buddhism" (1951) examines the arguments contained in these famous attacks on Buddhism, indicting what Fu I saw as the damage done to the economic foundations of Chinese society and the wild and masochistic features of Buddhist spirituality, which in his view encouraged delusions, negative obsessions, and depraved behavior in the false hope of spiritual reward. Fu I's violent and sometimes hysterical accusations were a warning sign that Buddhism always ran the danger of falling victim to its own success. That his proposal for the extirpation of Buddhism was rejected by the court testifies to the important place assumed by Buddhism in medieval Chinese society.

—Robert M. Somers

STUDIES IN

Chinese
Buddhism

1

BUDDHISM AND

CHINESE CULTURE

Phases of Interaction

En Chine, depuis les seconds Han (25–220 A.D.), en Corée, depuis le VIe siècle, au Japon, depuis Shōtoku (593), le Bouddhisme est partout: doctrines, systèmes croyances, institutions
politiques, architecture, sculpture, peinture, sur tous les do-
maines il est un facteur capital; sans lui, rien ne s'explique;
autour de lui, tout s'éclaire et s'ordonne.*—Sylvain Lévi.

The great French Orientalist stated with his usual clarity
the challenge which Buddhism presents to historians of China and its

Reprinted by permission from the *Journal of Asian Studies* 16, no. 1 (November 1957):
17–42.
* ["In China from the time of the Later Han (A.D. 25–220), in Korea from the sixth
century, in Japan from the time of Prince Shōtoku (593), Buddhism is everywhere:
(philosophical) doctrines, systems of belief, political institutions, architecture, sculpture,
painting—in all these areas it is a major factor. Without it, nothing can be explained;
with it, everything becomes clear and ordered."—Ed.]

cultural satellites. Western historians of China have, for a variety of reasons, been slow to respond to this challenge. They have been burdened with a vast range of ground-breaking tasks, with the effort to achieve a preliminary ordering of materials, events, and institutions. They have been understandably appalled at the ramifying complexity of Buddhist doctrines, texts, practices, and symbolism. And they have, until recently, been guided in their inquiries by the unseen hands of generations of Confucian historians—men who regarded Buddhism as an alien cultural excrescence, and the Buddhist periods of Chinese history as shameful chapters in the life of a great people.[1] Modern scholarship in China, in Japan, and in the West has made great strides over the last thirty years, and it is now possible for the historian to estimate the role and importance of Buddhism in the total development of Chinese civilization. It is possible for him to take account of the interaction of Buddhism and Chinese culture, and thus to order and clarify historical phenomena which have hitherto remained obscure or misunderstood.

The question then arises as to how he is to do this, what kinds of things will guide and foster this effort at understanding. The present paper seeks to make a modest contribution to this effort by suggesting a provisional historical outline of the interaction of Buddhism and Chinese culture. This outline is meant to aid the historian in two ways. It suggests a preliminary periodization of the interaction of Buddhism and Chinese culture, and thus reduces a long period of time, an inordinate variety of events, into segments that are susceptible of study. In doing this it offers a series of hypotheses on the process of cultural interaction through time—hypotheses which can be tested, modified, or discarded as empirical inquiry proceeds.

Several major problems complicate the study of this process of interaction and of the phases into which it falls. One is the problem of cultural levels. As Lévi's statement suggests, Buddhism interacted through the centuries with all levels of Chinese culture: with literary and philosophic traditions, with economic and political institutions, with mores and behavioral norms, with indigenous traditions in art and architecture, with the religions of all classes and of all the subcultures of China. This raises the question as to whether developments at one cultural level are to be taken as dominant in the process, as in some sense setting the pattern of interaction occurring at the other levels. Are we safe in saying that interaction seen, let us say, at the philosophic level, is a model for, or even a guide to, what goes on at the political or economic level? Clearly we are not, for each level of human activity has its specific character and dynamics, which will show a different pattern of interaction with elements introduced from an alien source. Yet in the extraordinarily homogeneous civilization of China, where we find institutions, ideas, and behavior reinforcing one another and reiterating the same themes, the various cultural levels are inevitably closely interrelated. And this would suggest that there may be certain major points in time where significant shifts or transitions in the process of interaction occur at all or most of the cultural levels. Lacking the encylopedic knowledge which would be needed to deal with each of these various cultural levels, I nonetheless believe that certain major shifts in this historic process can be discerned, and these provide the articulation in the provisional series of phases suggested below.

Another problem in developing such a historical schema is the problem of social classes, each with its distinctive and changing ethos, with different felt needs which condition the response a class will make to a foreign idea or institution, and thus the pattern of interaction which will emerge. Therefore, in the present inquiry we shall necessarily deal with the process of interaction among the elite and among the peasantry, while keeping in mind some of the characteristic ways in which these mutually interdependent classes affected one another.[2] It need hardly be said that our data for analyzing the process in the peasant villages is sadly deficient.

A further problem in establishing any series of phases or periods for a historical process lies in defining the points of transition from one phase to another. European historians, in their studies of the transition from the Middle Ages to the Renaissance, have made it clear that such transitions are neither sharp nor sudden. Rather they represent a discernible culmination of complex changes going on at many levels of society and culture. Elements from the preceding period linger on or find different expression in the age which follows; trends in one age prefigure a major transition which is to come. This is the view of historical change which I have taken in this paper.

In attempting a phasing of the interaction of Buddhism and Chinese culture, we are dealing with two culture complexes in continuous process of change. The Buddhism of the fifth century, both through new importations and continuous adaptations, is drastically different from that of the third century. In this same period Chinese culture and society undergo parallel but equally sweeping changes. Any historical analysis must therefore take account of both patterns of change and of the interactions between them. It should, perhaps, attempt to "weight" the two patterns, to discern which had a stronger influence on the other. My present impression is that Chinese institutional and cultural development had the greater weight in determining the successive phases of interaction which we shall consider. I shall call attention to those facts which seem to substantiate this relative weighting of determining forces. The provisional phasing presented in the following pages consists of the following periods:

Phase I. The Period of Preparation, 65–317
Phase II. The Period of Domestication, 317–589
Phase III. The Period of Acceptance and Independent Growth, 589–ca. 900
Phase IV. The Period of Appropriation, ca. 900 to the present

I. THE PERIOD OF PREPARATION, 65–317

The first period of the history of Buddhism in China, which we date from A.D. 65 to 317,[3] was preparatory in two respects: One is the evolution of those social and intellectual conditions which tended to make the Chinese responsive to a foreign religion and its cultural accompaniments. The other is the development of ways and means of translating the foreign religion into language, metaphor, and patterns of behavior which the Chinese could understand and adopt.

Let us first try to show how the political, social, and intellectual events of these years tended to create an atmosphere of receptivity, thus preparing the way for thorough domestication in the age that followed.

By the middle of the second century A.D. the great Han Empire was well on the way toward disintegration. Long years of peace had brought the growth of wealth, a trend toward the development of an exchange economy. The population had grown, but the social arrangements of a stable agricultural society were being steadily eroded as new groups struggled for power and wealth. The imperial power weakened, the great nobles lived lives of idleness and luxury supported by income from landed estates worked and managed by others. A succession of empresses' families used their positions for ruthless and rapacious drives for political and economic power. At the imperial court, which became ever more extravagant, incompetent and clique-ridden, the eunuchs occupied key positions— positions which they exploited to amass great power and huge fortunes.[4] The Confucian literati, as power slipped from them, formed yet another competing group banded together in their common opposition to the corruption of imperial power, the eunuchs, the idle nobility, and the nouveaux riches. We need not follow the course of the sordid power struggle among these groups in the capital and, increasingly, among the provincial warlords. What is important for our present purpose is the fact that the upper level of the Han sociopolitical order was riven by conflict, that the moral and political sanctions of an earlier day were undermined and discredited, that a mood of uncertainty and questioning developed within the elite.

Upon the peasantry fell the burden of supporting a corrupt and divided upper class; upon them fell the burden of military service, corvée, increasing taxation, and the exactions of the landed magnates. Peasant bitterness and resentment found expression in the mounting power of Taoist religious fraternities, which offered both religious consolation in a troubled age and a focus of organized opposition to intolerable oppression. The vast Yellow Turban revolt dramatized the extent of the alienation of the people from the state and the fanaticism of their devotion to new doctrines and new leaders.[5] The ferocious suppression of the rebellion did not unite the upper class around the decaying throne for the restoration of effective government but paved the way for the emergence of a series of military dictators whose wars, as Balazs has remarked, transformed China in one generation from a powerful empire into a vast cemetery.[6] The successor states of the Han were military dictatorships, and, even where they were able to exercise power at the local level, they did little to restore a stable and viable peasant economy. In the years before 317, therefore, the peasantry is sunk in misery and sullen discontent. The breakdown of their once stable life was complete, and they were readily drawn to those cults and organizations that promised some amelioration of their lot, some hope for the future. The breakup of the Han peasant society, then, is one of the factors that prepared the way in this period for the spread of an alien religion.

On the ideological and philosophic level, the Han Confucian synthesis was utterly discredited by the collapse of the order which it served and sanctioned. Indeed doubts about its coherence and validity had grown more insistent from the time of Wang Ch'ung (27–ca. 97), and when its formulae proved inapplicable or unworkable in time of crisis, the troubled Chinese upper class began to look elsewhere for the means of understanding what had befallen their society, and for prescriptions for its ills. In this, China's second great age of crisis and ' intellectual ferment, Taoism, Legalism, and the lesser doctrines of the age of the Warring States reappeared. Both Taoism and Legalism attracted interest because of their repudiation of Confucian tradition, by the very radicalness of their prescriptions for an age when old ways had been found wanting. Revived Legalism soon ceased to be protest, and often found itself sanctioning the absolute power of military dictators. Revived Taoism remained, then, the principal dissenting and protestant body of thought. Men found in the amorphous, loosely related concepts of the *Lao-tzu*, the *Chuang-tzu*, and the *I-ching* ways of talking about the individual and social malaise which afflicted them. They found a vocabulary of protest and a rationality of escape. Indeed an earlier mood of protest gave way, as the years of chaos and misery wore on, to an escapist mood, a sense of futility and a full retreat from responsibility.[7] *Ch'ing-t'an*, the dominant mode of discourse among the neo-Taoists, became less and less a speculative instrument and more and more a diversion of defeated men. I suggest that neo-Taoism had provided the Chinese upper class with some limited means of analyzing their sad individual and collective plight; it had enlarged the speculative range of their minds. But the vocabulary of the Taoist classics was limited, a primitive and poetic, dominantly negative vocabulary that could not fully satisfy the speculative interests it had aroused, nor suggest solutions for the problems it had raised. Arthur Waley's characterization of Wang Yen (266–311), prime minister at the end of the period we are discussing, suggests the atmosphere of futility and negation:

He belonged to one of the most distinguished families in China, the Wangs of Lang-yeh, and was descended from a long line of high officials. He was famous for his great beauty and in particular for the jade-like whiteness of his hands. He subscribed to the theory that though exceptional people can acquire transcendent powers through the cult of le néant (to use M. Sartre's convenient term), inferior people (among whom he modestly ranked himself) must be content if through their cult of the néant they manage (in a dangerous world) to save their own skins. He did his best to take a negative line towards everything, merely to drift with the tide of events.[8]

We have suggested some of the ways in which the breakup of the Han oekumené prepared the way for new ideas and institutions. Chinese self-confidence, the surest antitoxin against the viruses of innovation and xenophilia, had been seriously undermined. Yet the peasantry turned to religious Taoism, and the literate to neo-Taoist philosophy. The reason for this was not that Buddhism was not present in China but that it was still in the process of being translated and adapted—prepared for a Chinese clientele.[9] I shall now turn to this simultaneous phase of what I have called the period of preparation.

Everyone who has contemplated the process by which Indian ideas and institutions were made intelligible and, to a degree, acceptable to the Chinese has been struck by the breadth of the cultural gulf which had to be overcome. A paradigm of some of the points of divergence

will suggest the problems of "translation" which this age of preparation first began to deal with, and which were a major preoccupation in
the succeeding period of domestication:

	CHINESE	INDIAN BUDDHIST
Language	Uninflected, ideographic, and (in its written form) largely monosyllabic; no systematized grammar.	Highly inflected, alphabetic, polysyllabic, with a highly elaborated formal grammar.
Literary modes	Terseness, metaphors from familiar nature, limited imaginative range, concreteness.	Discursiveness, hyperbolic metaphor, unlimited imaginative flights, predilection for the abstract.
Psychology of the individual	No disposition to analyze the personality into its components.	A highly developed science of psychological analysis.
Time and space	Finite, life-time, milieu, and generation oriented.	Infinite, aeon-oriented.
Sociopolitical values	Familism, supremacy of the secular power, pursuit of the good society.	Individualism (in the Mahayana, universal salvationism), supremacy of spiritual power, pursuit of nonsocial goods.

The effort to bridge these gaps during the period of preparation was
carried on in scattered centers by a handful of missionaries who were
almost totally unprepared for the tasks they faced. Like the early
Christian missionaries centuries later, they knew virtually no Chinese,
and their few converts knew nothing of foreign languages. The first
translations were the product of a naive but touching optimism, of a
pooling of ignorance and enthusiasm. In the capitals of Han, Wu, Wei,
and Western Chin a succession of devoted Central Asian monks beginning with An Shih-kao labored at the work of textual translation, and
the corps of devoted Chinese collaborators gradually increased in
numbers and proficiency. Temples and clergy grew more numerous,

and one source states that in the years of the Western Chin (265–317), Buddhist establishments in Ch'ang-an and Loyang numbered 180, and clergy 3,700.[10] The following table gives a rough indication of the steadily increasing work of translation during the period we are considering.[11]

	Later Han, ca. 60–220 (about 160 years)	San-kuo Wei and Wu, 220–265, 220–280 (60 years)	Western Chin, 265–317 (52 years)
Number of known translators	13	11	16
Number of known titles, extant or lost	409	253	491

Yet the increasing number of translations indicates only one of the levels at which preparatory adaptation went forward. Small communities of believers began to develop at scattered points throughout China. At Tun-huang in the far northwest, at Loyang, in the Canton region of the far south, in Nanking and Wu-ch'ang on the Yangtze, in eastern Chekiang, possibly in Shantung. About 191 a numerous community was organized by a Chinese official in northern Kiangsu—an area which, significantly, had recently been a center of Yellow Turban dissidence and revolt; in this center religious observances were part of a wider social program that met some of the problems of a disorganized, impoverished, and demoralized peasantry.[12]

Throughout this period Buddhism develops outside the mainstream of Chinese philosophic life. The early, imperfect translations suggest that the scattered communities of Chinese neophytes were not interested in doctrine but in the practices leading to salvation. Demiéville suggests that Dharmarakṣa's translation, in 286, of one of the versions of the *Prajñā-pāramitā-sūtra* is the first to make the speculative ideas of Mahayana mysticism accessible and reasonably intelligible to literate Chinese; this appeared at a time when the revival of the study of the *Chuang-tzu* reflected a rising interest in an analogous range of indigenous ideas.[13] Although the translators invariably made use of Taoist terminology to render the basic ideas of Indian Buddhism, the *ch'ing-t'an* colloquies of the period show little evidence of the interaction between Indian and Chinese philosophies; the first Chinese Buddhist exegetical works are few and fumbling, outside the mainstream and the main centers of Chinese intellectual life.

Nonetheless during this period some of the issues in the competing claims of Buddhism, Taoism and Confucianism were given preliminary statement. Ts'ao Chih (192–232), prince of the Wei ruling house and pioneer experimenter with Chinese adaptations of Indian psalmody, wrote the first attack on Taoism from a Buddhist viewpoint. Mou-tzu's *Li-huo lun*, written at the end of the second century, is a kind of cyclopedia of the points at which Buddhism had to be reconciled with or adapted to Chinese tradition:[14] the alien versus the native, familism versus monasticism; Sinocentrism versus Indocentrism; the ritual and behavioral prescriptions of the Chinese Classics versus those of the Buddhist Canon; Chinese conceptions of a finite existence versus Buddhist ideas of transmigration. These are some of the problems which, stated in this period of preparation, are major themes in the period of domestication to follow.

The social and intellectual trends, the preliminary phases of Buddhist social activity, translation, intellectual development, and apologetics which have been outlined above suggest some of the lineaments of the age of preparation, and some of the reasons for its being so described. Let us now turn to the second phase.

II. THE PERIOD OF DOMESTICATION, 317–589

The pivotal character of the year 317 illustrates the suggestion made earlier that major turning points in Chinese social and political history seem to articulate the phases in the process of interaction which we are examining. This was the year in which the final stand of Chinese power in the north was made and failed. The first and probably decisive stage of the political cataclysm came in 313 when Loyang fell to the Huns, was sacked and destroyed, and the Chinese emperor was carried off to the barbarians' camp. One foreign observer's comments on the catastrophic Chinese defeat have been preserved. This is a fragmentary letter from the Sogdian merchant Nani-vandak to his colleague at Samarkand. He expresses astonishment that "those Huns who were yesterday the Emperor's vassals" should now have overthrown the empire. "And, Sir," he writes, "the last Emperor—so they say—fled from Saragh (Loyang) because of the famine, and his palace and walled city were set on fire. . . . So Saragh is no more, Ngap (Yeh, the great city in northern Honan) no more!"[15]

The Chinese had lost control of the heartland of their culture, of the most populous provinces, of the monuments and landmarks of their past; they had lost to disdained and hated barbarians. The psychological and intellectual impact of this debacle was enormous. Socially and politically the effects were far-reaching and long-lasting. During the next 272 years two widely different cultures developed in north and south; different institutions evolved in response to the different needs of the two areas. This meant that the domestication of Buddhist ideas and institutions proceeded along different lines in north and south. In considering domestication, therefore, we shall be obliged to consider the process of interaction between Buddhism and the two differently evolving cultures of south and north. We shall see that the two processes of domestication converge and culminate to usher in the period of acceptance and independent growth which begins with the reunification of the empire in 589.

Domestication of Buddhist Ideas and Institutions in the South

The Chinese ruling class which fled the north to establish a series of weak dynasties in Nanking had suffered a severe psychological shock. They found themselves in a rich but recently colonial area, much of it still populated by aborigines. They felt themselves exiles, and behaved like émigrés; their mood was a compound of chagrin, self-pity, and deep self-doubt. A scene in the country outside the new capital of Chien-k'ang recalls this mood. The leaders of the new government assembled, they sat on the grass, drank and feasted. Chou Hou sat down among them and said: "The scenery in general is no different, it is just that there are other mountains and rivers." They all looked at one another and wept. Only Wang Tao (the prime minister, brother of the ill-fated last prime minister of the Western Chin), his expression changing with deep emotion, said: "We should join forces with our royal house and reconquer our homeland. Why sit looking at one another like prisoners in chains?"[16]

Although the increasingly futile neo-Taoist colloquies continued to be a major pastime of the upper class, their recent bitter experience induced a more serious mood, a more urgent quest for some sort of certainty. Buddhism responded to this mood and this need, and more and more monks were to be found in the houses of the rich and the powerful. Many of these monks, such as Chih Tao-lin, were deeply versed in the concepts and the vocabulary of neo-Taoism and could present Buddhist ideas in the familiar *ch'ing-t'an* mode. Many of the leading monks were born members of the aristocracy; they tended to move from "Confucian" basic education to an interest in neo-Taoism, and thence to Buddhism.[17] These men knew intimately the mental and psychological preoccupations of their class. They expounded the neo-Taoist classics in terms of Buddhism, and Buddhism in terms of Taoism, and in this process Buddhist ideas were rapidly sinicized. They brought to their sophisticated but uneasy patrons a steady flow of new ideas gleaned from the increasing numbers of translated scriptures and Chinese exegetical writings.

The figure of Vimalakīrti was presented as an ideal model of character, overshadowing and outmoding the old ideals of the Confucian *chün-tzu* and the Taoist sage. Here was no bloodless moral paragon, no naked ascetic but a rich and powerful aristocrat, a brilliant talker, a respected householder and father, a pure and self-disciplined personality, yet a man who denied himself no luxury or pleasure while he changed all whom he met for the better.[18] Buddhism thus presented the southern aristocrats with a new model for a worldly life. At the same time, it began to attract more and more people to a monastic life. Taoism had long exalted the virtues of withdrawal and contemplation, and the social and political instability of the south encouraged escape from the frustrations of the world. Buddhism now provided a more highly sophisticated and aesthetically satisfying regimen for the meditative life, a richer and more diversified body of doctrine and philosophy, and—in the Bodhisattva ideal—a stronger ethical justification for such a life.

In the monasteries and temples which the rich and the pious endowed—from motives of piety, hope of salvation, fear of retribution, or love of ostentatious spending—an increasing clergy busied themselves with the study of the vast foreign literature that was coming to them in a steady flow of translation. Here in the south foreign missionaries were rare, and doctrinal discussions were carried on in Chinese by monks who seldom knew an Indian language. It is in this setting that many of the distinctive ideas of a domesticated Buddhism develop: a notion of the prime moving force of the universe that partakes of the qualities of the Chinese *tao* and the Buddhist *dharmakāya*; a rationalization of the celibate life that claims that the Vinaya is the counterpart of *li*; a rationalization of the monk's place in society that claims for him "higher forms" of both *hsiao* (filial submission) and *chung* (loyal devotion to authority); a conception of the soul and its salvation that owed much to the competing motions of both Taoism and Confucianism. The idea that Buddhism, if widely adopted, would bring about (that old Chinese ideal!) a harmonious and united society. Out of discussions and disputations, out of the struggle with the strange metaphors and vocabulary of a huge and heterogeneous sacred canon, Chinese monks developed special interests and emphases. It is these which prefigure the development of schools in the succeeding age. Meanwhile the whole effort of the clergy and of their lay patrons is to discover the "true" meaning of Indian Buddhism and to relate that meaning to the intellectual, spiritual, and social problems of their time and milieu.

Outside the temple walls the Chinese clergy moved freely in and out of the palaces of the rich and powerful. They also worked among the populace as a whole, and entered into a fierce competition with Taoist adepts—who had deeper local roots—for a popular following. The preaching of formulas of salvation, the elaboration of public ceremonies to compete with those of the Taoist religion, the performance of rituals invoking divine help against disease and natural disasters—all these means were used in their bid for popular support. By the sixth century, in north and south alike, the old village associations for fertility rites and other observances were being transformed into Buddhist organizations; thereafter they played an increasingly important role in making Buddhism an integral part of village life.[19] Yet one has the impression that the Buddhism of the south was more intellectual, more aristocratic, than that of the north, and that it had fewer adherents among the common people. And despite the growing populousness and prosperity of the south, the abuses of clerical privileges and immunities began to be noticed, and the burden of lavish temple building weighed heavily upon the common people. When an emperor of the Southern Ch'i attempted to outdo a predecessor in the building of lofty and richly ornamented pagodas a bold official remonstrated with him: "Your Majesty's building of this temple is entirely financed with money which the common people got by selling their sons and putting their wives in bond servitude. If the Buddha knew of this, he would be grieved and distressed. Your crime is higher than the pagoda. What religious merit does this have?"[20] Throughout this period there were attacks on Buddhism, but, though weak measures of regulation were taken, the attackers lacked real confidence in the Confucian formulas they affirmed, and thus offered no significant checks on the steady infiltration of Buddhism into court and culture.

Under all the short-lived southern dynasties, a series of fervently Buddhist emperors sponsored and promoted the growth of the alien religion. The performance of spectacular acts of penance, the building of splendid temples, the support of thousands of clergy—all motivated by belief in their efficacy as means to salvation—characterized several reigns. The best known of these Buddhist emperors is Liang Wu-ti. The festivals of the Buddhist year dominated his court calendar, he himself took Buddhist vows, and in 504, on the Buddha's birthday, he ordered the imperial relatives, the nobles, and the officials to forsake Taoism and embrace Buddhism. In 517 he ordered the temples of the Taoists—whose religion had steadily increased in power and influence (partly through its selective borrowing from Buddhism)—destroyed, and the Taoist clergy returned to lay life. In the titles which were given this pious ruler, we see the symbols of the domestication of Buddhism as an adjunct of imperial power. He was called Huang-ti p'u-sa (Emperor Bodhisattva), Chiu-shih p'u-sa (Savior Bodhisattva), and P'u-sa t'ien-tzu (Bodhisattva Son of Heaven).[21]

At many other levels, domestication went forward under the southern dynasties. New genres of Sino-Buddhist literature emerged, new architectural and art forms fused the native and the foreign, new music and musical instruments developed under foreign inspiration, new theories and practices in medicine merged with Chinese medical traditions, Buddhist principles were reflected in modifications of the penal code.

This brief survey suggests that domestication occurred at many levels in the south: at the level of thought and philosophy, of religious belief and practice, of social values and behavior, of state policy, and in the other cultural spheres just mentioned. We shall now examine the simultaneous but different process going on in the north.

Domestication of Buddhist Ideas and Institutions in the North

When north China fell to barbarian invaders in 317, this was the culmination of a long series of miscalculations and blunders on the part of the Chinese, and of a series of natural disasters that together left the north weakly administered, economically shattered, and, in certain key areas, virtually depopulated. Conquest of the north was accomplished by a coalition between those barbarians whom Chinese emperors had unwisely allowed to settle in the area and their cousins from beyond the great wall. In this vast area, from the decline of the Han onward, the institutions of settled agrarian life and the morale of the gentry and of the peasantry had been badly eroded. Now as the harsh, militaristic invaders set up their regimes, they encountered little coherent resistance. The breakup of well-ordered Chinese life and culture in the north is the precondition both for the continuance of barbarian control and for the spread and domestication of Buddhism in north China.

Buddhism found acceptance in all the strata of a deeply divided population: among the non-Chinese rulers and their kinsmen, among the surviving Chinese gentry, among the mass of the peasantry. At each stratum Buddhism, in the process of winning adherents and maintaining its dominance, underwent a process of adaptation. The configurations of this socially stratified process give us the pattern of domestication in the north.

Buddhism was appealing to the non-Chinese ruling groups in a variety of ways, and gifted missionaries such as Fo-t'u-teng and, later, resourceful native clerics exploited this receptivity to the full. Buddhism, notably in the persons of the great monks, offered the rulers charismatic and magical power which helped to ward off natural disasters, to win battles, to calculate future natural and human events. Thus we find the Buddhist clergy taking over the functions of rainmakers, calendar specialists, physicians, and general advisers. In performing these functions—and especially in meeting the rising challenge of their Taoist rivals—the monks domesticated Buddhism to its new environment and introduced it into realms of activity where it was to remain for centuries.

Buddhism commended itself to the rulers because it was not Chinese. As one of them remarked in an edict encouraging his subjects to become Buddhists, "We were born out of the marches, and though We are unworthy, We have complied with our appointed destiny and govern the Chinese as their prince. . . . Buddha being a barbarian god is the very one we should worship."[22] This foreign religion commended itself to the conquerors as a personal faith with its own means for quieting their superstitious fears and the spasms of remorse that occasionally shook them after some terrible slaughter of their subjects. Temples could be erected for the benefit of the souls of those who died in battle;[23] services of penance, donations to the clergy, and the commissioning of votive images could atone for their violent and ruthless acts. But in addition to these personal reassurances, Buddhism provided them, in the clergy, with a group of educated advisers totally dependent on the rulers' favor—a group as opposed as were their masters to the resurgence in the north of a Confucian-dominated Chinese state. Buddhism also appealed to them as a faith that was likely to induce submission and docility among the masses, to deepen their alienation from those older native patterns of belief and behavior which, if reasserted, might bring an end to alien domination. The favor of the rulers had far-reaching effects: it protected and encouraged the clergy as they proselytized among the population; it gave increasing economic support to temples and monasteries, making them, as never before, centers of trade, of money-lending, of milling, of a developing artisanry, and of large-scale agricultural enterprise.[24] The rulers also supported artists and artisans who, in the course of this period, transformed imported forms and motifs into a progressively domesticated Sino-Buddhist art—a process which is dramatized in the sequence of cave temples at Yün-kang and Lung-men. Buddhist organization developed to such a point that it required state controls, and there emerges in the Northern Wei a hierarchy of state-appointed Buddhist officials—the domestication of a loosely affiliated clergy into a Chinese-type bureaucratized organization.

When we turn to the Chinese gentry who remained in the north, we find that Buddhism offered some of the same appeals as it did to their émigré cousins south of the Yangtze. They too had felt the shattering blow of the conquest of the north by their enemies, and they lived uneasily and uncertainly under a succession of barbarian overlords. We find many of them turning to the alien faith for consolation, for the means of comprehending and enduring a life which Confucian formulae failed to explain and for which Taoism only prescribed escape. Many of them, as their fortunes improved, became generous lay patrons of Buddhism; in this they were motivated by hope of salvation but sometimes also by the desire to ingratiate themselves with their pious rulers and to secure tax exemption for their estates. Buddhism became part of their daily lives, of their thought, and of their family observances.

Other members of the gentry entered the monastic life, and many became leaders in the busy intellectual and ceremonial life of the northern capitals. These metropolitan clerics were in more regular contact with foreign missionaries than their southern counterparts and, through their own studies and through participation in great translation projects, they contributed notably to the domestication of Buddhist ideas in China. In the life and thought of Tao-an (312–385) one sees a growing awareness of the immense problems of translation and adaptation which Buddhism presented to the Chinese.[25] With him the easy "equivalence" of Buddhist and Taoist terms was shown to be delusive. Through his efforts and through those of Kumārajīva (in Ch'ang-an, 401–09) and his Chinese collaborators, Indian ideas were made intelligible to Chinese minds, and Buddhism entered decisively the mainstream of Chinese philosophy which it was to dominate for five centuries to come.

While the metropolitan clergy developed a way of life which was, in a sense, analogous to that of the Chinese official in its esteem for learning, its hierarchized bureaucracy, and its direct dependence on the state, the village clergy evolved along different lines.[26] Recruited from the peasantry, with scant pretensions to learning, often at odds with state authority, it was responsive to the needs of peasant life. The Buddhism which these men brought to the villages—against less opposition from religious Taoism than was encountered in the south —offered solace and formulas of easy salvation; it fused readily with local cults—particularly local earth and fertility cults; it provided, at the popular level, new and allegedly more efficacious observances for the repose of the ancestors—a striking instance of domestication through adaptation. The clergy were not only the local exorcists; when they were affiliated with an official temple they were also in a sense the representatives of state power; their influence and protection were often helpful, and the local temples offered relief grain and shelter in times of disaster. Though there are instances of gross exactions of labor and money from the peasantry for the temple building of the rich and powerful,[27] the mass of surviving inscriptions suggests that voluntary cooperation among villagers in pious building projects was far more common. The inscriptions of the period indicate the widespread practice of making votive objects which build up spiritual credit for the donors with the Bodhisattva invoked *and* seek his intervention on behalf of the souls of the ancestors and of living family members. Buddhism, then, became deeply interwoven with common life in the north, and this was the most important phase of its domestication at the popular level.

One of the trends which develops in the latter part of this period had far-reaching effects on the domestication of Buddhism. This was a trend, among the northern regimes, toward sinicization. It was produced by a number of factors, among which the following seem to be most important: The effort to get maximum productivity out of a Chinese agricultural region inevitably required the use of Chinese organizational and managerial techniques. The dream of a unified China under their domination obsessed many of the northern rulers, and this tended to make them increasingly interested in the Chinese statecraft, strategic knowledge, and political ideologies which the Chinese gentry monopolized; this, plus the revival of agriculture, increased the power of the gentry. The principal effort of the rising Taoist clergy—consciously or unconsciously leagued with those gentry who sought a revival of Chinese culture and power—was to attack and undermine Buddhism. The trend toward sinicization was accelerated in the reign of Emperor Hsiao-wen of the Northern Wei (471–99), who decreed that his own people should abandon the language and customs of their steppe ancestors, and moved his capital to the historic Chinese site of Loyang.

Toward the end of this period, therefore, the patterns of domestication in north and south tend to converge, and southern Chinese influence on the culture and the Buddhism of the north increases. The foreignness of Buddhism no longer commends it to monarchs who increasingly try to rule according to ancient Chinese patterns. Rather, the contradictions between a Chinese all-powerful state and a strong Buddhist community become clearer. In attempts to resolve these, one group urges the extirpation of Buddhism, while another stresses the uses of Buddhism as a sanction and bulwark of state power. Strangely enough both these views were expressed in support of the drastic suppression of Buddhism carried out by the northern Chou in 579. One group saw the extirpation of Buddhism as necessary to give credibility to the classical Confucian façade which the Chou was erecting as a means of laying claim to dominion over all China. The other argued that it was not Buddhism but the church—the *imperium in imperio*—that was bad, and that if temples and clergy were eliminated, the state would become one vast spiritual temple, P'ing-yen ta-ssu, with the Chou ruler presiding over his believing subjects as Tathāgata.[28] This second formula was a recognizable descendant of the Northern Wei solution to the problem of the conflict between secular and religious loyalties in an autocratic state: that the emperor *is* the Tathāgata. This solution contrasted with the southern pattern; there the Buddhists—living under an aristocratic rather than an autocratic regime—went no further than to persuade their monarchs to adopt the sanctified Indian model of the Cakravartin king who rules by and for the Buddhist faith, to become a lay patron, *mahādānapati*, rather than the deified monarch of a religious state. These are two of the solutions proposed to that most intractable problem of domestication: the relation of Buddhism to state power.

The two many-faceted processes of domestication in north and south met and merged in the reunified China of 589, and this begins a new phase in the history of Buddhism's interaction with Chinese culture.

III. THE PERIOD OF ACCEPTANCE AND INDEPENDENT GROWTH, 589–ca. 900

The years 581–89 are another one of the major turning points in Chinese history. In this period the Sui dynasty consolidated its hold on the north and planned and carried out its conquest of the south. With military conquest, its real task of institutional and cultural unification began. And in this massive and many-sided effort, the domesticated ideas and institutions of Buddhism were used and fostered by the dynasty to bring about cultural unity and to sanction the new Sui hegemony. We shall see that under the Sui and the T'ang those elements of Buddhism which had been domesticated in China were accepted—regardless of the predilections of individual rulers—as integral parts of social, political, economic, and cultural life; the prevalence of Buddhist belief in all classes of society made it essential for those in power to take account of this in formulating state policies at all levels. Acceptance by the populace and by the state—these are the conditions that make possible the notable development of Buddhism in this period of independent growth: the creation of a Buddhism by and for the Chinese. It may be useful to consider the modes of acceptance at various levels of state and society, and then to turn to some of the specific manifestations of independent growth. Let us first consider Buddhism in relation to state power.

The Sui dynasty adopted many policies which are characteristic of the state's relation to Buddhism throughout the T'ang.[29] A few of the more important of these might be briefly noted. The Buddhist clergy were close to the emperor, the center of power. As palace chaplains they ministered to the spiritual needs of the imperial family; as capital prelates they officiated in the imperially supported temples at great public services—for the relief of drought, for the peace of the realm, for the longevity of the reigning emperor (often on his birthday), for the repose of the souls of the imperial ancestors. In the provinces the Sui and the T'ang governments endowed special state temples (the Hsing-kuo ssu of the Sui, the Ta-yün ssu, Lung-hsing ssu, and K'ai-yüan ssu of the T'ang), and the bonds between the benign Buddha-sanctioned ruler and his pious subjects were dramatized for the local population. The Japanese monk-traveler Ennin reported that of the forty monasteries in Yang-chou, seven were classified as official.[30] The state advanced the fusion of Buddhism and indigenous cults by appointing Buddhist clergy to officiate at the shrines of the old tutelary deities of the sacred mountains, and these became major centers of Buddhist pilgrimage and religious activity.

The Sui and T'ang governments also reflected in a variety of social policies their acceptance of Buddhism. The state provided funds for the hospitals and the refuges for the sick and indigent which were attached to numerous temples. The suspension of state business was decreed for certain of the Buddhist holy days, and the state ordered the cessation of all executions, killing, and butchering during the days of special observances in the three months of Buddhist abstinence. The severity of the penal code was somewhat moderated, and the death penalty used more sparingly. The state also encouraged empirewide observance of such great festivals as the Feast of All Souls.

The great clerics were given special imperial honors and titles. Pu-k'ung or Amoghavajra (705–74) enjoyed the confidence of three emperors, was allowed to go in and out of the palace on horseback, was given a special court rank, and was enfeoffed as a duke; at his death court was suspended for three days.[31] Yet the great monks, besides being conspicuous objects of the government's solicitude for Buddhism, had a function: to control and regulate the clergy according to government regulations and to warn against the growth of heterodox or divisive beliefs. The hierarchy of clerical officials developed on the Northern Wei pattern was a bureaucracy responsible to the state for the maintenance of order, propriety, and conformity among believers, for the official ordination of monks, and for the chartering of Buddhist establishments. When Emperor Wen of the Sui said to the high clerical official Ling-tsang, "I, your disciple, am a lay Son of Heaven, while you, Vinaya Master, are a religious Son of Heaven," this was more than a flowery compliment; it clearly implied that the ranking clerical official had full and comprehensive responsibility for the Buddhist church.[32] The trend in the period we are considering is for Buddhism to become steadily more subordinated to state power. Takao has pointed out a vivid symbolic reflection of this process. In pre-T'ang times a monk addressing a monarch referred to himself by his name or as the śramaṇa (P'in-tao or Sha-men) so-and-so. In 760 a monk first used the word ch'en, "your subject," and by Sung times, the monks were using ch'en tun-shou, "your subject bows his head."[33]

Yet one of the indices of the clergy's power and importance in the T'ang was its ability to maintain its own religious norms. In 662 the great clerics of the realm were successful in getting the nullification of a government order that would have forced them to pay ceremonial homage to their parents and to their prince—acts consonant with li but contrary to the provisions of the Vinaya.[34]

In the life and culture of the upper class, Buddhism was everywhere accepted. Despite the revival of the examination system with an archaistic Confucian curriculum, Buddhism remained the dominant intellectual, spiritual, and aesthetic interest of the educated. Officials and nobles were munificent patrons of Buddhism, and the pattern of their donations shows the widespread acceptance of all the practices developed in north and south during the preceding period: the giving of alms to the monks and for charitable works, the giving of houses for temples, the donation of land for the endowment of monasteries and temples, the commissioning of greater or lesser votive images and paintings, the financing of special services and religious lectures, the conspicuous outpourings of treasure in the pursuit of religious merit. Withdrawal to a temple for contemplation and discourse with a learned monk was a favored way to use one's leisure. The prose and the poetry of the upper class reflect this pervasive interest in Buddhism. Approximately 8 percent of the poems in the most comprehensive collection of T'ang poetry have Buddhist references in their titles, and internal references occur in many times that number.[35] To study and collect Buddhist books or to become a specialist in Buddhist inscriptions—these were now scholarly avocations as respected as the study of the Chinese classics. Members of leading families often entered the clergy, sometimes through state-sponsored examinations; the ties between the metropolitan officials and clerics were close—those of social equals. In short Buddhism was an accepted part of the life of the elite; its ideas pervaded their thinking and shaped their views of life and destiny.

Among the peasantry too Buddhism was everywhere accepted. Although Taoist adepts continued to compete with Buddhists among the people as a whole and received sporadic encouagement from the Taoist-minded emperors of the T'ang, this is clearly the age of Buddhism as a common faith. Ennin's account of his travels in the years 838–47 gives a vivid picture of this acceptance of Buddhism among the people. Through the vast area he covered he met pious and hospitable laymen, witnessed mass gatherings for Buddhist festivals and services, watched the hosts of pilgrims on their way to the great shrines, noted the great crowds of temple visitors in Ch'ang-an and elsewhere.[36]

The clergy which served the peasants in the villages were often illiterate and lax in their religious observances; both in numbers and in the scope of their activities, they were often beyond the control of secular officials and of the official Buddhist hierarchy; in the T'ang many entered the clergy through the purchase of ordination certificates. But they brought a popular, thoroughly domesticated Buddhism into every aspect of peasant life. They organized local associations for pilgrimages, for the celebration of Sino-Buddhist festivals, for the building of votive images, and for the sponsorship of charitable works: the planting of shade trees along the pilgrimage routes, the building of hostels and bridges, etc. Many sold their medicinal and magical skills at temple fairs, and others subsisted on local alms. If these village clergy were a continuous source of official uneasiness, they helped to make Buddhism an integral part of Chinese rural culture; for the peasantry as for the gentry, Buddhism became an accepted part of individual and group life.

Having summarized the modes of acceptance of Buddhism by the state and by the two main classes of society, we shall turn briefly to some of the varieties of independent growth which characterize this period. Perhaps the most striking of these is the emergence of Chinese schools of Buddhism that bear little relation to the sects of Indian Buddhism. Some of these are culminations of developments which reach back into the age of domestication; each represents a peculiarly Chinese interpretation of one or more Buddhist doctrines—adapted to a particular emphasis or interest which already existed in Chinese thought. The emergence of these schools then should be regarded as a further development of the process of domestication within our period of acceptance and independent growth.

It should be noted first of all that certain sects and doctrines were outlawed by the governments of reunified China as "subversive." The growth of the new schools, then, is limited by what the resurgent and—compared to the Han—more centralized governments of this period regarded as conducive to the strengthening of state power and to the docile and submissive behavior of their subjects. Buddhist apocalypticism, for example, was recognized by the state as likely to provide an ideology of revolt, and even when a school was founded by a notable cleric and taught a number of socially salutary doctrines, the element of apocalypticism could bring suppression and the proscription of its books. An example of this is the San-chieh chiao. Its founder was an immensely popular preacher in the early Sui, and his patron was the most powerful minister of the period. It found a large following, but it taught that San-chieh chiao had the *sole* formula of salvation, and this was regarded as socially divisive; it taught that in the age of the apocalypse—the age of the extinction of the dharma—no government could exist which was worthy of the respect and cooperation of devout Buddhists, and this was regarded as utterly subversive. Hence the movement was ruthlessly suppressed.[37] The growth we shall consider, therefore, is growth within prescribed limits and growth from thoroughly domesticated roots.

The notion that religious faith, the capacity for fervent belief and for action based on belief, are untypical of the "rational" Chinese is one of those myths that die hard. The fervor and cohesion of the early communities of religious Taoism are well documented, and the life of faith was characteristic of mass culture during the period of disunion. The Pure Land sect which was finally organized and propagated in the T'ang had behind it centuries of Buddhist devotional practices and centuries of efforts to build a coherent doctrine of salvation by faith. Thousands of inscriptions attest the devotion of the Chinese to Maitreya and Amitābha and belief in the possibility of rebirth in their paradises. Generations of monks, going back to Tao-an and Hui-yüan in the fourth century, attempted to systematize the vision of salvation they had had. The work of devoted and brilliant clerics of the T'ang— Tao-ch'o (d. 645), Shan-tao (d. 681), and Fa-chao (active 766–805) built on these foundations of faith and doctrine a religion that was responsive to the spiritual needs of the ordinary Chinese. Fa-chao spread this faith from Ch'ang-an and from Wu-t'ai-shan in Shansi, and evidence of its influence has been found at Tun-huang.[38] This religion—a synthesis of beliefs which had been long accepted by the Chinese—had no scriptural links with primitive Buddhism; its doctrines claimed authority from those sections of assorted Mahayana sutras which stressed faith as a means to salvation. Forged sutras— written in Chinese for a Chinese audience—crystallize Pure Land teaching and testify to the fact of its indigeneity, its independent growth in China.

While a Sino-Buddhist salvationism was making its way with the people, other schools arose with more limited mass appeal but with influential followers and far-reaching effects on the development of Chinese culture. Ch'an Buddhism is one of these, and it is another of those manifestations of independent growth in the period we are considering. Again, the interest in meditation as a means to enlightenment and the notion of the immanence of Buddha-nature go back at least to the fourth century. So does the polarization of Ch'an Buddhism into "subitist" and "gradualist" schools—which reflects a perennial dichotomy in Chinese philosophy.[39] The Ch'an masters of the T'ang grafted much of their teaching on Taoist roots; they advocated quietistic withdrawal, the elimination of dualism, and the discovery of the Buddhanature within. In their writings the style, the metaphors, the form of argument bear a closer relation to Chinese philosophic traditions than to any Indian Buddhist text or school. And the methods of imparting their doctrine—the homely analogy, the concrete metaphor, the paradoxical question, the bibliophobic directness—all lack any Indian prototype. Indeed, as Jacques Gernet has suggested, the notion of enlightenment-salvation as being attainable in one lifetime or in one moment may be interpreted as the product of the relatively mobile society of China where, unlike caste-bound India, a man of merit could by his own efforts achieve status and recognition.[40] The Ch'an interest in natural phenomena and its glorification of intuition were two of the fundamental ingredients of the Chinese aesthetic outlook from T'ang times onward. Ch'an was to prove the most durable and influential of the Sino-Buddhist philosophies of this age of independent growth.

T'ien-t'ai Buddhism was another school whose interests and emphases were notably Chinese. Its founder was honored by the second Sui emperor, and its prelates were, in the T'ang period, clerics of great influence. It commended itself to the Sui rulers partly because it was gaining influence in the south, where the Sui had great difficulty in winning consent or support for its rule. But it had a further and broader appeal: this was its doctrine of "levels" of Buddhist teaching— a doctrine which reconciled the various and apparently contradictory Buddhist formulae of life and salvation which had come into China. This theory was responsive to a widespread and age-old Chinese predilection for harmony and dislike of conflict and exclusiveness. And it was particularly appealing to Chinese rulers who felt that only a harmonious and united society—riven neither by interpersonal conflicts nor by sectarian divisions—could testify to the success of their regimes. The means by which the T'ien-t'ai arrived at its reconciliation of conflicting doctrines seems to me Chinese in its appeal to historical principles of explanation: one doctrine was true for one period and one clientele, while another was suited for a second period, etc. This might be interpreted as a Chinese historicist theory inspired by, but going far beyond, suggestions made in the *Lotus Sūtra*.

Other schools were based on a metaphysical position or on a special emphasis on one text or a group of texts. An analysis would show that both groups developed a range of interpretations which was to a large degree independent of the Indian texts that inspired them, as Chinese as the language in which they wrote. The study of particular texts produced a scholasticism fundamentally little different in temper from that which characterized Han Confucianism. It was perhaps in the study and use of Vinaya texts that the Chinese developed the least independence; the failure to free themselves from Indian monastic rules and to develop a code specifically adapted to China, was, in Tsukamoto's view, one of the reasons for the inflexibility and the resulting decline of the Buddhist clergy.[41] But in general Buddhism in this period responded to a variety of political, spiritual, intellectual, and aesthetic needs. How then does this period of widespread acceptance and independent growth come to an end?

A number of developments slowly but certainly undermined Buddhism's dominant position. After the An Lu-shan rebellion, T'ang self-confidence and governmental effectiveness were not fully restored. The cosmopolitanism of the great days of T'ang slowly gave way, under the influence of barbarian attack and internal decay, to a cultural defensiveness which occasionally broke out into xenophobia. A foreign religion obviously suffered from this change. The T'ang economic order also weakened after An Lu-shan, and arguments as to the wastefulness of nonproductive clergy, temple building, tax exempt temple lands, and the like began to be given a more sympathetic hearing at court. Gernet suggests that social change in the course of the eighth century involved a realignment of economic and social groups, the growth of a money economy and a trend toward more impersonal relations between employer and employed, and that these changes were catastrophic for Buddhism, which had adapted itself to an older social order.[42] No doubt there lies in the social changes of this period a part of the explanation for Buddhism's subsequent decline, but I should have to know more of the social history of the period to give these factors their proper weight.

Yet it is doubtful if any or indeed all of these factors would by themselves have brought the decline of Buddhism in China. The decisive factor was the revival of the native tradition of Confucianism by an important segment of the Chinese elite. The Sui founder regarded Confucian teachings as arid and boring; many of the T'ang monarchs were personally Buddhists or Taoists. Yet from the time of reunification onward the rulers adopted more and more of those measures of traditional Chinese statecraft which are usually associated with Confucianism; neither Taoism nor Buddhism had developed any such arsenal of social and political formulae. And one of the measures which was taken was the restoration of the examination system for the recruitment of officials. The content of the examination questions was, throughout most of the T'ang, intellectually trivial, anachronistic, and—since Confucian texts represented many stages of China's philosophical development—remarkably heterogeneous. Yet from the beginning of the seventh century, young men were studying these texts in the hope of advancement, even though their intellectual interests might be in Buddhism or Taoism. And the people who studied and took examinations had been used by all the rulers from Emperor Yang of the Sui onward as a useful counterweight to the power of the old entrenched aristocratic families. This new group therefore had access to power, and it sought ideological sanctions for the maintenance and expansion of that power. The result of this—together with some of the factors noted above—was the gradual effort to bring coherence and consistency into the Confucian tradition, to make it intellectually competitive with the entrenched foreign religion. Another imponderable factor in the revival of Confucianism is that universal but seldom studied phenomenon: the obsolescence of ideas; ideas, after centuries in circulation, tend to become worn out, less interesting, and men long for something new. Perhaps this was beginning to happen to Buddhist ideas.

Han Yü's anti-Buddhist memorial of 819 contained few arguments that had not been heard before. But the arguments were put forward with a new confidence because there was now a growing body of people in power who shared its rationalistic and xenophobic sentiments. In his writings Han Yü put forward several of the ideas that were later to be central in organized neo-Confucianism; he began to glean from the Confucian tradition those ideas and formulae which answered, on the authority of native philosophers, many of the questions which Buddhism had raised in men's minds. The beginnings of the Confucian revival represent, in my view, the beginning of the end of the great age of Buddhism.

The persecution of 845 brought a massive, empirewide destruction of Buddhist establishments, the wholesale secularization of the clergy, and the loss of land, wealth, power, and prestige. Buddhism was later allowed to revive, but it never again was regarded as an essential adjunct of state power. The Chinese state which had made its peace with this *imperium in imperio* in the age of acceptance once again—with the help of revived Confucianism—reasserted its direct control over all institutions, mores, and ideas within the realm. As the educated elite turned toward the new Confucianism, Buddhist ideas ceased to be the common coin of intellectual life. And the power of nativist Taoism made slow but steady inroads on the following which Buddhism had won among the masses. All these are aspects of the transition to what I have called the age of appropriation. This is a gradual shift, but sometime in the years between 900 and 1000 the shift to this new and final mode of interaction between Buddhism and Chinese culture comes about.

IV. THE PERIOD OF APPROPRIATION, 900 TO THE PRESENT

In calling this the period of appropriation, I mean to suggest that the dominant mode of interaction between Buddhism and Chinese culture was the appropriation by the latter of those Buddhist elements which had, in the course of many centuries, been adapted and accepted in China. This is not to deny the sporadic revivals of Buddhism, for example, that in the late tenth and early eleventh centuries which was stimulated by the last Buddhist relations with India. Nor is it to deny the limited state-sponsored revivals of Buddhism in the Yüan and early Ch'ing dynasties—revivals motivated partly by considerations of Inner Asian policy and partly by the ideological requirements of alien rule. Throughout most of this period there were innumerable temples and millions of believers. But the trend was for Buddhist ideas to be appropriated by the revived Confucian orthodoxy of the official class and for Buddhist elements at other cultural levels to be appropriated by indigenous traditions.

One need not argue the fact that the neo-Confucian orthodoxy of the state and upper class from the Sung onward appropriated those Buddhist ideas which had by the tenth century become part of the intellectual heritage of educated Chinese. I am inclined to agree with the recent opinion of G. E. Sargent that Chu Hsi's effort was to consolidate the neo-Confucian position against that of Buddhism by proposing substitutes for Buddhist ideas, and that neo-Confucianism constitutes less an autonomous system than a complex of responses to Buddhist theories.[43] Yet the neo-Confucian effort to update the Chinese philosophic tradition, to give it, by reinterpretation and carefully disguised appropriations from Buddhism, a new coherence, consistency, and completeness, was a considerable success. It was a success because it was the first native movement in eight hundred years to provide a set of answers to those increasingly complex and sophisticated questions about life, time, history, and destiny which educated Chinese had asked themselves. Its answers were socially, politically, and morally oriented, and, if neo-Confucianism had ended with Chu Hsi, the tradition of Ch'an Buddhism—which Chu Hsi regarded as the most baneful of all—might have continued to be the sole recourse of those with a mystical, individualistic, or intuitionist bent. But another variety of neo-Confucianism, usually associated with the name of Wang Yang-ming but beginning long before him, developed as a native response to just those bents and interests which Ch'an Buddhism had served so long. Wang was attacked by the rationalist neo-Confucians as a Buddhist in disguise. Indeed he was, but the disguise was all-important, for in his neo-Confucianism Buddhist ideas are appropriated, given a native sanction and a cloak of respectability.

These two major schools of neo-Confucianism, maintained at the level of basic education and elite culture by the examination system, effectively eliminated Buddhist ideas from the spectrum of intellectual choice. Ch'an Buddhism, it is true, showed some continuing vitality, but it tended more and more to service the strictly aesthetic requirements of the upper class, and in this role it was tamed and academicized; as Levenson puts it, "the Ch'an intuitive nature-cult of the Ming painters was not an antithesis to Confucian humanism, but a tame, learned element in the Confucian humane culture—not a bold challenge to didacticism, but a cultural possession of didactically educated men."[44]

The appropriation of Buddhism at other levels can only be suggested here. The secret societies—organized for mutual aid and protection and often with a political purpose—show in their doctrines and practices the almost total amalgamation of popular Taoism and Buddhism. In the countryside, Buddhism's ability to fuse with local folk cults—a valuable quality in its days of vigor—slowly but surely brought its absorption into a general popular religion in which Buddhist elements are identified with difficulty. Father Grootaers' intensive investigation of the cults of an area in Chahar showed that only 19.7 percent of the local cult-units were identifiably Buddhist, and a number of the deities in these were tending to be confused with those of non-Buddhist origin.[45] Buddhist monks down to modern times have continued to serve as local shamans and exorcists, but with little organization and less education they have tended to become scarcely distinguishable from the shamans of popular religion.

Even as Buddhist words and phrases have long been appropriated as part of accepted Chinese vocabulary and its symbols for the meaningless decoration of ordinary objects, a number of Buddhist ideas linger on as part of the prevailing outlook on life. Karma, with its associated belief in some sort of retribution beyond the grave, is one of these. Two examples will show how, at different social levels, this notion has been appropriated. The first is the story of a peasant family. An old lady dies, and after a time her family inquires through a medium (not a Buddhist priest) as to her fate in the after life. She replies through the medium that she has now expiated her evil karma and has applied to the proper authorities for reincarnation in human form, that her papers are in order, and that she expects an early decision.[46] In this instance a Buddhist idea has been appropriated in such a way as to be almost unrecognizable. Popular belief in the supreme desirability of human life on earth and the Chinese-type bureaucratization of the nether world form with karma a complex that is more Chinese than Buddhist.

At the intellectual level karma has been so appropriated that even philosophers may be unaware that it is part of their outlook. Hu Shih, in a long essay in which he disposed of all foreign notions of immortality, reasserted what he felt to be the proper *Chinese* view: "Everything that we are, everything that we do, and everything that we say, is immortal in the sense that it has its effect somewhere in this world, and that effect in turn will have its effects somewhere else, and the thing goes on in infinite time and space."[47] Here is an unwitting but unmistakable restatement of the idea of karmic cause and effect!

The process of appropriation as it has proceeded down to yesterday may, finally, be illustrated by a statement from a recent political writer. Liu Shao-ch'i, in his essay on the training of a party member, paints the picture of the ideal Communist; in doing this he draws heavily on traditional moral idioms. At one point in the discourse he says that the true party member "grieves before all the rest of the world grieves and is happy only after all the rest of the world is happy."[48] A Confucian scholar might say that Liu was quoting the Sung statesman Fan Chung-yen (989–1052), but what he is really restating as an ideal of Communist conduct is the Bodhisattva ideal which Fan had appropriated into Confucianism 900 years ago.

The survey we have made of the four stages of Buddhism's interaction with Chinese culture makes it possible for us to draw, however tentatively, some general conclusions and to point to some specific lines of further study that would shed light on the process. A first and obvious conclusion is an underlining of Sylvain Lévi's statement with which this paper opened that an understanding of Buddhism in Chinese history helps to explain and clarify the whole of China's development, that without such an understanding much remains inexplicable. A second general conclusion is that the observation of Buddhism in interaction with Chinese cultural elements serves to bring into bold relief those institutions, points of view, and habits of mind which are most intractably and intransigently Chinese. Or, to use a chemical analogy, Buddhism is a precipitant which clarifies and brings to clearer notice the elements of the complex amalgam that is Chinese civilization.[49] A third general conclusion relates to the old problem of China's capacity to "absorb" foreign invaders—alien rulers and foreign cultures alike. Recent studies have shown that "absorption" does not describe the diverse fates of alien invaders. This paper suggests that it is equally inapplicable to the complexity of relationships through time between Chinese civilization and the invading Buddhist culture.

Modern scholarly knowledge of Buddhism in Chinese history is so uneven that it would be futile to attempt to list the unexplored fields and the unsolved problems. But it is possible to specify a few studies which would, at the present stage of knowledge, throw maximum light on the *process* with which this paper has been concerned. One is the study of the history of the relationship between Buddhism and Chinese law. Another is the history of the state policies and institutions for the control of Buddhism. A third is the history of the relation between Buddhism and religious Taoism—admittedly an enormously difficult undertaking even with the considerable amount of preliminary work that has been done. A fourth is the history of Buddhism in relation to Chinese philosophy; here the task is complicated by the Confucian apologetic bias of some of the sources, and by the Buddhist bias of the others. A fifth is not the study of a problem, of a facet of interaction through time, but rather the study of all aspects of Buddhism in relation to the total culture of a specific period. This is a plea to those historians with particular period interests to give fuller accounts—as Eberhard began to do in his sociological study of the Northern Wei—of Buddhism in the life and culture of an age.

The challenge is great, the obstacles formidable, but I hope I have been able to suggest some of the great increment of understanding that would come from a fuller and deeper knowledge of Buddhism in Chinese history.

2

FO-T'U-TENG 佛圖澄

A Biography

INTRODUCTION

In its long and turbulent history China has seldom presented such a picture of chaos and misery as it did in the early fourth century A.D. The seizure of power by the Ssu-ma family in 265, following a period of disunion, involved disorder and destruction on a large scale. The accession of the idiot emperor Hui in 290 brought on a struggle for the imperial succession—the twenty-one-year War of the Eight Princes—which further weakened the country.[1] Moreover the dangerous policy of settling non-Chinese within the empire was continued, despite the

Reprinted by permission from the *Harvard Journal of Asiatic Studies* 11, nos. 3, 4 (December 1948): 321–71. The Editor expresses his appreciation to the editors of the Journal.

34

Gilt bronze image of the Buddha Śākyamuni. Dated A.D. 338. Height: 15 inches. Collection of C. T. Loo and Company. This image was the subject of a paper read before the American Oriental Society in 1940 by John A. Pope, now of the Freer Gallery of Art, Smithsonian Institution, Washington, D.C. This paper, which has not been published, mentioned briefly the historical background, the images from India, Central Asia, and China which are related on chronological and stylistic grounds, and the microscopic examination of the bronze made by the technical section of the Fogg Museum of Art. All three factors point to the probable authenticity of the figure as dated; Mr. Pope informs me that he has examined it a number of times since then and has found nothing to upset his original conclusions. In the absence of definite proof to the contrary, this is the earliest known dated Buddhist image from China and the only one attributable to the time and place of Fo-t'u-teng's missionary activity.

protests of such farsighted statesmen as Chiang T'ung 江統.² Mass
migrations, resulting from the settlement policy and economic disintegration, left large areas of China with reduced and disorganized
Chinese populations.³

One of the first of the partly sinicized barbarians to take advantage
of this situation was Liu Yüan 劉淵, and by 316 his son, Liu Ts'ung
劉聰, had become master of North China.⁴ A loyal supporter of the
Liu family in their rise to power was Shih Lo 石勒.⁵ He was born a
member of the Chieh 羯 tribe, a subdivision of the Hsiung-nu;⁶ when
young he had served as a mercenary and as a slave. His rise as a gueril-
la leader with a large following of Hsiung-nu and homeless Chinese
attracted the attention of Liu Yüan, and the latter gave him wide powers in the areas he conquered for the house of Liu. Lo's strength increased when he destroyed Wang Mi 王彌 and absorbed the latter's
army. Late in 311 he could count himself master of Honan, Shantung,
and parts of Hopei. Several courses were open to him. In the end,
following the counsels of his great Chinese adviser, Chang Pin 張賓,⁷
he decided to consolidate his power in the territory he then controlled.
He established his capital at Hsiang-kuo 襄國 (southwest of the modern Hsing-t'ai 邢臺 county in southern Hopei), and from that time on
(312), though remaining a nominal feudatory of Lu Ts'ung, he became
more and more independent. After breaking with Ts'ung's successor,
Yao 曜,⁸ he gave himself, in 319, the title of prince of Chao 趙天王,
and in the course of the next ten years was constantly at war with Yao,
whom he defeated in 328 and executed in 329. After that Lo's power
was extended throughout Shensi and Shansi, though in the north of
the latter province he was threatened by the Toba. In 330, when he
was finally persuaded to take the imperial title—as emperor of the
Later Chao—he was master of most of North China.

Shih Lo was an illiterate soldier, but he was neither unintelligent nor
inhuman. He enjoyed hearing passages from the Chinese histories and
classics read to him and joined with his entourage in discussing the
ethical and political problems involved.⁹ His government, however,
was a failure. There are three main reasons for this: (1) in the area
which he ruled, agriculture and sericulture were at low ebb; the people
lived miserably, always on the verge of starvation; efforts to revive the

economy of the country were ineffectual because: (2) Shih Lo's government was not a civil administration but a war machine; (3) racial conflict, not only between the rulers and the Chinese, but between different non-Chinese groups, was a constant and disintegrating influence on all efforts to establish stable government.[10]

At Lo's death in 333, his son succeeded to the throne, but Lo's nephew and chief general, Shih Hu 石虎, long dissatisfied with his rewards, soon had the young ruler murdered and put himself on the throne.[11] The Chinese accounts present Shih Hu as a bestial tyrant, and even when due allowance is made for their prejudices, the picture of his reign is a terrible one. The factors which made Shih Lo's reign a failure still obtained. Their force was increasingly felt when Lo's common sense and political judgment were replaced by the vanity, extravagance, and political obtuseness of Shih Hu. Vast military undertakings and enormous building projects made demands on the country which led to widespread impoverishment and discontent.

While Shih Hu lay dying in 348, nationwide unrest and palace intrigue foretold the end of his dynasty. No sooner was he dead than Jan Min 冉閔, a Chinese adopted grandson, murdered all the remaining members of the Shih family and, as the center of a general uprising of the Chinese, started systematically to kill all the "barbarians."[12]

Fo-t'u-teng was a Buddhist monk, probably from Kucha. In the course of a long life of study he had visited Kashmir and other great Buddhist centers. He had come to China with the intention of starting a religious center in the imperial capital, and, had he reached there at a less disturbed time, he would no doubt have become a great translator and exegete. But with the instinct of a true missionary, he saw the possibilities which might lie in association with Shih Lo and, in the course of the next thirty-seven years, used the patronage of the Shih family to lay the foundations of a Buddhist church, passing on his great learning to his disciples, who, in the next generation, were greatly to expand the teachings of Buddhism in China.

In gaining and holding the support of the Shih family, Teng took into account both the condition of the country and the character of his patrons. He proceeded to demonstrate the fetish power of Buddhism in four fields: (1) Agriculture. He showed his prowess as a rainmaker, thus ingratiating himself with the rulers of a predominantly agricultural state.[13] (2) Warfare. The Later Chao was a military state, and its rulers expected Buddhism to give them an advantage in war, just as Constantine expected victory from the deployment of Christian fetish power. Fo-t'u-teng was successful in advising his patrons on their war plans, further increasing his prestige.[14] (3) Medicine. Buddhist missionaries had long used Indian medicine to cure and, in turn, to convert the Chinese.[15] When Teng effected cures, not only did the patients rejoice, but the rulers were pleased at the conserving of manpower in a depopulated, epidemic-ridden country. (4) Politics. Under the Later Chao dictatorship politics was largely a struggle for power among palace factions and racial groups. Teng, through the use of his "magical" powers and his intelligence, kept the confidence of the rulers and avoided alliances with groups or cliques which were usually destroyed by their rivals. Thus the monk won and kept the support of the Shih family for Buddhism so that he had both the time and the influence to spread his faith. The rulers, on their side, had a gifted and versatile adviser on whose loyalty and resourcefulness they could depend.

From the Western Chin onward there was a gradual penetration of Buddhism into intellectual circles. Philosophic Taoism had lost some of its appeal when, under the Wei, it became semiofficial. Its ideas had been discussed incessantly for decades and had lost their freshness. Educated people, dismayed at the fierce War of the Eight Princes and subsequent upheavals, were led to question the premises of their philosophy. Gifted monks, thoroughly versed in the ideas and vocabulary of Taoism, began to present to intellectuals a kind of Buddhism which would meet their spiritual needs and enliven their philosophic discussions.[16] This was a Buddhism of the cultured classes; it had no currency among the common people and few social consequences. When the Chin dynasty fled to the south in 317, this type of Buddhism for the most part went with it. In the decadent life of the southern capital Buddhism continued in vogue. Vivid personalities, brilliant (though seldom profound) ideas, scintillating conversation—these are the characteristics of Buddhist circles in the south. Far from the asceticism of Gautama, this type of Buddhism was a genuinely Chinese development. When this southern Buddhism in the course of time was blended with that of the north, we see at last the full maturity of sinicized Buddhism.

At the time of Fo-t'u-teng's arrival in 310, a Buddhism characteristic of the north had not emerged. Teng saw the oppressed and bewildered population with most of its traditional way of life destroyed and began, under the patronage of the rulers, to spread his religion. He trained disciples and built religious centers which would bring Buddhism into all parts of the country. He established Buddhism in a new relationship to the rulers. That relationship in a more developed form was characteristic of the Northern Wei. It involved Buddhist monks in all the activities of the court, both private and public, and it meant the creation, with state support, of a popular religion organized to work among the people; it also meant government sponsorship of temples, translators, artists, and exegetes. This development had a profound influence on the Buddhism of reunited China under the Sui and T'ang and affected the later history of state-church relations in China.

The edict tolerating monasticism which Teng extracted from Shih Hu was important at the time, since it enabled Teng to continue to develop a Buddhist church, unhampered by state control. It was later cited as a precedent by the church in its struggle against control and persecution.[17]

The historical significance of Teng's widespread temple building is as a symptom of the growth and spread of church organization. The real strength of that organization lay with a group of disciples whom Teng trained. They strengthened and expanded the church, and they ensured the continuance and further development of Buddhism in China. They reflect in their careers both the learning and the practical vision of Fo-t'u-teng:

1. Chu Fa-ya 竺法雅[18] was a Chinese monk who, like several of Teng's disciples, took the surname Chu out of respect for his master. Though he was a northerner, his contribution was to the development of the intellectual Buddhism of the south. He was a careful student of both Buddhism and Taoism. Far more earnest than most of the courtier monks of the south, he was dissatisfied with superficial resem-

blances between Taoist and Buddhist terms and concepts and sought to clarify and regularize the use of Taoist terms in Buddhist exegesis. He called his system ko-i.[19] In the end it contributed to the understanding of Buddhism among educated Chinese and was a step forward in the long process of the sinicization of Buddhism.

2. Tao-an[20] was a man of strong piety and profound scholarship; much of the latter he probably owed to his master. Tao-an worked a lifetime to elucidate Buddhist writings, to extract their true meaning, and to give that meaning wider currency. He compiled the first catalogue of translations and, through his own disciples, contributed to the success of the translations and the exegetical projects of Kumārajīva. Tao-an was one of the first to appreciate the devotional aspects of the Mahayana. It was through his great disciple, Hui-yüan 慧遠, that devotional Buddhism took root in China and began to have a real influence on the intellectual Buddhism of the south.

3. Chu Seng-lang 竺僧朗[21] is the first monk recorded as having founded a monastery in Shantung; in the course of a long life he built up a great center of Buddhism there. He was a man of strict piety and insisted on severe monastic discipline. His learning was considerable, and he had a strong influence on Seng-jui 僧叡, Kumārajīva's most prominent Chinese associate.

4. Chu Fa-t'ai 竺法汰[22] was a colleague of Tao-an. When the latter fled south after the fall of the Later Chao, he took Fa-t'ai with him, later sending him on a mission to the region of the lower Yangtze. Fa-t'ai eventually brought the more vigorous Buddhism of the north to the Chin capital and had an influential career as a preacher.

5. Fa-ho 法和,[23] after the fall of the Later Chao, took his disciples and went into Szechwan, and this is usually considered to mark the beginning of the expansion of Buddhism in that region. Later, in association with Tao-an and a foreign monk, he became a distinguished worker in translation and exegesis. He seems, late in life, to have known Kumārajīva.

6. Early nuns. The first two nuns mentioned in the *Pi-ch'iu-ni chuan* 比丘尼傳, Ching-chien 淨檢 and An-ling-shou 安令首, were associ-

ated with Fo-t'u-teng, the second having been converted by him.[24] Although the first full ordination did not take place until after his death, he contributed greatly to the establishment of the female order.

7. Shan Tao-k'ai 單 (or 善) 道開[25] was at the Later Chao court with Fo-t'u-teng and, like him, enjoyed the confidence of the rulers, partly because of his skill as a doctor. At the fall of the Later Chao, he fled south, reaching the imperial capital in 359. Shortly thereafter he went into Kwangtung, lived in the mountains as a hermit, and died there, "aged more than 100."

8. Chu Fo-t'iao 竺佛調[26] was another disciple who was skilled in medicine and won converts through his cures. He lived the life of an ascetic in a mountain retreat in Honan, instructing those who came to him.

The Sources for the Life of Fo-t'u-teng

1. The *Kao-seng chuan* by Hui-chiao, which appeared between 519 and 554.[27] Unlike many Chinese writers, Hui-chiao has left us, in the form of a preface, a valuable key to his method of compilation; this is supplemented by a postface by one of his disciples. From these sources we see that the *KSC* is a mosaic of material, refashioned by its author from a wide variety of earlier works. Some notion of Hui-chiao's method may be derived from the notes to the biography of Fo-t'u-teng, in which I have collected the fragments of works which may have contributed a fact, an incident, or a sentence to the composition of the biography. More than a century and a half elapsed between the death of Fo-t'u-teng and the completion of the *KSC*, and a considerable legend had developed during that period. Hui-chiao's efforts at an accurate account were hampered by the legend, and it should always be borne in mind that Hui-chiao, living in the south, did not have access to materials in the north, particularly inscriptions and private memoirs. Nevertheless this is the oldest extant biography of Fo-t'u-teng and remains, as will be seen, by far the most important.

2. The original *Shih-liu-kuo ch'un-ch'iu* written by Ts'ui Hung 崔鴻[28] during the Northern Wei period. This work, which appeared in 528, contained a biography of Fo-t'u-teng. The present work of this

name is a forgery,[29] and the only data on Fo-t'u-teng from the original *SLKCC* are found in quotations.

3. *Chin shu*. Chapter 95 contains the earliest extant secular biography of Fo-t'u-teng. A consideration of this biography clearly shows the weaknesses of the *CS*.[30] The account is often badly abridged, that is, the climax or denouement of an incident is omitted; all prodigies are retained while genuinely historical material is left out. As a result this biography has less historical value than Hui-chiao's account.

On the relation of the two earliest extant biographies of Fo-t'u-teng, Maspero took the view that all biographies of Fo-t'u-teng are based on the *KSC* account or indirectly on it through the *CS*.[31] Pelliot, on the other hand, believed that both the *CS* and *KSC* accounts were derived from a common original, probably a *pieh-chuan*, that is to say, a separate biography, which he believed dated from the second half of the fourth century.[32] In my opinion Maspero was more nearly correct. Eleven of the twenty-nine paragraphs into which I have divided the *CS* (see Appendix, p. 68) are the same as paragraphs in the *KSC*. Seven more are apparently abridged from paragraphs in the *KSC*. Of the remaining eleven, one is from the *Shih-shuo hsin-yü* 世說新語; all of another and parts of two more are probably from the *SLKCC*. Many sentences from the remainder are the same as sentences in the *KSC*, and there are no incidents in these remaining paragraphs which are not found in the *KSC*. Two more incidents from the *KSC* account are made into separate "biographies" in the *CS*.[33]

The postface to the *KSC* states that material on Fo-t'u-teng is scattered through works of the Chao period; neither the preface nor the postface mentions a *Teng pieh-chuan*, though they do specify such accounts for other monks.[34] While certain incidents in the *KSC* biography seem to be derived from one or more *Teng pieh-chuan*, surviving fragments of the latter do not always agree with each other nor with the *KSC*. For example the *KSC* differs from the longest surviving fragment (perhaps an abridgment) of a *pieh-chuan* on the vital points of Fo-t'u-teng's nationality and birthplace.[35] It thus would be incorrect to suppose that Hui-chiao depended for his account on any one earlier work. His biography of Fo-t'u-teng is his own synthesis of a variety of earlier sources,[36] while the CS account is largely based on that of the KSC.

On the basis of the above sources, and accounts derived from them, Europeans have written on various aspects of Fo-t'u-teng's career. The only complete biography is Abel Rémusat's account based on CS 95 which appeared in his *Nouveaux mélanges asiatiques* in 1829.[37] Chinese and Japanese scholars have treated Fo-t'u-teng in their accounts of Chinese Buddhism, though no study devoted exclusively to his life and work has yet appeared.[38]

Fo-t'u-teng's Name, Surname, and Origin

Fo-t'u-teng's name has not been successfully reconstructed. Pelliot long ago proposed *Buddhadāna*, but no further evidence has appeared to establish the equivalence.[39]

The problem of Fo-t'u-teng's surname is very complex, and there are three possibilities which must be considered:

1. Surname unknown. A *pieh-chuan*, quoted in the commentary to the *Shih-shuo hsin-yü*, says, "As to the monk Fo-t'u-teng, it is not known whence he came. He appeared in Tun-huang. He was devoted to Buddhism, left lay life, and became a śramaṇa."[40] This may be the earliest surviving data on this point, though, as we have seen, the *pieh-chuan* problem is not a simple one. The author of this notice may not have had access to information available to other writers known to Hui-chiao. West of Tun-huang was the Buddhist kingdom of Kucha, whose rulers sent tribute to the Chin and, when that became impossible, to the Liang Kingdom, nominally a feudatory of the Chin. This brings us to the second possibility.

2. Surname Po 帛. Both KSC and CS give this as Fo-t'u-teng's original surname, and since this was the surname of the kings of Kucha, it has long been held that he was from Kucha. Aside from the surname itself, there are several facts which support this hypothesis: (a) Kucha was a part of the "Western Regions," which Hui-chiao gives as Teng's native place. (b) Kucha was a great center of Buddhism, the language and the scholars of which acted as intermediaries between the Chinese and the Buddhist centers of India.[41] (c) Other monks from Kucha

played important roles in Chinese Buddhism, notably Śrīmitra and
Kumārajīva. It is therefore possible that Fo-t'u-teng was a native of
Kucha, though of unknown ancestry, and that he came to Central
China via Tun-huang as a missionary. It is also possible that those
who knew him in China did not know his birthplace but inferred from
the nature and range of his teachings that he had been trained in
Kucha and gave him the royal surname of that country.[42]

3. Surname Shih 濕 or T'a, anciently Śĭəp or T'ap. The *CS*, unlike
the *KSC*, gives India as Teng's native land. An anonymous manuscript
memoir of Fo-t'u-teng 佛圖澄和尚因緣 written on the verso of a
monastery memorandum dated 938 is in the Stein collection at the
British Museum.[43] This states that Teng was a native of "Central India" 中天竺. The *Ming-seng chuan*, the *KSC*, and the *Pi-ch'iu-ni
chuan* all place the prefix *chu*, which usually, but not always, signifies
an Indian origin, before his name. The inscription of 342 given in *SCC*
5.22a–b also has this prefix. This factor is not conclusive because of
the general practice of monks taking their masters' surnames.[44] This
leads, however, to the principal text which supports an Indian origin.
Feng Yen's 封演 *Feng-shih wen-chien chi* 封氏聞見記 (dating from the
eighth century) 8 has a note entitled "Fo-t'u-teng's surname" which
reads as follows:[45]

> To the west of Nei-ch'iu hsien, Hsing-chou 邢州內丘縣 [i.e., the
> modern Shun-te fu, southern Hopei] in the old city of Chung-
> ch'iu 中丘城, in a temple there is a stele which was erected in the
> fifth year of the Kuang-ch'u 光初 era of Shih Lo of the Later Chao
> [322]. The inscription reads, "the ta ho-shang 大和尚[46] Fo-t'u-
> teng was the eldest son of a minor prince of the great Indian coun-
> try of Chi-pin [Kashmir]. His original surname was Shih. The
> reason he was called Shih was that his thought gave order to the
> state and his benevolence pervaded the universe. For that reason
> he was called Shih." Now in the *Kao-seng chuan*, the *Ming-seng
> chuan*, and in the biographies of magicians in the *Chin shu*, there
> is no such surname. For one to say today that his surname is Shih
> would indeed be strange. During the Ta-li 大歷 era [766–80],

when I made inspection tours in the district of Nei-ch'iu, I rested in this temple, read the stele[47] and examined it.

The above text is very corrupt.[48] First of all the date is suspect. The era-name belongs to the Former Chao, Shih Lo's greatest rival. True, Lo in 322 had not yet begun his own era-names and may have had to use that of his rival, but the juxtaposition of the Later Chao ruler and a Former Chao era-name is most unlikely. Second, the use of the title *ta ho-shang* is anachronistic, for, while the stele is said to date from 322, the *KSC* indicates that Teng did not receive that title until after 328. The mention of Chi-pin is a corruption of the text. The *Chin-shih lu* 金石錄, dating from the first half of the twelfth century, reproduces the inscription as follows, with the remark that it agrees entirely with Feng's account:[49] "The t'ai ho-shang Chu Fo-t'u-teng was the eldest son of the prince of a minor vassal state of the great kingdom of India. His original surname was Shih."

Thus the date is doubtful, Chi-pin (though not India) is a textual corruption, and the absurd etymology for the surname given in the present text of the *Feng-shih wen-chien chi* is unlikely to have been part of the inscription. But there is no acceptable variant for the character *shih*, and one must assume that this was in fact given on the stele as Fo-t'u-teng's surname. It has been suggested that this may be a variant for *sai* 塞, used to transliterate Śaka, but this is not possible.[50] The original form of this surname is unknown, and it has thus far been impossible to locate it in one of the Central Asian kingdoms and thereby throw light on Fo-t'u-teng's origins.

Before concluding this introduction, we should note the range of Fo-t'u-teng's travels. He said of himself that he had been to Kashmir and had studied there under famous masters. The *Wei shu* remarks that Fo-t'u-teng was as a youth in Uḍḍiyāna,[51] and it is interesting to note that Hsüan-tsang, several centuries later, says that in Uḍḍiyāna they made a profession and an art of the use of magic spells,[52] in which we know Teng to have been particularly proficient. His knowledge of the Chieh language (see *KSC* 13) implies a previous residence among people speaking a Turkic language. All of these facts suggest that his wide knowledge was gained in the course of extensive travels.

It is difficult at this late date to reconcile the fragmentary data on his origins, but one might tentatively suggest some such hypothesis as the following:

He was born in Kucha, perhaps of Indian parents. While his parents' surname may have been Shih, the country of his origin led Chinese biographers to give him the only surname of that country known to them, Po. He joined the priesthood when very young, traveled through Central Asia for many years, and several times journeyed to Kashmir for special study. Sometime early in the fourth century he decided to do missionary work in China, perhaps paused in Tun-huang to improve his Chinese, and reached Loyang in 310 to begin the career which is recounted in the following pages.

KAO-SENG CHUAN 9.383B–387A[53]

Chu Fo-t'u-teng

1. Chu Fo-t'u-teng was a native of the Western Regions. His secular surname was Po. When young he left lay life. He was pure and true and devoted to study. He knew by heart several million words of sūtras and was good at explaining the meaning of texts. Although he had not yet read the Confucian works and the histories of this country, when he discussed difficult points with scholars, all [his arguments] in a mysterious way fitted [with our Chinese traditions] like the two parts of a tally,[54] and there was no one capable of humbling him [in debate].

2. He said of himself that he had gone twice to Chi-pin (Kashmir) and had there received instruction from famous masters. In the Western Regions, everyone called him the enlightened one.

3. In the fourth year of the Yung-chia 永嘉 era of Huai-ti 懷帝 of the Chin (310), he came to Loyang with the purpose of spreading the Great Teaching. He was proficient at intoning magic spells[55] and could make the spirits his servants. When he took sesame oil,[56] mixed it with rouge,[57] and smeared it on his palm, events more than 1,000 *li* distant were perfectly revealed in his palm as if he were face to face with them. He could also make those who kept the Buddhist regimen

see [events as reflected in his palm].⁵⁸ Moreover, when he heard the sound of bells, he would foretell events therefrom, and [these prophecies] were never once unfulfilled.

4. He wished to establish a temple in Loyang, but when there occurred the sack of Loyang by the invading armies of Liu Yao,⁵⁹ and the imperial capital was in turmoil, Teng's plan to found a temple could not then be realized. He therefore retired to the country and thus watched from afar the political upheaval. At the time Shih Lo encamped his army at Ko-pei⁶⁰ where they devoted themselves entirely to the slaughter [of the people]. The śramaṇas who met death were very numerous. Teng, out of his compassion for the people, wished to bring Lo under the influence of Buddhism. Thereupon, leaning on his priestly staff, he went to the headquarters. Lo's general, Kuo Hei-lüeh 郭黑略,⁶¹ had long honored the Dharma, so Teng went to stay [383c] at Lüeh's house. Lüeh, after accepting from him the Five Commandments, paid Teng the courtesies of a disciple. Afterwards, when on a punitive expedition under Lo, Lüeh always knew beforehand whether [an engagement] would be a victory or a defeat. Lo marveled at this and asked him, "I was not aware that you had such extraordinary discernment, yet you know every time whether a military expedition will be a success or a failure. How is this?" Lüeh replied, "General, your naturally extraordinary military prowess is being aided by supernatural influences. There is a certain śramaṇa whose knowledge of devices is exceptional. He said that you, my general, should conquer China and that he should be your teacher. All the things I have told you on various occasions were his words." Lo was delighted and said, "He is a gift from heaven." He summoned Teng and enquired, "What miraculous efficacy does Buddhism have?"⁶² Teng knew that Lo did not understand profound doctrines and would only be able to regard magic as evidence [of the power of Buddhism]. Accordingly he said, "Though the highest teachings are remote [from the general understanding], we can take nearby things as proof [of the efficacy of Buddhism]." Thereupon he took his begging bowl, filled it with water, burned incense, and said a spell over it. In a moment there sprang up blue lotus flowers whose brightness and color dazzled the eyes. Lo was

convinced by this, and Teng accordingly admonished him, saying, "Now when a king's virtuous influence pervades the universe, the four sacred creatures[63] appear as good omens. When government is corrupt, and the Way is neglected, then comets will appear in the heavens. When heavenly signs manifest themselves, fortune and misfortune come in their wake. This is the constant testimony of ancient and modern times and the clear rule for Heaven and man." Lo was very pleased at this. Of those remaining who were to have been executed, 80 or 90 percent benefited from this [intervention on the part of Fo-t'u-teng]. Thereupon almost all the barbarians and Chinese in Chung-chou 中州 worshiped the Buddha.

5. At this time there was a chronic illness which no one was able to cure. When Teng treated the disease, it was immediately cured. Those whom he secretly treated and who benefited in silence were uncountable.

6. Lo, returning to the north of the Yellow River from Ko-pei, passed through Fang-t'ou.[64] The people of Fang-t'ou planned to raid the camp during the night. Teng said to Hei-lüeh, "In a short time some brigands will arrive. I wanted to let you know." In fact it was as he had said, but since there were precautions taken, [the raid] did no damage.

7. Lo wished to test Teng. At night, putting on his helmet, donning his armor, and seizing his sword, he sat down [in his tent]. He sent a messenger to inform Teng saying, "We don't know where the general has been since nightfall." No sooner had the messenger arrived, and before he had spoken a word, Teng greeted him with the question, "When it is quiet and there are no attackers, why keep the night watch?" Lo honored him the more.

8. Later Lo, in a rage, planned to kill all the devotees, and he also planned to torment Teng. Teng then fled to Hei-lüeh's house and told his disciple, "If the general should send a messenger to ask where I am, answer that you don't know where I have gone." The messenger shortly arrived and searched for Teng in vain. When the messenger returned and reported this to Lo, Lo was frightened and said, "I had evil inten-

tions toward the holy man, and the holy man has abandoned me."
Throughout the night he did not sleep, wanting to see Teng. Teng
knew that Lo was repentant, and the next morning he visited Lo. The
latter said, "Why did you go away last night?" Teng said, "You had
an angry heart; last night, therefore, I deliberately stayed away. Since
you have now changed your attitude, I have dared [384a] to come."
Lo laughed heartily and said, "Monk, you are mistaken."

9. The source of the water for the moats of the city of Hsiang-kuo
was located below the T'uan-wan shrine, five *li* northwest of the
city.[65] This water had suddenly dried up. Lo inquired of Teng, "How
shall I get the water to flow?" Teng replied, "We should now get a
dragon to come." Lo, whose style was Shih-lung 世龍 (Dragon of the
Age), thought Teng was mocking him and replied, "It is precisely because the dragon could not make the water flow that you were asked."
Teng said, "This is a serious statement and not a jest. The source of the
stream certainly has a holy dragon living in it. Now if I go and speak
commandingly, water will surely be obtainable." Then, with a number
of disciples such as Fa-shou 法首,[66] he went up to the source of the
stream. At its source the old stream bed had been dry for a long time
and was cracked so as to look like cart tracks. His followers were
doubtful and afraid that water would be difficult to get. Teng sat down
on a corded bench,[67] burned Parthian incense,[68] chanted an invoca-
tion of several hundred words. When he had done like this for three
days, water seeped out a few drops at a time. There was a small dragon, about five or six inches long, which came out with the water. All
the monks rushed to go and look at it. Teng said, "That dragon is
poisonous. Do not go near it." In a little while the water came in
abundance, and the dry moats were all filled.

10. Teng, sitting at his ease, exclaimed, "Two days hence there will
be a common person who will disturb this neighborhood." Shortly
thereafter it happened that a man of Hsiang-kuo called Hsieh Ho
薛合 [69] had two sons; being both little and mischievous, they teased a
Hsien-pei slave. The slave became angry, took out a knife and slashed
the younger brother to death. He forcibly took the elder brother into
the house and with the knife pointed at the child's heart, [threatened]

that if anyone came into the house he would press the hand [that held the knife]. He said to Ho, "Send me back to my country and I will spare your son's life; otherwise both of us will die here." Everyone was horrified, and all went to watch. Lo then went in person to see this and said to Hsieh Ho, "To free the slave and thereby save your son would truly be a good thing, but if this practice is once known, it will make for trouble later on. If you can allay your paternal feelings, the state will maintain its usual laws [governing such cases]." He (Lo) ordered men to seize the slave. The slave died, having killed the elder son.

11. The Hsien-pei Tuan Po 段波[70] attacked Lo. The former's army was very numerous, and Lo, being frightened, questioned Teng. Teng said, "Yesterday the temple bells chimed, saying, 'Tomorrow at breakfast time they will make Tuan Po a prisoner.'" Lo ascended the city wall and looking out over Po's army, could not see the beginning or end of it. He blanched and said, "When the army moves, the ground tips; how can Po be captured! These are merely words by which [he means] to soothe me." He sent K'uei An 夔安[71] to question Teng again. Teng said, "They have already captured Po." At this time some soldiers in ambush north of the city came out and, meeting Po, captured him. Teng urged Lo to be indulgent toward Po and to send him back to his own country. Lo followed his advice and in the end obtained his (Po's) services.

12. At this time Liu Tsai 劉載 was already dead, and Tsai's younger cousin Yao usurped the false throne [of the Former Chao] and called the new era Kuang-ch'u 光初 (318–28). In the eighth year of Kuang-ch'u (325), Yao sent his younger cousin Yüeh, the false prince of Chung-shan 中山王岳[72] to lead an army in an attack on Lo. Lo sent Shih Hu at the head of the infantry and cavalry to oppose him. There was a great battle to the west of Lo[yang]. Yüeh was defeated and made the Shih-liang-wu[73] his defense. Hu [384b] built a stockade to invest him. At this time, Teng, with his disciples, was proceeding from the Kuan-ssu[74] to the Chung-ssu.[75] No sooner had they entered the gate of the [latter] temple than he exclaimed, "Liu Yüeh is in a pitiable state." The disciple Fa-tso 法祚[76] asked the reason for this [remark].

Teng said, "Yesterday at the hour of the boar 亥時 (9–11 P.M.) Yüeh was captured." In fact it was as he had said.

13. In the eleventh year of Kuang-ch'u (328), Yao himself led an army and attacked Loyang. Lo wanted to go in person to oppose Yao. Among all the officials there was no one who did not strongly admonish him [against this course]. Lo consulted Teng about it.[77] Teng said, "The sound of the bells of the *hsiang-lun*[78] said *Hsiu-chih t'i-li-kang pu-ku ch'u-t'u-tang*. This is Chieh language.[79] *Hsiu-chih* means 'army'; *t'i-li-kang* means 'to go out'; *pu-ku* means 'the barbarian throne of Liu Yao'; *ch'u-t'u-tang* means 'to seize.' These words mean that the army will go forth and capture Yao." At this time Hsü Kuang 徐光[80] understood Teng's interpretation of this and strongly urged Lo to go. Lo then left his eldest son Shih Hung 石弘[81] to govern Hsiang-kuo in cooperation with Teng, and himself led the main army of infantry and cavalry, going directly to the city of Lo[yang]. The two armies had barely made contact when Yao's army was completely routed. Yao's horse sank in the water, and Shih K'an 石堪[82] captured him (Yao) alive and sent him to Lo. Teng, at this time, smeared something on his palm and looked at it. He saw a man being bound in a great crowd and being tied about the elbows with a red silken cord.[83] [Teng] accordingly informed Hung of this. It was at that very hour that they were capturing Yao alive.[84]

14. After the submission of Yao, Lo presumed to call himself T'ien-wang of Chao 趙天王. He performed the imperial functions and changed the era-name to Chien-p'ing 建平 (330–33). This year was the fifth year of the Hsien-ho 咸和 era of the Emperor Ch'eng of the Chin dynasty 晉成帝. Once Lo had ascended the throne, his homage to Teng was still more ardent.

15. At this time Shih Ts'ung 石葱 was about to revolt.[85] The same year Teng warned Lo, "This year there will be insects among the onions. Eating them will certainly be harmful to people. You should order the people not to eat onions." Lo issued a general order that within the borders [the people] should take care not to eat onions. In

the eighth month Shih Ts'ung, in fact, fled. Lo's respect for Teng increased still more. When there was a problem, he invariably consulted [Teng], and only then did he act. He gave Teng the title of ta ho-shang.[86]

16. Shih Hu had a son named Pin 斌. Afterward Lo made him (Pin) his [foster] son[87] and loved him very dearly. He was unexpectedly taken ill and died. When two days had passed, Lo said, "We have heard that when the heir apparent of the state of Kuo 虢 died, Pien Ch'iao 扁鵲[88] was able to bring him to life. The Ta ho-shang is the most extraordinary man in this state. You should go quickly and inform him. He will surely be able to bring about a happy issue." Teng, [upon being informed], then took his toothpick and said a spell over it. In a moment [Pin] was able to get up and in a little while had fully recovered. As a result of this Lo had most of his young sons brought up in a Buddhist temple. On the eighth day of the fourth month of every year, Lo went to the temple, bathed the Buddha, and made a vow on behalf of his foster son.[89]

17. In the fourth month of the fourth year of Chien-p'ing (333), the sky was clear and there was no wind, yet on top of the pagoda a single bell sounded. Teng said to his followers, "The sound of the bell says, 'There will be a great mourning in the state, and it will not be later than this year.'" That year, in the seventh month, Lo died, and his son Hung succeeded to the throne. In a short time Shih Hu dethroned Hung and put himself on the throne. [384c] He moved the capital to Yeh 鄴[90] and named the era Chien-wu 建武 (335–48).

18. Hu's wholehearted esteem for Teng was greater than that of Lo, so he sent down an edict which said, "The Ho-shang is the great jewel of the state; honor and rank he will not accept, and great emoluments he will not receive. Since honors and emoluments are beneath his notice,[91] with what shall we do honor to his virtue? Hereafter and henceforward it is fitting that he be clothed in silk brocade and that he ride in a carved palanquin.[92] On the day of a court levee, when the Ho-shang ascends to the great hall, ministers from the Ch'ang-shih[93]

down are all to help to carry up his palanquin. The crown prince and the nobles are to assist him in ascending. When the chamberlain announces the Ta ho-shang, all those who are seated are to rise to show their reverence." Moreover Hu gave an order that the false Ssu-k'ung, Li Nung 李農,[94] was morning and evening to enquire personally [as to Teng's health], that "the crown prince and the nobles are to pay Teng a visit once every five days as a mark of our reverence for him."[95]

19. Teng at the time was staying in the Chung-ssu[96] within the city of Yeh. He sent his disciple Fa-ch'ang 法常[97] north to Hsiang-kuo. His disciple Fa-tso 法佐[98] was returning from Hsiang-kuo. They met each other and spent the night together outside the walls of Liang-chi.[99] From adjoining carts they conversed during the night, and their talk touched upon the Ho-shang. In the morning they both left. Fa-tso, as soon as he arrived [in Yeh], paid a visit to Teng. Teng received him with a laugh, saying, "Last night did not you and Fa-ch'ang in your adjoining carts discuss your master? The sages of antiquity had a saying, 'Is it not said of respect that in private it does not change; is it not said of caution that when one is alone it does not flag?'[100] Privacy and solitariness are the basis of respect and caution. Do you not understand?" Tso, in his amazement, was both ashamed and repentant. Thereupon the people of the land always said to each other, "Let no one have evil thoughts, for the Ho-shang knows you." Wherever Teng was no one dared to turn in his direction and clear his nose, spit, urinate or defecate.[101]

20. At the time the crown prince, Shih Sui 石邃,[102] had two sons living in Hsiang-kuo. Teng said to Sui, "Little A-mi 阿彌[103] will just have been taken ill. You should go and bring him back." Sui immediately sent a courier to go and look. It turned out that [the child] had already fallen ill. The great doctor Yin T'eng 殷騰[104] and some foreign exorcists said they could cure him. Teng told his disciple Fa-ya 法雅,[105] "Even if they caused a sage to appear once again, he could not cure this disease. How much less these [practitioners]." After three days, [the child] in fact did die.

21. Shih Sui, who had been drinking excessively, was making a plan to revolt. He said to a palace servant, "The Ho-shang, being supernaturally intelligent, will probably lay bare my plot. When he comes tomorrow, I shall get rid of him first of all." Teng, at the full moon, was about to go in to pay Hu a visit. He said to his disciple, Seng-hui 僧慧,[106] "Last night the spirits of heaven called to me, 'If tomorrow you go into [the palace], do not visit anyone.' If there is someone whom I am about to visit, you must stop me." Usually, when Teng went in, he invariably visited Sui. Sui knew that Teng had come into [the palace] and urged him strongly to visit him. Teng was about to go to the Nan-t'ai,[107] when Seng-hui pulled at his robe. Teng said, "This affair cannot be stopped." Before they were comfortably seated, they got up. Sui urged them to stay, but to no avail. In the end his plot [to murder Teng] went wrong. Upon returning to the temple, Teng said with a sigh, "The crown prince is about to revolt, and the shape of [his plans] is almost complete. Though I wish to speak, it is difficult to speak; though I wish to ignore it, it is difficult to ignore it." In the course of discussing other matters, he did however indirectly [385a] give Hu a warning, but Hu, in the end, did not understand it. When presently the affair was discovered, he awoke to the import of Teng's words.

22. Afterward Kuo Hei-lüeh[108] led an army in a punitive expedition against the Ch'iang people in the mountains north of Ch'ang-an, and fell into an ambush of Ch'iang warriors. At this time Teng was sitting at the head of the hall with his disciple, Fa-ch'ang,[109] at his side. Teng, in anguish, blanched and said, "Mr. Kuo is now in danger." He called out, "Let all the monks offer prayers." Moreover Teng himself offered a prayer. After a short time he spoke again, "If he escapes on the southeast, he will survive; if in any other direction, he will be in difficulties." And once again he prayed. After some time, he said, "He has escaped." More than a month afterward Hei-lüeh returned. He himself recounted how they had fallen into an encirclement of the Ch'iang and had fled to the southeast.[110] Just as his horse was exhausted, he encountered an aide who gave up his own horse to him, saying, "You, sir, ride this horse, and I shall ride your horse. Whether

one is saved or not depends on fate." Lüeh took his horse, and for that reason made good his escape. When they compared the day and the hour, it was just at the time that Teng was praying.

23. Shih Hu's son, the false Ta Ssu-ma, Shih Pin, duke of Yen 大司馬燕公石斌, was appointed by Hu as governor of Yu-chou.[111] A band of evil men had collected in Chi, and because of this Shih Pin was indulging in outrageous cruelty. Teng warned Hu, saying, "Last night the spirits of heaven said, 'Quickly round up your horses and return. In the autumn Ch'i 齊 will putrefy.'" Hu did not understand these words, but he immediately gave an order that all localities were to round up their horses and send them back [to him]. This autumn a certain man censured Pin to Hu. Hu summoned Pin and had him whipped three hundred lashes. He killed Ch'i, the mother who bore him (Pin). He flexed a bow, fitted an arrow, and himself supervised the infliction of Pin's punishment. When the punishment [seemed] light, Hu struck him five hundred lashes with his own hand.[112] Teng admonished him, saying, "The feelings should not be unconstrained; the dead cannot be brought to life. The rule is that one should not administer chastisement in person, which would thereby violate [the principle of parental] mercy. How can it be that the emperor with his own hands carries out a punishment?" Hu then ceased.

24. Afterward a Chin army advanced to the Huai and the Ssu. The walled cities of Lung, Pi, and Fan were all raided.[113] The three localities informed [Hu] of their distress. The people felt uneasy. Hu then said with an angry look, "I worship the Buddha and contribute to the monks; in spite of this I still draw foreign invaders. Buddha has no divine power!" Teng early the next morning went into [the palace]. Hu questioned Teng about the affair. Teng accordingly admonished him, saying, "Your Majesty, in ages past, was born as a great merchant. Coming to a temple in Chi-pin (Kashmir), he once provided for a great congregation [of monks]; in it were sixty arhats. I, my humble self, also took part in this meeting. At this time a man who had attained arhatship said to me, 'This merchant, when his life is ended, will take the body of a chicken, and after that he will be king of the

land of Chin.' Now that you have become king, is that not a blessing? Armed raids on its border regions are usual for a state. Why revile the Three Treasures (*triratna*) and allow evil thoughts to arise in the night?" Hu then believed and understood, knelt and gave thanks to him.[114]

25. Hu once asked Teng, "Buddha's teaching is against the taking of life. I am the head of the empire, and without capital punishment, there is no means of keeping the country quiet. I have already violated the vows in putting living beings to death. Even though I still worship the Buddha, how shall I obtain blessings?" Teng said, (385b] "Worship of the Buddha on the part of emperors and kings lies in their being reverent in their persons and obedient in their hearts and in glorifying the Three Treasures. [It lies in] not making cruel oppressions and not killing the innocent. As to the rogues and irresponsibles whom the civilizing influence does not reform, when they are guilty of a crime, they must be put to death, and if they are guilty of an evil deed, they must be punished. You should execute only those who should be executed and punish only those who should be punished. If, cruelly and willfully, you put the innocent to death, then, even if you should pour out your wealth and devote yourself to the Dharma, there will be no escaping a bad end. I wish that the emperor might eliminate desire and cultivate compassion. If [your compassion] is broad and all pervading, then Buddhism will long prosper, and your good fortune will be prolonged." Although Hu was unable to comply entirely with this admonition, still benefits from it were not few.[115]

26. Hu's shang-shu 尙書, Chang Liang 張艮 and Chang Li 張離,[116] were wealthy and worshiped Buddha; each erected a large pagoda. Teng said to them, "Worshiping the Buddha lies in pure tranquility and desirelessness and in making [works of] mercy your chief concern. Although you almsgivers pay ceremonial honor to the Great Teaching, nevertheless your covetousness is insatiable and your indulgence in hunting is without limit. Your accumulations of wealth are inexhaustible. You are precisely the sort who should receive punishment in this world, so how do you expect a happy reward [in the next life]?" Li and others were afterward all put to death.

27. At this time there was again a prolonged drought; it lasted from the first month to the sixth month. Hu sent the crown prince[117] to Fu-k'ou, west of Lin-chang, to pray for rain.[118] After a long time there was still no rainfall. Hu ordered Teng himself to go. Straightway two white dragons descended on the place of worship, and on this very day there was a heavy rain over an area several thousand *li* square, and that year there was a great harvest.

28. The Jung 戎 and Mo 貊 peoples at first did not know about the Dharma. When they heard of Teng's supernatural effects, they all, from a distance, turned toward him and worshiped, and, without words, they were transformed by him.

29. Teng once sent a disciple to the Western Regions to buy incense. When he had already gone, Teng informed the rest of his disciples, saying, "In my palm I see that the incense-buying disciple is in a certain place and at the point of death at the hands of brigands." Accordingly he burned incense and said prayers that he might save him from afar. The disciple afterward returned and said, "On such and such a day of such and such a month in such and such a place I was attacked by brigands. When I was about to be killed, I suddenly smelled the fragrance of incense. The brigands for no [apparent] reason were frightened and said, 'Rescuing troops have arrived,' and they left me and fled."

30. Hu was repairing an old pagoda in Lin-chang but lacked dew dishes.[119] Teng said, "In the city of Lin-tzu[120] there is an old stupa of King Aśoka. In the earth there are dew dishes and a Buddha image. Above this site trees grow luxuriantly. You might excavate and get them out." He immediately drew a plan and gave it to a messenger. They excavated according to what he had said, and did in fact get the dishes and the image.

31. Hu often wanted to attack Yen. Teng admonished him, "The allotted span of the Yen state has not yet come to a close. In the end it will be difficult to succeed in conquering it." Hu attacked many times and was defeated. Hu then believed Teng's warning.[121]

32. When Teng's program for bringing [the people] under the influence of Buddhism had been put into effect, many people worshiped Buddha; in every case they built temples and shrines or rushed to leave lay life. The true and the false were confused, and this gave rise to much misconduct. Hu issued an edict asking the opinions of the secretaries [*chung-shu*] 中書, saying, "The Buddha is called the world-honored one and is worshiped by the ruler. As for the lesser people of the villages [385c] and those without official rank, whether they should be allowed to worship the Buddha or not [is the question]. Moreover the śramaṇas should all be of the highest integrity and uprightness; their capabilities should be of the best. Only after that can they become proper devotees. At present the śramaṇas are very numerous. Some are troublemakers and avoid their state service. Many are not such men [as to meet the qualifications We have outlined above]. You may examine the matter and advise as to [the distinctions to be made between] the true and the false." The *chung-shu chu-tso-lang*, Wang Tu 王度,[122] submitted a memorial saying, "That kings make the suburban sacrifices to Heaven and Earth and worship the myriad deities is recorded in the canons of sacrifice. The *Book of Rites* contains the regular sacrifices. Buddha, having been born in the Western Regions, is a foreign god. His merit does not help the people, and he is not one whom the emperor and the Chinese should sacrificially worship. Formerly when [the emperor] Ming of the Han 漢明 had his dream and they first passed on this teaching, they only permitted men of the Western Regions to build temples in the capitals wherein to worship their god.[123] No Chinese of this period were permitted to leave lay life. Wei 魏 adopted the Han regulations and followed the precedent. Now the Great Chao has received the mandate and follows the ancient statutes. Institutions for Chinese and barbarians differ, and the spheres of men and of gods are different [among them]. What is alien differs from what is native, and sacrifices are different in ceremonial procedure [among them]. As to the clothing and ritual of the Chinese, it is not proper to intermingle them [with foreignisms]. The ruler should decide to forbid the people of Chao from going to temples, burning incense and worshiping, and thereby he will conform to the ancient laws. From the lords and ministers down to the lowest

classes, forbid them all by law. If there be those who transgress [this prohibition], let them be meted out the same punishment as those guilty of unauthorized worship. As for those men of Chao who have become śramaṇas, let them return and follow the occupations of the four classes of civilians." The chung-shu ling, Wang Po 王波,[124] agreed with what Tu had memorialized. Hu issued an edict, saying, "Tu's argument is that Buddha is a deity of foreign lands and is not one whom it is proper for the emperor and the Chinese to worship. We were born out of the marches, and though We are unworthy, We have complied with our appointed destiny and govern the Chinese as their prince. As to sacrifices, we should follow our own customs, equally [with those of the Chinese]. Buddha being a barbarian god is the very one we should worship. Now regulations are carried into effect from above and for long ages serve as precepts [for posterity]. If a thing be truly without fault, why keep narrowly to the rules of former times? As for the I 夷, the Chao, and the myriad barbarians,[125] if there are those who abandon their unauthorized worship and take pleasure in worshipping Buddha, We hereby permit all of them to become adherents."[126] Thereupon the people who were lax in keeping the precepts were encouraged by this.

33. In the Yellow River for a long time there had been no seagoing tortoises. Unexpectedly someone caught one and sent it to Hu as a present. Teng saw it and exclaimed, "Huan Wen's 桓溫 invasion of the Yellow River [region] is not far off."[127] Huan Wen's style was Yüan-tzu.[128] Afterward it was in fact as he had said.

34. At the time in Wei-hsien[129] there was a wanderer. No one knew who his family were. He always wore a hempen tunic and a cloth skirt. He begged in the Wei-hsien market, and the people of the time called him "Hemp Tunic." His speech was extraordinary, and he looked like a madman. He begged and got cereals, [yet] did not eat them but always scattered them on the highroad, saying, "Feed the heavenly horse."[130] Chi Pa 籍拔, the prefect of Chao-hsing,[131] seized him and sent him to Hu. Before this Teng had said to Hu, "Two hundred li to the east of the capital, on a certain day of a certain month, they will send you an extraordinary man. Do not put him to death."

At the appointed time, in fact, [386a] he did arrive. When Hu talked with him, there were no strange words whatever, except for the statement, "The emperor will end up at the foot of a one-pillared palace."[132] Hu did not understand these words and ordered him to be sent to Teng. Hemp Tunic said to Teng, "Long ago, during the Kuang-ho 光和 era (A.D. 178–84), we met. In due course, coming to the present day, the Hsi Jung[133] have received the mandate of Heaven. There is a time for all successions to end. The metal will be scattered, dissipated over the earth.[134] The frontier peoples are not to be followed, for they will destroy the traces of the goodly period,[135] without the merit of [knowing how to] stop. Yet their descendants, numerous as leaves, will in the future accumulate. The time of rest will be in what period? Long shall we rejoice at its arrival."[136] Teng said, "The heavens revolve and mandates end; evil will not endure. Nine-trees-water[137] will make trouble, and there will be no pacifying it by artifice. Even if saints remain in the world, there will be no one able to support that which must fall.[138] For a long time we have wandered about this world. It is tumultuous, and there is much of this kind of calamity. Soon we shall ascend to the higher world and shall meet in the region of the eternal." Teng discoursed with Hemp Tunic to the end of the day; there was no one able to understand. There were some people who secretly listened, but they only got these few words. In pondering [this dialogue] it seems as if they were discussing events of several hundred years [past and future]. Hu sent a post-horse to return [Hemp Tunic] to his own district (i.e., Wei-hsien). When he got outside the city walls, he refused the horse, [saying that he] was able to go on foot. He said, "I have other places to visit. It is not convenient for me to start yet. When you reach Ho-k'ou bridge,[139] you might stop and wait for me." The messenger went rapidly away as he was told. Before he reached Ho-k'ou, Hemp Tunic was already on the bridge. The way he traveled on foot was like flying.[140]

35. Teng had a disciple, Tao-chin 道進.[141] His learning comprehended both Buddhist and non-Buddhist [subjects], and he was highly esteemed by Hu. Once their talk touched upon the subject of hermits. Hu said to Chin, "There is a certain Yang K'o 楊軻;[142] he is one of our subjects. We have summoned him for more than ten years, with-

out his heeding the royal commands. We therefore went personally to pay our respects, and he, most disrespectfully, was lying down. Even though We are not virtuous, still We govern the myriad kingdoms. Whither our chariot turns, the heavens are in turmoil, and the earth gushes forth water. Though We cannot make the trees and stones bow down, how is it that a mere commoner persists in his arrogance? Long ago when T'ai-kung 太公 went to Ch'i, he first of all punished Hua Shih 華士 with death.[143] T'ai-kung was a sage. Was he in error this time?" Chin replied, "Of old Shun 舜 treated P'u I 蒲衣 liberally.[144] Yü 禹 visited Po Ch'eng 伯成,[145] [Lord Wen of] Wei saluted Kan-mu 干木.[146] [Kuang-wu ti of the] Han praised Chou Tang 周黨.[147] Kuan Ning 管寧 did not obey the Ts'ao 曹 family.[148] The Huang-fu 皇甫 did not submit to the Chin dynasty.[149] As for the two sages and the four monarchs, they all rewarded the purity of these men, because they wished to encourage emulation and thereby exalt chaste behavior. I wish that your majesty would follow the virtuous [example] of Shun and Yü and not imitate T'ai-kung's use of punishment. Whenever a prince acts, it will surely be written down. Is it desirable to make it so that the record of the house of Chao will have no biographies of hermits?" Hu was pleased with these words and straightway had K'o returned to his home. He ordered ten households to provide for his needs. Chin returned and told Teng all about this. Teng smiled and said with a laugh, "Your words were appropriate, but in K'o's fate there is that which is contingent upon [other factors]." Afterward in Ch'in-chou there was an armed uprising.[150] One of K'o's disciples led an ox, bearing K'o on its back, and fled westward [386b]. The rebel troops pursued and captured them, and both were put to death.

36. Hu was once taking a nap and saw in a dream a herd of sheep carrying fish on their backs, coming from the northeast. When he woke up he asked Teng about it. Teng said, "It is not a good omen. The Hsien-pei shall have the central plain!"[151] The Mu-jung family later did make their capital there.

37. Teng once ascended the Chung-t'ai with Hu.[152] Teng suddenly started and said, "Calamity! Calamity! In Yu-chou there will be a

conflagration."[153] He accordingly took some wine and sprinkled it. After a considerable time, he laughed and said, "A rescue has been effected." Hu sent a messenger to verify this, and [the report from] Yu-chou said, "On that day fires broke out from the four gates. On the southwest were black clouds rolling up, and a sudden shower extinguished them. Also the rain had somewhat the aroma of wine."

38. In the seventh month of the fourteenth year of Hu's Chien-wu era (348), Shih Hsüan 石宣 and Shih T'ao 石韜 were making plans to kill each other.[154] Hsüan at the time came to the temple and sat with Teng. On the pagoda a single bell chimed. Teng said to Hsüan, "Do you understand the sound of the bell? The bell says, 'The barbarian's sons will fall from grace.'" Hsüan blanched and said, "What does this mean?" Teng lied and said, "I (the old barbarian)[155] as a religious man am unable to dwell apart and keep silent. As for thick matting and fine clothes, are they not [evidence of] my fall from grace?" Later Shih T'ao came. Teng looked at him attentively for a long time. T'ao was frightened and questioned Teng. Teng said, "I am wondering at the smell of blood on you; that is the reason I have been watching you." In the eighth month (of 348) Teng ordered ten of his disciples to go into retreat in a separate apartment. Teng suddenly entered the Eastern Palace.[156] Hu and the empress Tu 杜[157] questioned Teng. Teng said, "There are rebels near you, and [the outbreak of rebellion] is no more than ten days away. From the pagoda to the west and from this palace to the east, there will be streams of blood. Take care not to go to the east." The empress Tu said, "The Ho-shang is senile. Where are there any rebels?" Teng then changed his manner of speaking and said, "The experience of my six sense organs is of nothing but rebels.[158] An old man is naturally subject to senile decay; but I [seek to] make the young not muddle-headed." He then used a metaphor without further explaining the point [of his remarks]. Two days afterward Hsüan in fact sent a man to kill T'ao in a Buddhist temple. He planned to take advantage of Hu's participation in the mourning [for T'ao] to carry out his great revolt. Hu, because of Teng's previous warning, made good his escape. When Hsüan's activities came to light he was taken prisoner. Teng admonished Hu, "He is still your majes-

ty's son, so why add to your woes [by executing him]? If your majesty will restrain his anger and be merciful, you will still have [a life of] more than sixty years. If you insist on putting him to death, Hsüan will become a comet, and falling, will sweep away the palaces of Yeh." He did not follow this advice. He took an iron chain, ran it through Hsüan's cheeks, led him up to a pyre and burned him alive. He gathered up his (Hsüan's) official subordinates, more than three hundred of them,[159] had them all quartered by chariots and had their [remains] thrown into the Chang River.[160] Teng then ordered his disciples to cease their retreat in a separate apartment. A little more than a month later there was a monstrous horse. Its mane and tail both had a burnt appearance. It came in the Chung-yang gate[161] and went out the Hsien-yang gate.[162] It headed east to the Eastern Palace,[163] but could nowhere gain [386c] entrance. It fled toward the northeast and suddenly disappeared. Teng heard about this and exclaimed, "A disaster is imminent."

39. In the eleventh month Hu gave a great feast for the ministers in the T'ai-wu ch'ien-tien.[164] Teng chanted, "Oh the palace, oh the palace! Thorny bushes will become a forest and will spoil men's clothes."[165] Hu ordered them to raise the paving stones of the palace and looked under them, and there were thorny bushes growing there. Teng returned to the temple and, looking at the Buddha image, said, "What a pity you will not be given adornment." He said to himself, "Will there be three years [more]?" and he himself replied, "There won't be, there won't be." Moreover he said, "Will there be two years, one year, a hundred days, a month?" He answered himself, "There won't be." Then, without further speech, he returned to his room and spoke to his disciple Fa-tso 法祚,[166] saying, "In the wu-shen 戊申 year (348) terrible disorders will begin to break out. In the chi-yu 己酉 year (349) the Shih family will perish. While there are still no disturbances, I shall first conform to the order of nature." He straightway sent a man to take leave of Hu, saying, "It is the nature of things inevitably to change; bodily life is not to be preserved. Mine[167] is an ephemeral body, and the time of change has come. Your kindness to me has been very great, and therefore I am informing you of this in

advance." Hu sadly said, "I did not know that the Ho-shang was ill, and he suddenly announces his death." He immediately left the palace, went to the temple and remonstrated with him. Teng said to Hu, "To leave life and enter death is the constant principle of the Way. Whether a man's life be long or short is determined, and it cannot be prolonged. Now the Way is to emphasize perfect conduct, while Virtue is to exalt tirelessness. If one has fulfilled his obligations without fault, then, though he dies, it is as if he lived. To depart from this and prolong [my life] is not my wish. As for those ideals which have not been fully realized: whereas the ruler has preserved Buddhist principles in his heart, has accepted the Dharma without reservations, and, in building temples and shrines has displayed magnificence, and one may call this Virtue, and he should [therefore] enjoy good fortune, but, when government is tyrannical, and extreme punishments are too viciously [meted out], it is outwardly a violation of the code of the sages and inwardly a contradiction of the precepts of Buddhism. If he does not himself stop and reform [all this], in the end there will be no good fortune. If you compose your mind, change your preoccupations, and treat your subjects kindly, then the prosperity of the state will be prolonged, and the clergy and laity will be happy to depend on you, and when, at last, my life shall end, I will die without regrets." Hu cried out in grief, and, knowing that he (Teng) would surely die, at once gave orders that a sepulcher be hewn out for him. On the eighth day of the twelfth month he died in the Palace Temple in Yeh.[168] This year was the fourth year of the Yung-ho 永和 era of the emperor Mu 穆 of the Chin. The officials and common people were grieved and loudly lamented him. The rush [to mourn him] shook the country. He was 117 years old. They then interred him at Tzu-mo, west of Linchang.[169] It was the tomb which Hu had built.

40. Shortly thereafter Liang Tu 梁犢 rebelled,[170] and the next year Hu died. Jan Min continued the slaughter, and the Shih line was totally extinguished.[171] Min's childhood appellation was Chi-nu. This was what Teng had meant when he previously said that the thorny bushes would become a forest.[172]

41. On the left side of Teng's breast in front there was a hole four or five inches round. It connected with the inside of his abdomen. Sometimes his intestines came out from inside, and sometimes he stopped up the hole with silk waste.[173] If in the night he wanted to read a book, he always removed the silk waste, and then the whole room was thoroughly lighted. [387a] Moreover on fast days he always went to the bank of a stream, took out his intestines and washed them and put them back inside.[174] Teng was eight [Chinese] feet tall;[175] his demeanor was refined. He had a subtle understanding of profound sūtras and besides could comprehend secular writings. On the day of a lecture, he simply laid bare the principles, making the whole text clearly understandable. Moreover his compassion was extended to all living creatures and saved them from danger and suffering. The two Shih (i.e., Lo and Hu) were brutal, and their oppression [of the people] was [utterly] unprincipled. If they had not been contemporaries of Teng, who could say [how much worse it might have been]? But the people were benefited, and though daily profiting [from his influence] were not aware of it. Fo-t'iao,[176] Hsü-p'u-t'i 須菩提,[177] and others, to the number of several tens of famous monks, came from India and Sogdiana. They did not consider the journey of tens of thousands of li too long; trekking across the deserts, they came to Teng and received instruction. Shih Tao-an of Fan-mien,[178] Chu Fa-ya of Chung-shan[179] both crossed the passes and the rivers to listen to Teng's discourses. All of them thoroughly understood the basic principles and comprehended the subtleties.

42. Teng said of himself that his birthplace was more than ninety thousand li from Yeh, that, since leaving lay life and entering upon a religious career, 109 years had passed, that wine had not passed his teeth, that he had not eaten after noon, that he had never acted without reference to his vows, that he was desireless and unseeking.

43. Those who received instruction and followed him about always numbered several hundred. His disciples all told were nearly ten thousand. In the provinces 州 and prefectures 郡 through which he passed, he erected Buddhist temples to the number of 893.[180] Such a

flourishing condition of the propagation of Buddhism was unprecedented.

44. When Hu first dressed Teng's body for burial, he took his priestly staff and alms bowl which [Teng had used] when alive and put them into the coffin. Afterward, when Jan Min usurped the throne, he opened the coffin but found only the alms bowl and staff and did not see the corpse.[181] Some say that in the month of Teng's death, someone saw him in the desert. Hu, suspecting that he was not dead, opened the coffin but did not find a corpse.[182]

45. Afterward Mu-jung Chün 慕容儁[183] made his capital at Yeh and lived in Shih Hu's palace. He often saw in a dream a tiger gnawing his arms. This meant that Shih Hu was a malevolent ghost. He then organized a group to hunt for Hu's corpse. In the Tung-ming kuan[184] they excavated and found it. The corpse had not yet decomposed. Chün kicked it and cursed it saying, "Oh dead barbarian, how dare you frighten the living emperor. You built the palaces to perfection, but you were plotted against by your own son. How much the more should others [mistreat you]!" He whipped, trampled, and dishonored the corpse and threw it into the Chang River. The corpse came up against a support of a bridge and did not move on. General Wang Meng 王猛[185] of the Ch'in 秦 took it out and buried it. This was what Hemp Tunic had meant by a "one-pillared palace."[186] Afterward Fu Chien 符堅[187] attacked Yeh; Chün's son, Wei 暐,[188] was captured by Chien's general, Kuo Shen-hu 郭神虎.[189] This was in fact the fulfillment of his former tiger dream.[190]

46. T'ien Jung's 田融 *Chao-chi* 趙記[191] says, "Several years before his death Teng himself built his tomb." Now since Teng knew beforehand that the tomb would surely be opened and that the corpse would not be inside it, why should he have prepared it beforehand? Perhaps it is an error of Jung's. Teng was also called Fo-t'u-teng 磴, Fo-t'u-teng 橙, and Fo-t'u-teng 蹬; all are variants of the Sanskrit sound.

The critical estimate [*lun*] 論 (at the end of the section on miracle workers, *KSC* 10.395a) says:

Earlier [Liu] Yüan and [Liu] Yao were usurpatious and oppressive. Later [Shih] Lo and [Shih] Hu were usurpatious and cruel. The whole country was divided and in a state of collapse, while the people were afflicted with misery and misfortune. The noble Teng deplored the outbreak of warfare and grieved at the unending punishments and murder. Consequently he manifested his supernatural powers at Ko-pei and displayed [his skill at] foretelling the future[192] in Hsiang [-kuo] and Yeh. Using secret spells, he saved those on the point of death; using the fragrance of incense, he rescued those on the verge of disaster. Contemplating [the sound of] bells and producing reflections in his palm, he easily determined good and evil portents. In the end he caused the two Shih [rulers] to pay him homage, the barbarians to come to him like sons. There is indeed no way of estimating the benefits he conferred on the masses.

APPENDIX

The derivation of the *Chin shu* 95 biography of Fo-t'u-teng

CS paragraph	Chin-shu chiao-chu	T'ung-wen CS, 1894	Derivation
1	24b1–25a3	19a4–19a10	*KSC* 1,3,4,41,42
2	25a5–25b5	19a10–19b6	abridged from *KSC* 4
3	25b5–25b7	19b6–19b8	*KSC* 6
4	25b7–25b9	19b8–20a1	*KSC* 7
5	25b10–26a6	20a1–20a6	*KSC* 8
6	26a6–26b1	20a6–20b1	abridged from *KSC* 9
7	26b7–27a2	20b1–20b5	*KSC* 11
8	27a2–27a6	20b5–20b8	abridged from *KSC* 12
9	27a6–27b9	20b8–21a5	*KSC* 13; the last 2 sentences from *KSC* 14
10	27b9–28a2	21a6–21a8	*KSC* 15
11	28a2–28a6	21a8–21b2	abridged from *KSC* 16
12	28a6–28a8	21b2–21b4	abridged from *KSC* 17
13	28a8–28b4	21b4–21b8	abridged from *KSC* 18
14	28b4–28b5	21b8–21b9	*Shih-shuo hsin-yü* 1A, 19 (see note 95)
15	28b5–29b1	21b9–22a8	much abridged from *KSC* 32
16	29b1–30a1	22a8–22b3	except for the second sentence, abridged from *KSC* 19
17	30a1–30a5	22b3–22b6	*KSC* 20
18	30a5–30b2	22b6–23a3	*KSC* 21
19	30b2–30b9	23a3–23a9	*KSC* 22
20	30b9–31a1	23a10–23b2	abridged from *KSC* 27
21	31a3–31a6	23b2–23b5	*KSC* 29
22	31a6–31a8	23b5–23b7	*KSC* 33
23	31a8–31a10	23b7–23b9	slightly abridged from *KSC* 26
24	31a10–31b3	23b9–24a2	*KSC* 37
25	31b3–32a10	24a2–24b7	abridged from *KSC* 28; the dream and its interpretation from *SLKCC*. Cf. *TPYL* 120.6b
26	32a10–32b2	24b8–24b10	first part of *KSC* 39
27	32b2–32b5	24b10–25a3	*Yu-ming lu* or *Yeh-chung chi*. See note 164
28	32b9–33a2	25a3–25a6	much abridged from *KSC* 29
29	33a5–33a10	25a6–25a8	from Shih Hu's biography in original *SLKCC*. Cf. *TPYL* 120.7a, 697.2b

3

BIOGRAPHY OF THE NUN

AN-LING-SHOU 安令首

The following biography is translated from the *Pi-ch'iu-ni chuan* (Lives of the Nuns) by the monk Pao-ch'ang 寶唱.[1] An-ling-shou's is the second biography in the first *chüan* of that collection.

The historical setting of this biography has been sketched in my study of Fo-t'u-teng (died 349).[2] An-ling-shou is, indeed, the only nun whose "ordination" is recorded as having been performed by Fo-t'u-teng, during his long career as a missionary.[3]

The principal historical interest of this short account is its vivid statement of the conflict between Chinese social morality and the ethics of Buddhism. The girl's first reply to her father's objections to the clerical life contains a formula for the resolution of that conflict

Reprinted by permission from the *Harvard Journal of Asiatic Studies* 15, nos. 1, 2 (June 1952): 193–96. The Editor expresses his appreciation to the editors of the Journal.

which one finds on many votive inscriptions of the fifth and sixth centuries: "this act of piety is performed for the salvation of all living beings, especially our parents, grandparents, etc."⁴

The judicious appeal to the authority of the Chinese Classics to win a point for Buddhism was a technique which went back to the beginnings of Chinese apologetics in the *Mou-tzu*. According to his biographer, Fo-t'u-teng was skilled in this device, and one suspects that he may have coached his young convert in its use against her father. The great missionary's suggestion that the father's consent would bring "wealth and honor" is but another example of the varied tactics which the monk's strong position at court enabled him to use in the interests of his religion.

Finally, how authentic is this account? This raises the larger question of the historical accuracy of Chinese Buddhist hagiography. Here it might be said that, in general, Chinese hagiographers adopted the methods and some of the standards of Chinese historians. Pao-ch'ang's preface sounds like an echo of Ssu-ma Ch'ien's preface to the *Shih-chi* when he says, "I began by making a catholic collection of stone inscriptions and eulogies and collecting on a wide scale records and collectanea [—all concerned with nuns]. I questioned those with broad knowledge about them and queried old people concerning them. Having selected and classified [these materials] from beginning to end, I wrote biographies of them."⁵

His purpose was to immortalize exemplary Buddhists, just as secular historians sought to preserve the virtuous deeds of statesmen and princes. The collected materials were edited and woven into continuous narratives, but the hagiographer, like the secular historian, seldom intruded himself. Pao-ch'ang, unlike his junior contemporary Hui-chiao, author of the *Kao-seng chuan*, did not list the earlier works on which he drew. We can only guess that the material included in this and the other biographies met the rather naive standards of authenticity recognized by Chinese historians and hagiographers alike.

TRANSLATION OF THE BIOGRAPHY OF THE NUN
AN-LING-SHOU OF THE CHIEN-HSIEN TEMPLE,[6] WHO
LIVED UNDER THE ILLEGITIMATE CHAO DYNASTY

An-ling-shou's secular surname was Hsü. She was a native of Tung-kuan.[7] Her father [Hsü] Ch'ung served the illegitimate Chao dynasty as *Wai-ping-lang*.[8] Ling-shou, when young, was intelligent and fond of study. Her discourse was clear and elegant, and her gentle nature was of limpid purity. She did not take pleasure in worldly affairs but was predisposed to quietism. She occupied herself with Buddhist teachings and did not wish [her family] to seek a marital engagement for her. Her father said, "You should marry. How is it that you behave like this?" Shou said, "I take work for religion to be my basic propensity; I take spiritual matters to be the exclusive [object of my] thought. Blame or praise will not move me, for purity and uprightness are their own reward. Why must I thrice submit and only then be regarded as [a person of] propriety?"[9] Her father said, "You wish to do good for yourself alone. How can you at the same time help your parents?" Shou said, "When I establish myself in life and walk the path of religion, I want to bring salvation to all. How much more to my parents!"[10]

Her father asked Fo-t'u-teng about it. Teng said, "You return home and keep to maigre fare; at the end of three days you may come [to me again]." Ch'ung agreed to this. [When he returned] Teng ground sesame oil with safflower and spread it on Ch'ung's right palm.[11] When he ordered Ch'ung to look at it, the latter saw a śramaṇa in the midst of a large gathering, preaching the dharma. In appearance [this śramaṇa] resembled a woman. When he told Teng all about this, Teng said, "This is a former incarnation of your daughter; leaving lay life, helping living creatures—her past deeds were of this sort. If you consent to her [present] plan, she will raise her relatives to glory and bring you wealth and honor. As to the great sea of suffering of births and deaths, she will direct you toward attaining its farther shore."[12] Ch'ung returned home and permitted her [to become a nun].

Shou then cut off her hair and received the vows from Teng and the nun Ching-chien.[13] She built the Chien-hsien temple. Teng took a flower-embroidered vestment,[14] a seven-striped inner vestment,[15] a vestment tie,[16] and a water pitcher[17] which had been given him by Shih Lo and gave them to her.

She read widely in all sorts of books, and having once seen a book she invariably knew it by heart. Her thought penetrated the deepest profundities, and her spirit illumined the subtle and the remote. In the religious communities there were none who did not revere her. Those who left lay life on account of her numbered more than two hundred. Moreover she built five or six monasteries (or nunneries). She had no fear of hard work and brought them all to completion. Shih Hu paid her honor and promoted her father Ch'ung to be *Huang-men shih-lang*[18] and prefect of Ch'ing-ho.[19]

4

BIOGRAPHY AND

HAGIOGRAPHY

Hui-chiao's Lives of Eminent Monks

PART I: INTRODUCTION*

The *Kao-seng chuan*, Lives of Eminent Monks, written in the first half of the sixth century by the monk Hui-chiao, has long been of interest to scholars of China everywhere. Viewed as literature it is a masterpiece of Six Dynasties prose. When used as a historical source, it is a

Reprinted by permission from the *Silver Jubilee Volume of the Jimbun-Kagaku-Kenkyusho* (1954).
* This study was begun at the Tōhō Bunka Kenkyūjo in 1940–41 and was completed there on a second visit, under a Guggenheim grant, in 1954. I am deeply grateful to all the members of the Institute who have given generously of their learning and advice, particularly to Professors Tsukamoto Zenryū and Yoshikawa Kōjirō. I am also indebted to Mr. Achilles Fang, who read and corrected my draft translations many years ago. These scholars must share the credit for whatever value the present study may have, while the mistakes and shortcomings are the author's alone.

vital record of the great figures in the history of the first five centuries of Chinese Buddhism and a valuable corrective to secular histories of the period A.D. 67–519. Seen as hagiography, it reveals the developing norms of Chinese clerical behavior and the growth of new standards—alien in origin—for evaluating men's actions. It is rich in the lore and traditions of the Chinese Buddhist church, a record of developments in ritual, literature, and the arts. Moreover it established the form and style for the major series of Chinese clerical biographies which have been continued down to recent times.

For many decades Western scholars have drawn on this rich and important source. They have translated a few of its biographies and have used the data it provides on a variety of subjects.[1] But the translations and citations have generally been accompanied by the briefest of bibliographic notices, and no attempt has been made to subject the *Kao-seng chuan* as a whole to critical examination. In view of the interest and usefulness of the book, I propose to attempt such a study here.

In the introduction I shall deal with those general features of the work which are of interest to modern scholarship: the author's motivation, his methods of work and critical standards, the derivation of his formal organization, his attitudes and prejudices. In a sense the introduction is a summing up and an interpretation of the findings presented in the sections which follow it. Part 2 is devoted to the life of Hui-chiao in an effort to discern something of his time and milieu. Part 3 is a translation of Hui-chiao's preface in which he tells us a good deal about his sources, his methods, and his aims. The final section is a study of the sources he used and the ways in which he used them.

Motivation

Hui-chiao undertook the long and arduous task of compiling the biographies of eminent monks with a variety of motives. Some of these are explicit in his preface; others may be inferred from his biography and from the *Kao-seng chuan* itself. In the preface he expressed his dissatisfaction with the treatment of monks' lives in non-Buddhist writings. He felt that in such works their biographies were often omitted or subordinated when the subjects were of major importance in the general history of the period.[2] If he was dissatisfied with secular accounts, he was also highly critical of previous attempts at clerical biographies. The most comprehensive earlier work was the object of an anonymous but biting attack.[3] The defects of earlier works which moved him to write his own were, in general, these: they lacked breadth and scope; they were poor in organization and style; they used imperfect standards for the inclusion and exclusion of material; they were uncritical in their allocation of praise and blame. These manifold dissatisfactions are in a sense the negative motivation for the writing of the *Kao-seng chuan* and an indication of the standards he set himself.

In positive terms, Hui-chiao's dominant motive was his Buddhist piety. For him, in the words of his preface, "other religions are to Buddhism like the myriad rivers making their way to the sea, like the galaxies of stars turning toward the pole star." It seemed to him that those who had made striking contributions to the introduction and spread of his faith deserved, like other great figures of China's past, to be commemorated in a collection of reliable and well-written biographies. In his own words, "I reflect that the Dharma depends upon men for its dissemination, that principles depend upon teaching for their manifestation. In propagating the Dharma and explaining the teachings, none excel the eminent monks. Therefore, from its inception, they have illumined the Dharma bequeathed by Buddha. Since their extraordinary merit and wonderful accomplishments have flourished throughout the ages and provide an inspiration to posterity, it is reasonable and proper to write a comprehensive and connected account of them."[4] To the extent that he conceived and wrote the lives of the monks within the conventions of Chinese historiography, he was a biographer. To the degree that his biographies sought to demonstrate the rewards of piety and faith, the working of Buddhism's universal laws in the lives of eminent monks, he was a hagiographer. It is this ambivalence of purpose which has suggested the title of the present paper.

In the following discussion of the methodology, the style, and the organization of the *Kao-seng chuan* it will be apparent not only that Hui-chiao was steeped in Chinese historiographical traditions but also that he consciously sought to write a work within that tradition, one that would meet the prevailing standards for secular literary and historical writing. I venture to suggest that his adoption of the conventions of an established genre of Chinese literature was motivated by a desire—conscious or unconscious—to rescue Buddhist biography from the limbo of the exotic, the bizarre, and give to the lives of the monks a place of honor in the cultural history of China. In short, one of his motives—in writing this book and in writing it the way he did— was to advance the naturalization of monks and monasticism in Chinese history and society. It may be of interest to explore somewhat further the evidences of such a motive.

The lives of the great figures of the Indian Buddhist tradition are to be classified as hagiography; their subjects move through a sequence of supernatural events with the majesty of demigods.[5] The biographical element—the chronological record of the commonplace events and actions of mundane existence—is lacking or subordinate. In contrast, Hui-chiao's subjects pass through the usual phases of human life from birth to death; they yield to the temptations of the flesh, they suffer from stammering and dysentery, they are buffeted by the social and political upheavals of their times. Miracles punctuate but do not dominate the sequence of events. Indeed miraculous happenings are no more frequent than in many secular biographies of the period.[6] In adopting the sober and judicious manner of a Chinese historian, Hui-chiao not only rejected the patterns of Indian hagiography. He also turned away from a popular Chinese literary genre—typified by the *Sou-shen chi* 搜神記 —whose highly colored stories were intended to entertain, with "morals" thrown in for those with a taste for them. It seems to me that in his choice of a genre and a style Hui-chiao was seeking to reach—with a polished example of Chinese historical literature—an educated, upper-class audience. He was less concerned to awe the simple with accounts of miracles than to persuade the nobles and literati that Buddhism was intellectually respectable and that its clergy had led useful, creative, and well-disciplined lives.

Hui-chiao is at pains to establish not only his subjects' religious eminence but the prestige they enjoyed in the Chinese society of their times. He describes in detail the gifts and homage which the monks received from princes, officials, and intellectual leaders. He stresses the friendships between his subjects and the leading political and literary figures of their times, and he often mentions the grief of some distinguished person on the occasion of a monk's death. The index to laymen mentioned in the *Kao-seng chuan* reads like a *Who's Who* of the period it covers. A comparison between this list and the very short list of monks in a secular work such as the *Shih-shuo hsin-yü* 世說新語 makes one somewhat sceptical of some of the monks' recorded friendships with the great, but it serves to underscore one of Hui-chiao's purposes: the habilitation of Buddhism and the Buddhist clergy in the Chinese upper class.

It is consistent with such an aim—as well as with his own background and interests—that Hui-chiao lays great emphasis on literary abilities and accomplishments. Out of 257 major biographies, 35 are devoted to translators and 101 to exegetes; of 259 subordinate biographies, 196 are in these two categories. These two groups are given the place of honor at the beginning of the work.[7] It is widely agreed that the principal focus of interest of the Buddhist communities in the first five centuries of their history in China was on the translation and explication of Indian and Central Asian Buddhist texts. Yet even when due allowance is made for this historical fact and for the fact that Hui-chiao was himself an exegete, the emphasis on literary activity is overwhelming. It seems to me that this may be interpreted as a reflection of Hui-chiao's broader aim, that of gaining for the clergy status and recognition in the favored class of Chinese society. Such an interpretation is supported by the recurrence on every page of the *Kao-seng chuan* of the set phrases used in Chinese biography to describe literary precocity and brilliance. Again and again monks are described as having memorized the classics at an early age, as being able to memorize every page they read, as being proficient in prose or poetic writing or in calligraphy. Dozens are described as "widely read in Buddhist and non-Buddhist writings." Through stress on such accomplishments Hui-chiao established the standing of his subjects in terms of the values of the literate upper class of his time.

Sources and Methods

In part 4 I shall discuss the specific sources Hui-chiao is known to have used and the different types of materials he drew upon. And, like Ssu-ma Ch'ien and other Chinese historians, he supplemented his documents with interviews.[8] He says that he carefully compared and collated these accounts, attempting to get as full and accurate a biography as possible. At the same time one finds him reproducing in toto an earlier account, and in this, too, he followed an established historical practice, namely, to take over bodily an earlier record that seemed to be the best available. Occasionally he discusses problems of dating and consistency, emerging from impersonality with the traditional "I" 余 [*yü*] or "In my judgment" 余案 [*yü-an*].[9] When he repeats an oral tradition or a local legend he identifies it as such.[10] And, for his completed work he makes the same demurrer that had long ago been made for the *Shih-chi*; it is, he says, a transmission of the records of the past and not a creative work.[11]

In using the Chinese historian's principal device for the expression of personal judgment—inclusion and exclusion—Hui-chiao behaved in a way consistent with the aims suggested above and with the various attitudes to be discussed below. In reducing the number of major biographies from the 425 which had appeared in his principal source to 257, he actually increased the number of biographies of translators from 29 to 35, added 11 biographies of exegetes who had not been noticed in the earlier work and concentrated the bulk of his subordinate biographies in these two categories. His reductions were made in the other categories. For example, he reduced the biographies of self-immolators from 19 to 11, of builders or sponsors of religious works from 32 to 14; among the more recent specialists, biographies of hymnodists were reduced from 17 to 11, of sermonizers from 13 to 10.[12]

In sorting and collating, in rejecting some documents and accepting others, what were his standards? At one point he discusses the inconsistency of an account which reported that a monk had built a tomb for himself, but after his burial was found to be no longer occupying it. Hui-chiao asks the commonsense question: if the monk knew he was not going to use a tomb, why did he prepare one?[13] Yet in the same biography Hui-chiao recounts without question or qualification a series of incidents—evidence of this monk's prescience and supernatural powers—which commonsense judgment would certainly reject. In another biography he argues that it is not likely that a monk lived to the age of 130 and goes on to show that a more natural life span was probably his lot.[14] Yet elsewhere in the *Kao-seng chuan* ages such as "over 100," "117" are recorded without qualification. And, while Hui-chiao takes great pains to give exact dates and to be precise about where an event occurred, the events themselves may be highly improbable. What then were his standards of credibility?

First of all he was a man of his age, and he adopted prevailing standards. It was not until two centuries later that "fiction," in the sense of works of the imagination written to entertain, was clearly differentiated from "history."[15] Thus Hui-chiao regards such works as the *Sou-shen hou-chi* and the *Hsüan-yen chi* 宣驗記 —prototypes of the frankly imaginative collections of later date—as credible sources, and he draws on them. Further, he believed with his contemporaries in the intimate interaction of human and natural events, and it is not surprising that he reports soberly and circumstantially the timely appearance of portents and the manifestations—climatic and astronomical—of Heaven's favor or disfavor. The neo-Taoist ideas which had developed in the centuries following the fall of the Han had a strong influence on Hui-chiao and his contemporaries. On the one hand neo-Taoism had tended to enhance the sense of mystery and wonder toward nature; on the other it elevated the individual to a new level and continually suggested the capacity of individual man to transcend the usual patterns of human existence. Under the influence of such ideas Hui-chiao, along with the secular historians of his time, took the attitude toward a seemingly unnatural event which asked, "Who can say that this did not happen to this man?" And, one might add, he also shared with his fellow historians respect for all books that had come down from the past, a respect that is at once veneration for the past as the repository of experience and wisdom and an esteem for all writings which approaches bibliolatry.

Hui-chiao's standards of credibility were affected by another factor—one that he did not share with the secular historians of his time. This was his faith in Buddhism. To him the law of Karma was profoundly true and universally operative. Thus a document which described the working of that law in the life history of a man was prima facie worthy of credence. To him the intervention of the Bodhi-sattvas in the lives of men was an article of faith, and records of such interventions were inherently credible. Given his general outlook and his particular faith, he found no difficulty in believing and recording the extraordinary deeds of great men who in the first place were cap-able of transcending the patterns of ordinary life and in the second were aided in these deeds by interested and potent supernatural beings. To sum up, he worked with all the care and judiciousness of superior Chinese historians of his day. Yet while they found in history the manifestation of certain moral principles, he found in the lives of the great monks exemplification of the working of Buddhist laws and the potency of Buddhist deities. In this context too he may justly be called both biographer and hagiographer.

Formal Organization

Some of the ways in which Hui-chiao used the conventions of Chinese historiography have been suggested. In the formal organization of his work this is even more striking. The grouping of biographies in terms of the dominant activities of their subjects was used in a limited way by Ssu-ma Ch'ien and more consistently by Pan Ku. In Fan Yeh's *Hou Han-shu* the categories are further elaborated, particularly to provide for grouping the biographies of nonofficial individuals.[16] In Hui-chiao's day this device was widely used for the organization of biog-raphies in collections of limited focus, such as the *Chung-ch'en chuan* 忠臣傳 by Hui-chiao's contemporary the prince of Hsiang-tung 相東王 —later Emperor Yüan of the Liang.[17] Although, as will be shown in part 4, Hui-chiao was not the first Buddhist biographer to use this traditional device, he was the first to adapt it successfully to the requirements of Buddhist history.

The use of the subordinate 附 [*fu*] biography, appended to a major one, also had its origins in secular historiography. In secular biographies, with some exceptions, these subordinate biographies tended to treat of the sons and grandsons of the principal subject; this arrangement came, later, to be most extensively used in the *Nan-shih* 南史 and the *Pei-shih* 北史.[18] In Hui-chiao's work the minor subjects are linked to the major by the disciple-master relationship, by some common activity, or by geographical propinquity.

The *lun* 論 or critical estimates which are placed at the end of each group of biographies also have the sanction of great antiquity. According to the *Shih-t'ung* 史通 this convention originates with those comments in the *Tso-chuan* which are introduced with the phrase "The superior mans says [*chün-tzu yüeh* 君子曰]."[19] These comments were in later historical works introduced in a variety of ways, but their purpose was always to sum up the historian's view of the meaning of the preceding narrative and to point up its moral significance. Often, as in the *Shih-chi*—in which they were called *tsan* 贊 —they were the means by which the historian also discussed his standards of judgment, problems of credibility, and the like. In the sequence of dynastic histories it is with the *History of the Later Han* that these discourses came to be introduced impersonally, as they are in the *Kao seng chuan*, with the phrase *lun-yüeh* 論曰, "The critical estimate says." In that work, however, many groups of biographies are introduced with a preface which serves the same purpose as the *lun*. Hui-chiao states in his preface his reasons for concentrating all his own comments in one essay at the end of each group of biographies. His essays are brilliant short accounts of the various aspects of Buddhist history which are the rubrics for his groups of biographies. As Yamanouchi pointed out, they serve the same purpose as the *chih* 志, topical treatises, in the dynastic histories.[20] They point out the special contribution which each form of activity made to the spread of Buddhism, using brief references to individuals to illustrate the different phases of that activity. Occasionally Hui-chiao discusses a problem of credibility and judgment; for example, his life of Chu Fa-tu 竺法度 is short and circumstantial, but in the critical estimate he points out that some of this monk's pretensions were very dubious, that some of the religious practices he advocated were not in accord with the Vinaya, that he was in fact a charlatan who victimized a good many people.[21] These *lun*, then, are in purpose, form, and content patterned on the models of secular historiography.

The *tsan* 贊 are short poems appended to the first eight critical estimates, and it is possible that two more have dropped out of the text.[22] It was Pan Ku who first consistently put his historical judgments into verse of four-word lines, though he called them *shu* 述 and grouped them, with cross-references, at the end of his work. And it was Fan Yeh 范曄, in his *History of the Later Han*, who gave these poetical pieces the name *tsan*.[23] When Fan Yeh appended a *lun*, his *tsan* immediately followed it. It is this convention which Hui-chiao follows. A *tsan* is most often a eulogy or encomium of an individual, and Huichiao's *tsan* might be termed "appreciations" of the work of the men whose biographies precede them. They are, in short, compact, allusive verse of four words per line, the summing up of Hui-chiao's estimate of the contribution of a group of monks to the spread of Buddhism. In secular biography a *tsan* often follows the biography of an individual and crystallizes the historian's judgment of him. In the body of the *Kao-seng chuan* Hui-chiao did not write *tsan* to individual biographies but he frequently quoted those of other authors.

These brief remarks on the formal aspects of the *Kao-seng chuan* may serve to suggest Hui-chiao's relation to Chinese historiographical traditions, his conscious adoption, for reasons I have outlined, of the accepted style and conventions of the historians of his time.

Attitudes

One of Hui-chiao's biases—in favor of literary activity—has been suggested. And this is reflected in the temper of his whole work. He was an educated member of the Chinese upper class, and he obviously believed in the possibility of a comfortable adjustment between the norms of Chinese society and the truths of his religion. He was steeped in the classics of Confucianism and Taoism, and every page of his book is full of apt allusions to them. He was willing to go so far as to say that the Vinaya was basic for monastic life but that *Li* 禮 and *I* 義, the rules of proper behavior and the principle of righteousness, should govern the lives of the laity.[24] He then goes on to quote the *Li-chi* on the fundamental importance of *Li* in moral and social life. At the same time he was somewhat dubious, as his critical estimate suggests, about such un-Chinese behavior as self-immolation.[25] He had a profound respect for Chinese culture and social norms and a concomitant distaste for the more radical and disruptive forms of religious activity.

This attitude is reflected in his treatment of popular Taoism and is intensified by his religious conviction that popular Taoism was an utterly false and socially harmful religion. The Taoist adepts who appear in his narratives are invariably represented as evil and corrupt, the proper objects of the disdain of all true Chinese gentlemen and all devout Buddhists. In his biographies Taoist adepts invariably suffer defeat when they measure their "fetish power" against that of an eminent monk.[26] Biased as his accounts are, they nonetheless suggest the dimensions of the struggle that was to continue for many centuries for religious dominion over the holders of power and over the masses in the countryside.

Hui-chiao had strong views about the dignity and independence of the clergy. In the preface he expressed these views both directly and obliquely. He says, "Some say that a person who leaves lay life is yet a resident of the state and a guest of its ruler, and that he is not obliged to be austere and withdrawn. . . . Yet to renounce worldly honors and cast off emotional ties is really the way a person differentiates himself from the commonalty and comes to be regarded as a worthy." This passage is, in my view, an attack on the worldly and sycophantic clergy who surrounded the pious emperor Wu. Hui-chiao's preface, in contrast to those of his older contemporaries in the capital,[27] contains not a word of obsequious praise for the Liang dynasty nor for the reigning emperor, fervent Buddhist though he was. I suspect that Hui-chiao's attitude toward secular authority was much like that of Hui-yüan 慧遠, whose discourse "Śramaṇas should not pay homage to princes" is quoted at length in the *Kao-seng chuan*.[28] In explaining his choice of the word *kao* 高, "eminent," for his title Hui-chiao says, "If men of real achievement conceal their brilliance, then they are eminent (*kao*) but not famous (名 *ming*); when men of slight virtue happen to be in accord with their times, then they are famous but not eminent." When one recalls the overtones of meaning of the word *kao* in the

Kao-shih chuan 高士傳 "Biographies of Eminent Worthies," connoting unworldliness, moral austerity, rigid adherence to principle, etc.,[29] the impression is strengthened that Hui-chiao was expressing in various ways his opposition to the worldlings, the opportunists, and the sycophants among the clergy of his day. The obliquity of these statements was probably prompted by a realistic appreciation of the autocratic power of the emperor in the state and the influence of the palace clerics in the Buddhist church.

An attitude which is closely related to this is his coolness toward the great metropolitan clerics who were his senior contemporaries and to whose writings he was greatly in debt. This is something one senses in his anonymous attack on Pao-ch'ang's 寶唱 work, in his depreciation of the word *ming*, which was part of the title of that work, and in his rather meager biography of the great Seng-yu 僧祐.[30] What the personal basis may have been we cannot know. Was it the mixed envy and disapproval of the provincial cleric toward his urbane and worldly brethren in the capital? Was there an element of local pride—the sort of sentiment that prompts the Belgian Catholic clerics to say, "A doctor in Rome is an ass in Louvain"? Whatever the reason may be, the effect of this attitude on the *Kao-seng chuan* was, as Tao-hsüan 道宣 pointed out, inadequate coverage of the great clerics of the Liang dynasty.[31]

When we come to the regional bias of the *Kao-seng chuan* we are on firmer ground. No great weight is to be given to Hui-chiao's use of *wei* 偽 "illegitimate" as a prefix to the names and official nomenclature of the non-Chinese dynasties in the north. By his time this had become an automatic convention among writers south of the Yangtze. But when one looks at the geographical distribution of those monks whose geographic origins or place of work are identified in the *Kao-seng chuan*, the emphasis on Central China—particularly the area of the modern Kiangsi, Kiangsu, and Chekiang—is striking. Yamazaki has shown that out of 151 monks whose geographical connections are specified in the *Kao-seng chuan*, 121 are from this region.[32] Now this emphasis— which is one of the generally acknowledged weaknesses of the *Kao-seng chuan*[33]—is the result of many factors. First, there is the simple fact that this region was the area where Hui-chiao had his roots, the area in which he worked, traveled, and had his friends. Second, although Buddhist monks moved between north and south, easy or casual travel was not possible; information on the history of the church—amid the wars and upheavals of the northern dynasties—was not readily accessible, and adequate records were not available.[34] Third, Hui-chiao's background and interests did not make him sympathetic to the demagogic missionaries, the mass religious movements, and the monarcho-centric Buddhism of the north. These factors in sum mean that Hui-chiao, by inclination and circumstances, favored the intellectual upper class Buddhism which was a part of the flourishing cultural life of the Chinese dynasties south of the Yangtze. His biographies clearly reflect this, and works on the history of the church written after the reunification of China have been at pains to redress the balance.[35]

PART 2: A BIOGRAPHICAL SKETCH OF HUI-CHIAO

Hui-chiao was a native of K'uai-chi 會稽, in his day an administrative district (chün 郡) lying south of Hangchow Bay.[36] This region was then, as it is today, prosperous and famed for its superb scenery. Its rapid development as a major center of culture dates from the influx of upper-class refugees following the disastrous loss of North China to the Huns in the years 321–17. As one chronicler describes it, "When the Chin moved to the east of the Yangtze, the flower of the gentry of the Central Plain all gathered in Yüeh. It became the major cultural center of six provinces. Distinguished men and literary worthies came together in clouds, one attracting another."[37]

Throughout the period of division between north and south K'uai-chi was one of the principal centers of intellectual and cultural life. As Hui-chiao grew up in the early years of the sixth century, its local traditions had been enriched by the names of two centuries of scholar-statesmen, philosophers, and great clerics. Here were the honored tombs of scholar-officials famed for their Confucian learning.[38] Here too were the graves of many great figures of neo-Taoism *hsüan-hsüeh* 玄學 and of the cult of repartee *ch'ing-tan* 清談: Juan Yü 阮裕, Hsieh An 謝安, Hsieh Ling-yün 謝靈運, the great calligrapher Wang Hsi-chih 王羲之, the witty philosopher-monk Chih Tun 支遁.[39] K'uai-chi and neighboring sites were peculiarly attractive to the neo-Taoists because of the exquisite scenery—ideal settings for the refined contemplation of nature. While Hui-chiao's writing shows his thorough knowledge of the Confucian Classics, of the major literary and historical traditions, the ideas and the "classics" of neo-Taoism—the *Chuang-tzu*, the *Lao-tzu* and the *I-ching*—had a pervasive influence on his thought and style. By Hui-chiao's time, neo-Taoism's creative period had long passed, but its ideas and its principal mode of discourse—*ch'ing-t'an*—still dominated upper-class intellectual life. It is not surprising that Hui-chiao's lay disciple, in complimenting him on the *Kao-seng chuan*, refers to four famous *ch'ing-t'an* colloquies, two of which involve great figures in the history of K'uai-chi.[40]

The Buddhism of K'uai-chi had grown and developed through two centuries of material prosperity and cultural brilliance. Its temples and monasteries, many of them set in the midst of great natural beauty, had been richly endowed and patronized. Imperial patronage had built some. For others great officials had donated lands or their own homes.[41] There was, by Hui-chiao's day, an old and rich tradition of Buddhist scholarship and religious activity, and during the Liang dynasty Buddhism increasingly prospered.[42] K'uai-chi Buddhism was largely, though not exclusively, an upper-class interest. The scenic temples and monasteries provided delightful retreats for the rich and the powerful; the discourses of learned and cultivated monks appealed to them in their scholarly and reflective moods; the building of temples, shrines, and monasteries gave them pious satisfaction, accumulated merit for the future, and increased their prestige in the community. The Chia-hsiang Temple 嘉祥寺 at which Hui-chiao lived and worked had been built by a fourth-century governor of K'uai-chi who was also the patron of its first abbot.[43] It was within this well-endowed, upper-class, officially patronized Buddhist community that Hui-chiao lived his life as monk and scholar.

We do not know Hui-chiao's secular surname or anything of his family connections. Yet it is possible to infer that he was either rich and wellborn or came very early under generous patronage. He has only one thing to say of his own youth—that he was not over-diligent at study and self-cultivation—and this is probably no more than a rhetorical flourish.[44] However, the richness of his style and the breadth of his learning as they are revealed in his preface and essays can only have been the product of long years of reading and practice. The leisure to acquire such accomplishments is, in China, only to be found in the homes of the gentry or under their patronage. Two facts support, though they do not prove, the hypothesis that he was the son of a gentry family. One is the richness of his non-Buddhist learning, which, one suspects, he began to acquire in a secular environment. Another is his fame as a book collector. Book collecting has ever been the hobby of the literate gentry, but Hui-chiao must have been un- usually well off to build a library that would attract the attention of the bibliophile prince of Hsiang-tung, later the emperor Yüan.[45]

Hui-chiao's life at the Chia-hsiang Temple, west of the administra- tive city of K'uai-chi, was, according to one biographer, divided into two phases. In the spring and summer he propagated Buddhism, and the autumn and winter he devoted to writing.[46] His historical research was a subsidiary interest, and he found time for it whenever he was not reading religious texts or attending lectures.[47] He was regarded by his contemporaries and by his seventh-century biographer as primarily an exegete, a specialist in sūtra and vinaya texts.[48] He left a commen- tary to the *Nirvāṇa sūtra* in 10 chüan and a commentary to the section on monastic rules in the *Brahmajāla sūtra*.[49] Both of these were still widely read in the early Sui but have since been lost.[50] The study of the *Nirvāṇa sūtra* was a major preoccupation of Buddhist clerics in the north and the south throughout the Liang period. Among the galaxy of brilliant specialists on this sūtra, Hui-chiao was probably a relative- ly minor figure.[51] It has often been pointed out that exegesis was the major activity of the Buddhist clergy up to the Sui dynasty—that the effort of Chinese Buddhists was centered on discovering the meaning of the ideas of Indian Buddhism. Hui-chiao shared this prevailing in- terest and probably saw himself as making his principal contribution through the interpretation of key texts.

Of Hui-chiao's contacts with his contemporaries we know very little. We have suggested in the introduction the coolness of Hui-chiao toward certain of his clerical contemporaries. Yet the fact that the book collecting prince of the ruling house knew of him and his library suggests that he may have had some renown at the capital, Chien-k'ang 建康 (Nanking); perhaps he occasionally visited the capital. It is likely that his search for biographical materials and his practice of interviewing historical informants—as well as his annual period of "spreading the Dharma"—took him to other regions of central and south China.[52]

We have the record of an exchange of letters with the lay Buddhist Wang Man-ying 王曼穎.[53] The letters are couched in the conventional phrases of compliment and self-deprecation. They contain, as will be seen in part 4, useful material on Hui-chiao's sources but little biographical data. This exchange shows only that Hui-chiao was on friendly terms with a cultivated layman, that the two men lived in the same "universe of discourse," and that both were steeped in the traditions of southern intellectual life, particularly neo-Taoism and *ch'ing-t'an*. The third contemporary who knew Hui-chiao and left a record is Seng-kuo 僧果, to whose memoirs we are indebted for details on Hui-chiao's last years.

Early in 550 K'uai-chi fell to the rebel forces of Hou Ching 侯景: a year later a Liang loyalist revolt broke out in K'uai-chi and was forcibly suppressed.[54] To escape involvement in further disorders, Hui-chiao in 553 fled his native place and, according to Seng-kuo, took refuge in P'en-ch'eng 湓城, near the modern Kiukiang, Kiangsi.[55] There he lectured for a short time. "In the second moon of the chia-hsü 甲戌 year [March 10–April 17, 554], he died aged fifty-eight (歲). The abbot 僧正 Hui-kung 慧恭 of Chiang-chou 江州[56] was in charge of the arrangements, and they buried him in the graveyard of the Ch'an-ko Temple 禪閣寺 on Lu-shan. I, Seng-kuo of the Lung-kuang Temple 龍光寺,[57] having likewise fled from the troubles and lived in the same temple, happened to observe an event of the time and make this brief record of it."[58]

Hui-chiao is remembered for his biographies, and it is important to establish when these were completed. It has often been assumed that since he chose the year 519 as the terminal date for the biographies the work was completed at that time.[59] Yet, if Seng-kuo's note is correct—and I believe it is—Hui-chiao would have been only twenty-two years old at that time. Yet the *Kao-seng chuan* does not impress one as the work of a precocious youth; it is clearly the product of long study and reflection. In his preface Hui-chiao says that the years since the introduction of Buddhism number "nearly five hundred," while he specifies the years covered by his biographies as 453. This is the slightest of suggestions that the preface was written and the work completed sometime after 519.[60] Wang Man-ying, to whom Hui-chiao sent the completed biographies, and later the *lun* and *tsan*, for criticism, died sometime before 533. His household was poor, and his friend Chiang Ko 江革, on the widow's behalf, sought the charity of the prince of Nan-p'ing 南平王.[61] This kindly prince himself died in 533,[62] although he is mentioned in a *Kao-seng chuan* biography as "the present prince of Nan-p'ing."[63] Thus the evidence is strong that the work was finished before 533. Another fact suggests that the completion date should be placed toward the end of the period 519–33. This is that the *Ming-seng chuan*, which, as will be shown in part 4, was used as a basis for much of the *Kao-seng chuan*, was completed—nine years after its conception—in 519.[64] It is doubtful if the young Hui-chiao, twenty-two in that year, could immediately have secured a copy of this imperially commissioned work. It is certain that the time he required to get a copy, to master its contents, to collate these with his other written and interview materials, and then to organize and write his own book—all this in the midst of other religious duties—was not a year or two, but more likely ten or a dozen years. If we say that the *Kao-seng chuan* was completed "about 530" we do violence neither to the facts nor to probability.

PART 3: THE AUTHOR'S PREFACE

The ultimate principle is profound and broad: only through media is it revealed.[65] The mysterious ultimate is deep and impermeable; only through preceptors does it achieve usefulness.[66] Hence the sagely traditions, as they are handed down, prosper, and men of wisdom and men of ability play different roles. Some have discussed loyalty and probity, filial piety and paternal kindliness, thereby establishing a Way for princes and fathers;[67] they explain the *Book of Songs*, the *Book of*

History, the books of ritual and the *Classic of Music*, thereby perfecting the precepts of good custom. Others are oblivious to honors, ignore ordinary affairs, and esteem an otherworldly calm.[68] Still others bring themselves to accept the fact of growth and decay and value the understanding of their mortal fate.[69] But with all these, their doctrines are limited to China, and their merit lies in immediate benefits. It may be that such methods of gradual adjustment [to the world and its ills] have neither probed nor fulfilled the divine nature in man.[70]

As to the precepts which Śākyamuni[71] formulated: when he examined the mysterious minuteness of [the working of] cause and effect,[72] [he saw that] they came in orderly alternation throughout past, present, and future time; when he spoke of the lofty sublimity of the ultimate principle, [he said that] it interpenetrated all creation. He revealed the ten stages[73] and thereby elucidated the essential doctrine of prajñā;[74] he made manifest the two truths[75] and thereby explained the storehouse of jñāna.[76] For the purpose of probing the essence of the divine and fully realizing man's nature and for bringing about control of the cardinal points of the universe, other religions are to Buddhism like the myriad rivers making their way to the sea,[77] like the galaxies of stars turning toward the polar star.[78] How great it is! How profound! In truth it is difficult to praise it adequately in mere words.

Moreover Buddha's teachings fill the three thousand worlds,[79] and his form pervades the six classes of beings.[80] For all [creatures, Buddha's teachings] are the means of saving the ignorant and of conferring great blessings. But, because the pure and the impure hear differently and because those whose [state of life] is rising and those whose [state of life] is falling see differently, the Western quarter was the first to be blessed with the sound and form [of Buddha and his teaching],[81] while the eastern kingdoms later had the benefit of seeing and hearing them.[82] A cloud dragon appeared at midnight, and a wind tiger was manifested in a nocturnal vision.[83] The mighty wind [of Buddhism] then blew, and its great transforming power was then diffused.

From that time on famous monks of the western lands came constantly to China. Some introduced the teachings of the scriptures; others taught the principles of meditation. Some converted people with magic, while others saved living beings through supernatural powers. From the Han to the Liang the time is long indeed; the state has been subject to six successive dynasties, and the years number nearly five hundred.[84] Among the śramaṇas of this land, men endowed with talents have appeared in abundance, and heroes have frequently come forth. Time and again there have been such men.

Accounts [of these monks] given in the narratives of various authors differ one from another.* The Śramana Fa-chi gave accounts of a single class only—the eminent recluses.[I] The Śramana Fa-an set forth only [the lives] of a single group—those who were strict in keeping their vows.[II] The Śramaṇa Seng-pao gave only the lives of a single category—the pilgrims.[III] The Śramaṇa Fa-chin composed essays and narratives on a comprehensive scale, but in treatment and in matter there were omissions and undue abridgments.[IV] In all of these [the accounts] are sometimes too long and sometimes too brief; they differ in what they include and what they omit. When we examine the activities [narrated] in them, we fail to see their purport.[85]

All [the following works] mention in passing many monks and describe their characters, but these are all subsidiary notices and frequently have many lacunae: the *Hsüan-yen chi*[V] and *Yu-ming lu*[VI] by the Sung Prince of Lin-ch'uan [Liu] I-ch'ing, who was canonized as K'ang; the *Ming-hsiang chi*[VII] by Wang Yen of T'ai-yüan; the *I-pu ssu chi*[VIII] by Liu Chün of P'eng-ch'eng; the *Ching-shih ssu chi*[IX] by the Śramaṇa T'an-tsung; the *Kan-ying chuan*[X] by Wang Yen-hsiu of T'ai-yüan; the *Cheng-ying chuan*[XI] by Chu Chün-t'ai; and the *Sou-shen lu*[XII] by T'ao Yüan-ming.

The *San-pao chi-chuan* by the Ch'i prince of Ching-ling, who was canonized as Wen-hsüan, is sometimes called the *Fo-shih* or the *Seng-lu*.[XIII] The Three Treasures (Buddha, his teaching, and his order) are recounted together. Treatment and ideas [on the three topics] are intertwined, so it is confused and difficult to draw upon, even more unclear [than other works discussed]. As to the *Seng-shih* compiled by Wang Chin of Lang-ya, its aim seems to be comprehensiveness, but the literary form is inadequate.[XIV] When the Śramaṇa Seng-yu com-

---

* Roman numerals placed after the book titles in the following paragraphs refer to the numbered paragraphs in part 4 which discuss these sources and their authors.

piled the *San-tsang chi*, he included only [biographies of] thirty odd monks, and those left out are very numerous.^{XV}

[Of the following works,] each either strives to exalt a single region without covering both the modern and the ancient or concentrates on single good deeds without touching on other activities [of its subjects]: the *Tung-shan seng-chuan* by the Chung-shu 中書 Hsi Ching-hsing;^{XVI} the *Lu shan chung-shu* by the Chih-chung 治中 Chang Hsiao-hsiu;^{XVII} and the *Sha-men chuan* by the Chung-shu 中書 Lu Ming-hsia.^{XVIII}

Right down to the present day there continue to be writers [of such works]. Some, in their encomiums, praise to excess; others, in their narratives, profitlessly set down a plethora of meaningless words. When one looks for their real meaning, they lack any reliability worth mentioning.[86] Still others, out of an aversion to multiplicity and breadth, abridge their data, and remarkable [instances of] exemplary conduct are often omitted or cut short.[87]

Some say that a person who leaves lay life is yet a resident of the state and a guest of its ruler, and that he is not obliged to be austere and withdrawn, to become a hermit[88] and live in solitude, cut off from ordinary life.[89] [Yet] to renounce worldly honors and cast off emotional ties is really the way a person differentiates himself from the commonalty and comes to be regarded as a worthy.[90] If such as these are excluded, what in the end would there be to record?

I was wont in my leisure time to examine a large number of writings. I made a point of investigating the miscellaneous accounts of several tens of authors together with the chronicles and histories of the Chin, Sung, Ch'i, and Liang dynasties, the heterodox histories of the frontier dynasties of Ch'in, Chao, Yen, and Liang, geographical miscellanies, isolated pieces, and fragmentary accounts. In addition I made extensive interrogations of experienced ancients, and I widely questioned those more learned than myself. I collated what was included with what was excluded and found where they agreed and where they differed.

[My biographies] begin with the tenth year of the Yung-p'ing 永平 era of the emperor Ming of the Han (A.D. 67)[91] and end with the eighteenth year of the T'ien-chien 天監 era of the Liang (519), including in all 453 years and 257 men. Moreover those who appear collaterally in subordinate notices number more than 200. In setting forth their virtuous deeds I have made ten broad categories: 1. Translators 譯經, 2. Exegetes 義解, 3. Theurgists 神異, 4. Meditators 習禪, 5. Disciplinarians 明律, 6. Self-immolators 遺身,[92] 7. Cantors 誦經, 8. Promoters of works of merit 興福,[93] 9. Hymnodists 經師,[94] and 10. Sermonists 唱導.[95]

Yet it would seem that the flow of Buddhism into China was due to the meritorious work of the translators. Some went through the perils of desert wastes; others were tossed about on tempestuous seas. All were forgetful of self in their devotion to religion, heedless of their lives in the propagation of the Dharma. The enlightenment of China[96] was wholly dependent on them. Such merit being worthy of deep respect, I have placed them at the beginning of the book.

And, when the wise explanations [of the Exegetes] revealed divine [truth], Buddhism encompassed a myriad myriad [worlds]. When the supernatural power [of the Theurgists] made itself opportunely felt, violent men were thereby pacified. When [the Meditators] composed their thoughts and entered into meditation, achievement and virtue came to full flower. When [the Disciplinarians] propagated the Vinaya, conduct in accord with the prohibitions was of limpid purity. When [the Self-immolators], forgetful of self, sacrificed their bodies, the prideful and avaricious experienced a change of heart. When [the Cantors] intoned the words of the teaching, the invisible and visible worlds tasted blessedness. When [the Promoters of works of merit] created works of religious merit, then the symbols bequeathed by Buddha could be passed on to posterity. [The monks] in all these eight categories, even though their legacies of good deeds were not all the same, and though their beneficent influences were markedly different, nonetheless were all endowed with virtue like that of the four classes of saints,[97] and their achievement lay in meritorious acts of body, mouth, and mind.[98] Therefore they are praised by all the scriptures and extolled by all the saints.

Concerning my investigations of origins and developments, my decisions as to what to accept and what to reject, I have stated all this in the *tsan* and *lun*;[99] these I have put as appendices [to the various

groups of biographies]. At the beginning [of the *lun*] I have set forth
the general meaning [of the group of biographies]; in type this resembles [the usual] preface. At the end [of the *lun*] I have discussed [spe-
cific] dates and men; in matter this is identical with [the usual] postface. If I had placed [these two discourses] at the beginning and end [of
each section] it might have been considered confusing. Therefore I
have placed them together at the end of each category and have given
them the general name of *lun*.

The Hymnodists[100] and the Sermonists,[101] although their origins
are not in the distant past, have nevertheless taken advantage of their
opportunities to awaken the laity and in truth have some merit. Therefore the miscellaneous records of the Ch'i and Sung dynasties have
generally given accounts of the superior ones. Those whom I now
select are of course those whose achievements were outstanding and
who had some pervasive religious influence; I have given accounts of
them at the end of this work. Those who deviate from this standard are
not included here.

What I have related in all the ten categories [of biographies] was all
scattered in multitudinous records. Now I have simply condensed and
collected these in one place. Hence this is a transmission [of what has
come down from the past] and not a creative work.[102] To enable one
to get a general view within the limits of one book, it should contain
all the essential points. [Passages which] are wordy and vainly eulogistic and [accounts of] those whose merit was unworthy of mention
have been completely eliminated. Thus I have given an account of the
worthies of six dynasties and have written only thirteen rolls, counting
the preface and table of contents, fourteen rolls.

I have called my work the *Lives of Eminent Monks*. Compilations
from earlier times have mostly spoken of "famous monks."[103] But
fame (or name) is basically the guest of reality.[104] If men of real
achievement conceal their brilliance, then they are eminent but not
famous; when men of slight virtue happen to be in accord with their
times, then they are famous but not eminent. Those who are famous
but not eminent are, of course, not recorded here; those who are eminent but not famous have been fully treated in the present work. For
these reasons I have avoided the word *famous* and used instead the

word *eminent*. Here and there I was writing [on certain subjects] for the first time, and there may be some omissions. Now these fourteen rolls, complete with *tsan* and *lun* are, in my opinion, in final form. If there be things that have not been brought into line with accepted standards,[105] the reader will please exercise his judgment on them.

PART 4: THE SOURCES OF THE *KAO-SENG CHUAN*

The Problem of the Ming-seng chuan　名僧傳

Tao-hsüan, in his famous continuation of the *Kao-seng chuan*, suggested the special relation of Hui-chiao to the work of his older contemporary Pao-ch'ang 寶唱, the *Ming-seng chuan*. Hui-chiao, he says, "regarded the *Ming-seng* compiled by the Honorable Ch'ang as prolix and erratic. Accordingly he set up his own principles, consolidated its scope [?], and wrote his *Kao-seng chuan* in fourteen rolls."[106] Hui-chiao does not specify the *Ming-seng chuan* in his discussion of sources, but since Tao-hsüan it has been assumed that he was criticizing Pao-ch'ang in the passage of his preface where he says, "others [i.e., among contemporary biographers of the monks] in their narratives profitlessly set down a plethora of meaningless words. When one seeks their real meaning, they lack any reliability worth mentioning."[107] Wang Man-ying, in his letter to Hui-chiao, mentions Pao-ch'ang's work, saying, "Ch'ang's compilation most truly approaches [the ideal], but in my humble opinion it is regrettable that it is so very verbose."[108] There is no doubt that both Hui-chiao and his lay disciple were familiar with the earlier work.

The *Ming-seng chuan* was begun on the basis of a vow taken in 510, its material was first organized in 514, and it was completed in 519.[109] From Pao-ch'ang's other biographical work, the *Pi-ch'iu-ni chuan* 比丘尼傳 , we know that he was an adequate compiler and historian. His methods and standards in the writing of clerical biography were not strikingly different from Hui-chiao's.[110] His *Ming-seng chuan*, however, was completed under pressure in most adverse circumstances. The author had been accused of some crime and was under sentence of exile to the far south. In this period he made hurried, last-minute efforts to reorganize and condense his biographical collection.[111] This may account in part for the negative opinions of later writers and for the fact that the work was never included in the Canon.[112] Nevertheless this was a substantial and widely read work, and Hui-chiao clearly made extensive use of it.

We are handicapped in appraising the extent and nature of Hui-chiao's debt by the fact that the *Ming-seng chuan* has long been lost.[113] All that is available is a table of contents and a few excerpts copied in haste by a thirteenth-century Japanese monk[114] plus two quotations—from the preface and postface—in Tao-hsüan's biography of Pao-ch'ang. Yet it is possible from these fragments to make some observations on Hui-chiao's debt to Pao-ch'ang, though many questions will remain unanswered.

Hui-chiao's debt to the earlier work might be considered in terms of formal elements and then in terms of content. If the surviving table of contents is to be trusted, Pao-ch'ang divided his biographies into eighteen categories, whereas Hui-chiao used ten. Although Pao-ch'ang's categories seem somewhat overlapping and unwieldy, there are striking resemblances between his eighteen groups and Hui-chiao's ten.[115] For example, Hui-chiao's last two categories are the same as Pao-ch'ang's, though the order is reversed. Hui-chiao's category 8 combines Pao-ch'ang's 15 and 16. Hui-chiao's category 6 has the same heading as Pao-ch'ang's category 12.[116] In terms of category breakdown, it is difficult to escape the conclusion that Hui-chiao's ten groups represent a reorganization and rationalization of Pao-ch'ang's eighteen. This does not mean that Hui-chiao derived the idea of grouping biographies into categories from Pao-ch'ang. Rather, both adopted a time-honored convention of Chinese historiography, and Hui-chiao profited from Pao-ch'ang's experiment in adapting it to the purposes of a Buddhist biographical collection.

A second formal element is the comment, in preface or *lun*, on a group of biographies. Here much the same relation between the two works can again be seen. Both authors were indebted to Chinese secular tradition, but Pao-ch'ang's use of this device in Buddhist biographies preceded and probably influenced Hui-chiao's. When one examines the one preface or *lun* which survives from Pao-ch'ang's work—a discourse on the history of the Vinaya—one finds that, though it is of inferior literary quality, it does not differ in general purport and tone from Hui-chiao's *lun* on the same subject.[117] I doubt that it is a coincidence that the two essays, in their opening passages make the same point—that vinaya is to the Buddhists what *Li* is to the Confucians.[118]

The subordinate biography was apparently not a feature of the *Ming-seng chuan*, and Hui-chiao, in using this device, is indebted to secular historiography but not to Pao-ch'ang.

When we turn from form to content, Hui-chiao's debt to his predecessor is more striking. Of the 257 major biographies in the *Kao-seng chuan*, 216 had been the subjects of biographies in the *Ming-seng chuan*. Of 245 subordinate biographies in the *Kao-seng chuan*, 78 were represented in the earlier work.[119]

Unfortunately no text is extant which can be certainly identified as a complete biography from the *Ming-seng chuan*. The Japanese copyist was mainly interested in certain religious themes, and in the case of biographies of major figures, the accounts are far briefer than those in the *Kao seng chuan*. However, the biography of a lesser monk, Fa-yü 法遇 , gives evidence of being rather full; it is possible that this is a complete biography. When one compares the contents of this with the contents of Hui-chiao's life of the same monk, the similarities suggest the derivation of the later biography from the earlier.[120] The length is very nearly the same, 275 characters in the *Kao-seng chuan* to 286 in the *Ming-seng chuan*. Both biographies consist of nine incidents or items, and the order of these is identical. The longest incident, the case of a bibulous monk, is told in virtually the same words in the two accounts. In no case does Hui-chiao *add* a fact which is not in the earlier account. (The difference of one year in the monk's age at death seems to me insignificant.) Rather, Hui-chiao omits certain details, for example, illustrations of the monk's pride in youth, the date of the monk's flight from Hsiang-yang and the names of his companions in flight, the fact that the congregation was assembled "by striking chimes." Hui-chiao adds the conventional ending to the longest incident: "Those who were moved to religious work by this were very numerous." While the *Ming-seng chuan* account is somewhat loosely written, Hui-chiao's is more concise and more smooth, and words of transition and subordination are introduced to advantage. From what we know, through critical opinion, of the *Ming-seng chuan* and from this comparison of two biographies, it seems highly probable that this is the manner in which Hui-chiao used and reworked biographies in the earlier collection.

Other Biographical Compendia

The *Sui-shu* attributes a "*Kao-seng chuan* in 14 chüan" to Seng-yu 僧祐 (d. 518).[121] No such notice appears in any of the Buddhist catalogues, and it is clear that Seng-yu did not compile a *Kao-seng chuan*.[122] Yamanouchi suggests that the error in the *Sui-shu* may have come from the legend that Tao-hsüan's mother, before his birth, had a dream in which she was informed that her son would be a reincarnation of Seng-yu. Since, in many respects, Tao-hsüan's activities did parallel those of his great predecessor, it was someone's inference that since Tao-hsüan compiled a *Hsü Kao-seng chuan*, Seng-yu must have written a *Kao-seng chuan*.[123]

"The title *Kao-seng chuan* originated with the monk Hui-min 惠敏 of the Liang dynasty, who [wrote a work of that name] and divided it into two parts, 'translators' and 'exegetes.' Shih Hui-chiao in turn expanded this and divided his work into ten categories."[124] This statement by the *Ssu-k'u* editors would suggest that both the title and the first two—and by far the most important—category headings of the *Kao-seng chuan* were derived from another slightly earlier or contemporary work. Yet Hui-chiao's preface is evidence that he at least believed himself to be the first person to use this title, and the large and meticulous Buddhist catalogues of successive periods do not mention this supposed prototype. On the other hand, the *Sui-shu*, *Hsin T'ang-shu*, and *Chiu T'ang-shu* all mention a "*Kao-seng chuan* in 6 chüan by Yü Hsiao-ching."[125] Yü Hsiao-ching 虞孝敬 served as secretary to the prince of Hsiang-tung and later entered the priesthood and took the name of Hui-ming 惠命.[126] I suspect that the *Ssu-k'u* editors took the notice in the *Chün-chai tu-shu chih* 郡齋讀書志 by Ch'ao Kung-wu 晁公武 —a twelfth-century work—as the basis of their note.[127]

There is no evidence as to where Ch'ao got his statement that Hui-min's (or -ming's) *Kao-seng chuan* was divided into two categories. And, so far as I know, there are no quotations of such a work in later commentaries and compendia. There is a quotation, however, of a *Kao-shih chuan* 高士傳 by Yü Hsiao-ching.[128] Yao Chen-tsung makes an effort to reconcile these data, suggesting that, because of the biography of the one subject known to have been mentioned in the work, it may have been called alternatively a *Kao-shih chuan* or a *Kao-seng chuan*.[129] This seems to me forced, and I am driven by the evidence to suggest another hypothesis: (a) Yü Hsiao-ching wrote a *Kao-shih chuan* which survived at least until the latter part of the seventh century.[130] (b) The *Sui-shu* editors cited this incorrectly, and their placing it both under secular biography and with the Buddhist works is evidence of uncertainty. (c) The two *T'ang-shu* perpetuated the error. (d) Ch'ao Kung-wu, in the twelfth century, added further misinformation from an unknown source. (e) The *Ssu-k'u* editors accepted the accuracy of Ch'ao's notices, drew the obvious inference from the similarities between the work of Hui-min and of Hui-chiao and said that the latter was based on the former. For the purposes of this discussion, there is insufficient evidence that there was such a *Kao-seng chuan* and no evidence whatever that, if there was, it was a source used by Hui-chiao.

Tao-hsüan, in his biography of Hui-chiao, remarks, "Beyond the Yangtze there were numerous copies of P'ei Tzu-yeh's 裴子野 *Kao-seng chuan*, ten rolls in one case. Its text was very abbreviated, and it fell short of being a complete mirror. Therefore its repute declined."[131] The title here is an error of Tao-hsüan's. No *Kao-seng chuan* by this author is mentioned in any secular or Buddhist bibliography. However, P'ei Tzu-yeh, who lived from 467 to 528 and was a distinguished Liang official and historian, did write a *Chung-seng chuan* 衆僧傳 in 20 chüan at the command of Emperor Wu.[132] I have suggested that Hui-chiao may have been criticizing this work in his preface when, in commenting on contemporary biographers of the monks, he says, "Still others, out of an aversion to multiplicity and breadth, abridge their data, and remarkable [instances] of exemplary conduct are often omitted or cut short."[133] As late as 664 P'ei's work survived and then included a supplement in 10 chüan by the Liang official Liu Ch'iu 劉虬.[134] There are no surviving quotations which would make it possible to appraise it or to estimate Hui-chiao's indebtedness to it. It is likely that he did use it, but he did not, as Tao-hsüan's note might suggest, take the title *Kao-seng chuan* from it.

Sources Mentioned by Title in Hui-chiao's Preface (In Order of Occurrence)

I. *Kao-i sha-men chuan* 高逸沙門傳 by Fa-chi 法濟, Hui-chiao states that Fa-chi gave accounts only of a single class of monks—the eminent recluses—and Wang Man-ying's letter echoes this.[135] It is nowhere cited as a source in the *Kao-seng chuan* itself, although Hui-chiao mentions the title in his brief biographical note on Fa-chi.[136] The *Li-tai san-pao chi* notices the work, states that it was in one chüan and that it was written during the reign of Emperor Hsiao-wu of the Chin (373–96).[137] The longest surviving fragments are found in Liu Chün's 劉峻 (465–521) commentary to the *Shih-shuo hsin-yü*.[138] These are anecdotes about Chih Tun 支遁 (314–66) and Chu Ch'ien 竺潛 (286–374), and these do no more than suggest the nature of the *Kao-i sha-men chuan*. Both these monks periodically withdrew from the society of the wealthy and powerful, and this is consistent with Fa-chi's title. The stories of Chih Tun's triumphs in *ch'ing-t'an* society also appear in his biography in the *Kao-seng chuan*. Hui-chiao may have drawn on Fa-chi's work for these or he may have drawn on the *Shih-shuo hsin-yü*. This is not mentioned in the preface, although two other works of its author are noted. (See below, V and VI.) The only striking difference in fact between the surviving fragments of the *Kao-i sha-men chuan* and the *Kao-seng chuan* is that the former states that Chih Tun died in Loyang, the latter at his mountain retreat in Chekiang.[139]

II. A *Seng-chuan* 僧傳 by Fa-an 法安. Hui-chiao states that Fa-an's record was limited to a single category, those who were strict in keeping their vows. Wang simply echoes this comment.[140] The only mention of the work in the *Kao-seng chuan* simply states that Fa-an wrote a *Seng-chuan* in five chüan.[141] There is some doubt as to whether this is in fact a notice of a specific title; it may mean, rather, "monastic biographies." Yamanouchi assumes that the title was *Chih-chieh chuan* 志節傳,[142] but this is hypothetical. Nothing further is known of the work. The author lived from 454 to 498.[143]

III. Biographies of pilgrims *yu-fang* 遊方 by Seng-pao 僧寶. Hui-chiao says that Seng-pao's biographies were limited to this category of monks, and Wang again simply restates this.[144] The work is not mentioned in the *Kao-seng chuan*, in which there are brief biographies of three monks named Seng-pao;[145] no biographical work of any kind is mentioned in connection with any of them. No more is known about this book. As will be noted below, Hui-chiao was well read in the travel accounts of pilgrims, but we have no way of knowing what use he made of this particular work.

IV. A work by Fa-chin 法進. Hui-chiao says "The Śramaṇa Fa-chin composed essays and narratives on a comprehensive scale, but in treatment and in matter there were omissions and [undue] abridgments." Wang groups this book with that of Wang Chin (see XIII below) and says, "Only Fa-chin's work and Wang Chin's book are comprehensive in their conception and worthy to be considered [the works of] authors of some standing. But though Fa-chin's list of names is extensive, it is not broad (geographically? in terms of various types of clerical activity?); though Wang Chin's literary form is well set up, his [aim] is unrealized."[146] Wang Man-ying's judgment might be helpful if Wang Chin's book, with which he groups Fa-chin's, had survived, but a formalistic comparison of two unknowns provides little basis for inference. The *Sui-shu* lists a *Chiang-tung ming-te chuan* 江東名德傳 in 3 chüan by Shih Fa-chin 釋法進,[147] and T'ang identifies this with the present work.[148] However, I am inclined to agree with Yao Chen-tsung that the attribution of the *Chiang-tung*...to Fa-chin is incorrect, though I am not convinced that this work is by the famous eulogist Sun Ch'o 孫綽.[149] Biographical notices of two monks named Fa-chin in the *Kao-seng chuan* do not indicate that either was a writer, nor, from their activities, does it appear likely that either wrote clerical biographies.[150]

V. The *Hsüan-yen chi* 宣驗記 by Liu I-ch'ing, prince of Lin-ch'uan under the Sung dynasty 宋臨川王劉義慶 who was canonized as K'ang

康 (403–44).[151] Hui-chiao makes no separate criticism of this work or of nos. VI to XII which follow. For the entire group he says that they "mention in passing many monks and describe their characters. But these are all subsidiary notices and frequently have many lacunae."[152] Wang Man-ying does not comment on the *Hsüan-yen chi*. The work is cited once, by author and title, in the *Kao-seng chuan*.[153] It is noticed as a work in 30 chüan in the *Sui-shu* and is widely quoted in later encyclopedias and compendia, sometimes under the title *Ming-yen chi* 冥驗記.[154] From Lu Hsün's collection of surviving quotations, it is clear that this was a book of prodigies and that many of the stories show the rewards of piety and faith and describe the powers of the monks in dealing with natural and human events.[155] It seems likely that some of Hui-chiao's incidents in this vein were drawn from the *Hsüan-yen chi*, although the extent of his use of it cannot be determined.[156]

VI. The *Yu-ming lu* 幽明 (or 冥) 錄, also by Liu I-ch'ing. Wang Man-ying remarks that this work does not lack brief accounts of monks, but he comments that in the *Yu-ming lu*, as in nos. X, XI, and XII below, the monks appear in subsidiary passages that are not very revealing and that these biographies are not up to accepted literary standards.[157] The *Yu-ming lu* is noticed in the *Sui-shu* as a work in 20 chüan and is extensively quoted in later compendia.[158] The late Ch'ing scholar Hu T'ing 胡珽 published an old incomplete MS of uncertain date and provenance together with collations with other surviving fragments.[159] The most complete collection of fragments was published by Lu Hsün.[160] From these materials it is clear that the *Yu-ming lu* was a collection of stories of prodigies, shamanistic feats, marvels of clairvoyance, etc. It is likely that Hui-chiao drew some of his accounts of such wonders from this book.[161]

VII. The *Ming-hsiang chi* 冥祥記 by Wang Yen 王琰. Wang Man-ying makes no specific comment, despite the fact that he was the author of a *Hsü ming-hsiang chi* 續冥祥記.[162] Wang Yen's work is noticed in the *Sui-shu* as a book in 10 chüan.[163] It is widely quoted in later compendia, particularly in the *Fa-yüan chu-lin* 法苑珠林, and Lu Hsün brought together surviving quotations.[164] Wang Yen was a pious Buddhist layman and a devotee of Kuan-yin. Some time after

479 he wrote this book,[165] and it was intended to edify the reader with accounts of the rewards of piety and faith and of the ills that overtook unbelievers and opponents of Buddhism. From the extant quotations it would appear that the accounts of monks were somewhat longer and more detailed than those in nos. V and VI above. It is highly probable that Hui-chiao drew on this work for many of the pious anecdotes in his biographies, particularly those of the "theurgists."[166] Maspero believed that Wang Yen's account of Kāśyapa Mātaṅga formed the basis of that missionary's biography in the *Kao-seng chuan.*[167]

VIII. The *I-pu-ssu chi* 益部寺記 by Liu Ch'uan 劉俊. Wang has no comment. It was written by a high Ch'i official who was governor of I-chou 益州 (Szechwan) from early 491 to late in 493.[168] From its title it would appear to have been an account of the temples of Szechwan, and it is perhaps safe to infer that it was written during or after Liu's governorship. No notice or quotation is to be found.

IX. The *Ching-shih ssu-chi* 京師寺記 by the Śramaṇa T'an-tsung 曇宗. Wang Man-ying does not mention this work. Its writing is recorded in the *Kao-seng chuan* biography of T'an-tsung, and it is there noticed as *Ching-shih t'a-ssu chi* 京師塔寺記 in 2 chüan.[169] It is cited by Hui-chiao in his discussion of the date of An Shih-kao's death.[170] It is noticed in the *Sui-shu* as a work in 2 chüan, but the author's name is incorrectly given as T'an-ching 景.[171] Although a Liang work with the same title survives in quotations,[172] no trace of T'an-tsung's work is to be found. The author was something of a favorite of the emperor Hsiao-wu of the Sung (reigned 454–64) and lived some time at the capital. From this and from the title of the work we may infer that it was an account of the temples and pagodas of the capital, Chien-k'ang.

X. The *Kan-ying chuan* 感應傳 by Wang Yen-hsiu 王延秀. Wang Man-ying remarks that some monks are discussed in this work.[173] It is noticed in the *Sui-shu* as a work in 8 chüan.[174] Wang is mentioned as participating in a neo-Taoist study group in 436[175] and as serving the Sung as a ritual specialist during the T'ai-shih 泰始 era (465–71).[176] The *Kan-ying chuan* has disappeared. We can only surmise, from knowledge of other works of this kind, that it was a collection of stories of divine responses to appeals for help, to vows of the faithful, or to deeds of religious merit.

XI. The *Cheng-ying chuan* 徵應傳 by Chu Chün-t'ai 朱君台. Wang's remarks on this and the following work have been noted under VI above.[177] No such work is noticed in the *Sui-shu*, but a *Cheng-ying chi* 徵應集 in 2 chüan is listed, without an author's name, in both T'ang histories.[178] This may be Chu Chün-t'ai's book.[179] Nothing is known of the author save that he was a native of Wu-hsing 吳興, the modern *hsien* of that name in Chekiang.[180] The meaning of *cheng-ying* is close to that of *kan-ying* and, in default of more evidence, we may surmise that this work was a collection of the same type as no. X above.

XII. The *Sou-shen lu* 搜神錄 by T'ao Yüan-ming 陶淵明 (T'ao Ch'ien 陶潛). Wang Man-ying makes the comment noted under VI above. The *Sui-shu* lists a *Sou-shen hou-chi* 搜神後記 in 10 chüan by T'ao Ch'ien.[181] It has long been recognized that the surviving work of this title could not have been written by the famous poet since it contains accounts of incidents that happened after his death in 427.[182] Yet it is not a late forgery, and Hui-chiao's listing is evidence that such a work, attributed to T'ao Ch'ien, existed in the early part of the sixth century. This book is a popular account of prodigious feats and unnatural events. Hui-chiao may have drawn from it his account of Fo-t'u-teng's ability to remove and wash his intestines.[183] He cites "T'ao Yüan-ming's account 記" in connection with the biography of Shih-tsung 史宗.[184]

XIII. The *San-pao chi-chuan* 三寶記傳 by the Ch'i prince of Ching-ling 竟陵王, who was canonized as Wen-hsüan 文宣. Hui-chiao remarks that this work was sometimes called the *Fo-shih* 佛史 and sometimes the *Seng-lu* 僧錄 and, "The Three Treasures are recounted together. Treatment and ideas [on these topics] are intertwined so it is confused and difficult to draw upon, even more unclear [than other works discussed]."[185] Hsiao Tzu-liang 蕭子良, prince of Ching-ling, lived from 406 to 494; he was a pious Buddhist and a lifelong patron of learning.[186] Seventeen of his Buddhist writings, in a total of 295 chüan, are noticed as surviving in the Sui, but neither these works nor the twenty unlisted sūtra texts were held in very high esteem.[187] Among the seventeen works listed is the *San-pao chi* 三寶記 in 10 chüan. It was divided into three sections: (1) Fo-shih 佛史, history of the Buddhas, (2) Fa-chuan 法傳, history of the Dharma, and (3) Seng-lu 僧錄, history of the saṁgha.[188] Nothing has survived on which to base an estimate of Hui-chiao's possible use of this work.

XIV. The *Seng-shih* 僧史 by Wang Chin 王巾. Hui-chiao remarks, "its aim seems to be comprehensiveness, but the literary form is inadequate."[189] Wang Man-ying's comparison between this work and Fa-chin's book has been noted under IV above. The *Sui-shu* notices a *Fa-shih chuan* 法師傳 in 10 chüan by Wang Chin, and this is probably the same as the *Seng-shih* in 10 chüan noticed in the *Li-tai san-pao chi*.[190] Wang Chin, a literary figure and official under the Ch'i, died in 505.[191] He held the office of 記室, secretary, under the prince of Ching-ling, author of no. XIII above.[192] Since Wang Chin was associated with the prince, whose many literary enterprises were what we would now call cooperative projects, the suspicion is strong that Wang used the third part of the prince's book—on which he may have worked—as the basis for his own history of the saṁgha.[193] There are no surviving fragments.

XV. The *Ch'u-san-tsang chi-chi* 出三藏記集 by Seng-yu 僧祐. Hui-chiao remarks that Seng-yu included only the lives of thirty-odd monks and that those left out were very numerous.[194] Wang states that Seng-yu's work shares the criticism accorded Fa-chi's book—presumably that it included only a single class of monks.[195] This is the only major source of the *Kao-seng chuan* that has survived intact. It was written by the great Vinaya master Seng-yu and is the oldest surviving account of the history and content of the Chinese Tripiṭaka.[196] Seng-yu completed this work late in life, sometime between 510 and 518.[197] The fourth section is devoted to the lives of translators and exegetes, although these classifications are not used. There are 32 principal biographies which include a number of subsidiary accounts of lesser figures. All 32 subjects are given biographies in the *Kao-seng chuan*. According to the existing table of contents, the *Ming-seng chuan* contained only 27 out of the 32; this is somewhat surprising in

view of the fact that Pao-ch'ang was a disciple of Seng-yu and regarded the *Ming-seng chuan* as, in a sense, a continuation and expansion of his revered master's work.[198]

Hui-chiao made considerable use of the biographies in the *Ch'u-
san-tsang chi-chi*, and he did so in two different ways.[199] The first is
the use of a Seng-yu biography for the basic data and sequence of a
Kao-seng chuan biography—as in the biographies of Chu Shih-hsing
朱士行, T'an-wu-ch'an 曇無讖, and Kumārajīva—supplementing and
expanding these, to a greater or lesser degree, from other sources.[200]
The second pattern is the copying verbatim of an entire biography.
This is exemplified by the biography of Po Yüan 帛遠, wherein the
differences between the *Kao-seng chuan* and the *Ch'u-san-tsang chi-
chi* are no more than would creep into the transmission of a single
text.[201] This is a rather striking case of the unaltered use of an earlier
text, especially so since its muddy sequence, interpolated incidents,
and loosely relevant subsidiary accounts make it a most untidy piece
of biographical writing. I can only hazard the not very confident guess
that Hui-chiao took over such an account in toto because he did not
have access to other materials on Po Yüan's life in the far northwest a
century and a half earlier.[202]

XVI. The *Tung-shan seng-chuan* 東山僧傳 by Hsi Ch'ao 郗超, *tzu*
Ching-hsing 景興. Concerning this work and nos. XVII and XVIII
below Hui-chiao comments: "each either strives to exalt a single region without covering both the modern and the ancient or concentrates on preserving single good deeds without touching on other activities [of its subjects]."[203] On Hsi Ch'ao's work Wang remarks that it
collected only the lives of those who dwelt in the mountains.[204] Hsi
Ch'ao was a noted Chin dynasty official, a *ch'ing-t'an* adept, and a
pious Buddhist layman who lived from 336 to 377.[205] The mountains
referred to in the title were those in the then Yen hsien 剡縣 in the
Shao-hsing area of Chekiang. They were filled with noted Buddhist
temples.[206]

XVII. The *Lu-shan seng-chuan* 盧山僧傳 by Chang Hsiao-hsiu
張孝秀. Wang remarks that this work is subject to the same adverse
criticism as that of Hsi Ch'ao, namely, that it collected only the biographies of those who lived in the mountains.[207] The author, who lived

from 479 to 520, had a brief official career and then withdrew to the Tung-lin 東林 Temple at Lu-shan. He worked his fields and his "serfs" 部曲 for the support of the monastic community. He cultivated a rustic manner but was learned in Buddhism—particularly Vinaya—and an expert dialectician.[208] Nothing has survived of his monastic chronicle of Lu-shan.[209]

XVIII. The *Sha-men chuan* 沙門傳 by Lu Kao 陸杲 *tzu* Ming-hsia 明霞 . Wang makes no comment. Lu Kao, who lived from 450 to 523, was a respected official under the Liang.[210] He was a fervent Buddhist and was strict in keeping the precepts.[211] He and Chang Hsiao-hsiu mentioned above took instruction in the Vinaya from the monk Fa-t'ung 法通.[212] Lu is said to have donated his house, in 503, for the building of a Buddhist temple.[213] His *Sha-men chuan* is mentioned in both his biographies as a work in 30 chüan.[214] The Shören-in 青蓮院 in Kyoto has a late Heian or early Kamakura MS copy of a work by Lu entitled *Hsi Kuan-shih-yin ying-yen* 繫觀世音應驗. This is a collection of excerpts from earlier works showing the power of faith in Avalokiteśvara. Although it falls in the same category as nos. X and XI discussed above, it most closely resembles no. VIII, Wang Yen's *Ming-hsiang chi*. Both authors were devotees of Kuan-yin, and in both works the pious incidents are set in rather full historical and biographical contexts.[215] It is likely that Lu Kao drew heavily on his predecessor's compilation. From the nature of this work of Lu Kao and from his interests, we may infer that the *Sha-men chuan* emphasized those monks' lives which illustrated the power of faith or in which some divine intervention occurred. It may have been such an emphasis—on a single type of worthy action—that made the book the object of the second part of Hui-chiao's criticism quoted under XVI above. No quotations of the *Sha-men chuan* have survived.

In addition to the authors and titles mentioned in his preface, Hui-chiao specifies five broad types of writings which he used. It may be useful, in completing this study of his sources, to deal briefly with these types. To trace every title in these five groups is unnecessary for our present purposes, and to do so would protract this paper to inordinate length. Therefore I propose to illustrate each type of material by reference to a few of the sources Hui-chiao made use of. The general qualification should be made that he sometimes "used" these sources indirectly, taking over references to them and quotations from them when he copied or followed closely an earlier biography.[216] For a full bibliography of the titles mentioned in the *Kao-seng chuan* the reader is referred to Makita, *Ryō kōsōden sakuin*, pp. 323–70.

A. "Miscellaneous accounts" 雜錄. This refers to such works as the *Yu-ming lu*, the *Ming-hsiang chi*, etc., which have been described under nos. V–VII and X–XI above.[217] From Hui-chiao's reference to reading "several tens of authors" in this category, it was obviously a much larger group than the titles discussed, but no other works of this general type are mentioned in the *Kao-seng chuan* itself.

B. "Chronicles and histories of the Chin, Sung, Ch'i, and Liang dynasties" 晉宋齊梁春秋書記. From the wealth of, on the whole, accurate detail on secular events in the *Kao-seng chuan* itself it is clear that Hui-chiao was widely read in this historical literature. However he mentions only three works of secular history by title: the *Wu-chih* 吳志 of the *San-kuo chih* 三國志,[218] a *Sung-shih* 宋史 of unspecified authorship,[219] and a *Sung-shu* 宋書 mentioned in a reported admonition from the Sung emperor Hsiao-wu (ruled 454–65) to its author.[220] The dearth of citations is of course not surprising, for in freely using, but not citing, earlier works, Hui-chiao followed the accepted practices of Chinese historiography.

C. "The heterodox histories of the frontier dynasties of Ch'in, Chao, Yen, and Liang" 秦趙燕涼荒朝僞歷. Again there is evidence that Hui-chiao made considerable use of such sources, yet there is only one citation, that of T'ien Jung's 田融 *Chao-chi* 趙記.[221] I have elsewhere pointed out his probable use of several other works in this category.[222] Research on individual biographies will eventually reveal the full range of Hui-chiao's use of these materials.

D. "Geographical miscellanies" 地理雜篇. These include biographies on a regional basis such as VIII, IX, XVI, and XVII discussed above. They also include geographical and travel works descriptive of a region. The *Shan-hai ching* 山海經 is cited once,[223] Yü Chung-yung's 庾仲雍 *Ching-chou chi* 荊州記 is directly quoted on the life of

An Shih-kao.[224] Hui-chiao also mentions the travel and descriptive writings of pilgrim monks, and it is probably from such works that he got much of his knowledge of areas outside China.[225] The *Kao-seng chuan* shows that its author had an excellent knowledge of geography and local history. Works in this category, supplemented by travel, are the sources of that knowledge.

E. "Isolated pieces and fragmentary accounts" 孤文片記. This is so large a body of literature that it may be convenient to discuss it in four groups:

1. Separate biographies, *pieh-chuan* 別傳 or *pieh-chi* 別記.[226] This is a large class of writings of which Hui-chiao made extensive use. He most often makes no acknowledgment of these sources, and their use can be detected only through close study of individual biographies.[227] In other cases he simply says, "A separate biography states. . . . ," leaving the precise identity of the work and its author in doubt.[228] In a very few instances Hui-chiao mentions either the author or the title or both for a separate biography.[229] When he mentions the existence of such an account for one of the monks, we may assume that he used it as a source of that monk's biography. Wang Man-ying, in his letter to Hui-chiao, singles out four separate biographies with which he and his master were no doubt familiar.[230] These were a *Shan Tao-k'ai pieh-chuan* 善道開別傳,[231] a *Kao-tso pieh-chuan* 高座別傳,[232] a biography of Seng-yü 僧瑜,[233] and a biography of Hsüan-ch'ang 玄暢.[234] These represent only a few examples, of whose existence we know Hui-chiao to have been aware, of one of the most important groups of sources for his work.

2. Inscriptions 碑文. Hui-chiao frequently mentions the erection of a monument to the memory of an eminent monk; sometimes he names the donor, and often he specifies the writer or writers of the inscription.[235] Although the texts of such inscriptions abound in the conventional ornaments of eulogistic writing, they often contain vital biographical data put down in permanent form soon after the subject's death.[236] Hui-chiao unquestionably made use of these materials, either through visiting the monuments, or through copies made by travelers or collectors of such writings. We are perhaps safe in assum-

ing that as a general rule, when he mentions the existence of a memorial inscription as a biographical fact, he had access to the data it contained.

Hui-chiao's work contains an immense amount of historical detail on temples and monasteries: their donors and patrons, their outstanding monks, their building, their repair and expansion, their changes of name, their images and stūpas, etc. It is likely that Hui-chiao drew such information not only from such books as nos. VIII and IX discussed above, but also from the inscribed monuments erected to celebrate important events in the history of various Buddhist establishments.[237]

The relative inaccessibility of North China and the fact that Hui-chiao did not, so far as we know, travel there probably limited the amount of this type of material available to him from that area.[238]

3. Doctrinal treatises and discussions. Over sixty works of this general type are mentioned in the *Kao-seng chuan*. Sometimes the treatises are merely listed among the monk's writings. More often they are noted to illustrate a monk's position on a doctrinal point or in the religious controversies of his time. In a few cases the argument is summarized,[239] and occasionally a passage of the work is quoted.[240] These are among Hui-chiao's basic sources on the intellectual and doctrinal history of the Buddhist church and on the relations between the clergy and secular authority.

4. Miscellaneous. Prefaces to the translations of Buddhist works often not only describe the particular translation project but contain valuable biographical data on individuals. This is especially true for the translators. As we have seen, Hui-chiao relied heavily on the *Ch'u-san-tsang chi-chi* for these biographies, but he clearly made use of certain of the prefaces.[241]

Another valuable source were letters, in which the monks often discussed important doctrinal questions and occasionally touched on their personal activities. Hui-chiao drew on these for biographical data and quoted them at length to illustrate a monk's thought and literary ability.[242]

Eulogies, *tsan* 贊, are among the most frequently quoted short pieces in Hui-chiao's book. Since he did not, as many Chinese biographers did, write his own *tsan*, he quotes those of others to round out a biography with an appreciation of its subject. The most frequently quoted author of *tsan* is Sun Ch'o 孫綽, whose favorite device was comparing a monk to a noted *ch'ing-t'an* adept.[243] These eulogies were particularly suited to Hui-chiao's inclination to seek for his subjects status in the intellectual life of their times.

Poems in various styles are occasionally quoted. Sometimes they serve to recapture the atmosphere of an important moment in a monk's life or to express, in elegant form, his doctrinal views or his piety. Most often, perhaps, they are quoted to demonstrate a monk's virtuosity in a given verse form.[244]

5

FU I AND THE

REJECTION OF

BUDDHISM

I. HISTORICAL BACKGROUND

Fu I, the subject of this paper, lived from A.D. 555 to 639. During his lifetime China came to the end of a long period of disunion and was reunited under the Sui Dynasty; that reunification was consolidated by the T'ang. Behind political reunification there lay a complex of fundamental changes which had been taking place simultaneously but along divergent lines in north and south China. There were marked changes in material culture, shifts in population, new developments in economic and intellectual life. While Fu I's proposal for the extirpation of Buddhism is part of the history of the early T'ang, the roots and

Reprinted by permission from the *Journal of the History of Ideas* 12, no. 1 (January 1951): 33–47. Copyright © by the Journal of the History of Ideas.

motives of that proposal are to be found in the history of the Northern Chou and the Sui.

North China had been dominated by non-Chinese rulers for more than 250 years. Toward the end of that period two developments prefigured reunification. On the one hand the north Chinese gentry, at first impotent, had gradually fought their way back to political power; they had made judicious marriages with the families of alien overlords; they had served these same princes as military and civil officials. Most important, they had exerted unremitting pressure on their masters to reconstitute a Chinese-type state and society. On the other hand, the alien rulers themselves had become convinced of the superiority of the Chinese system. This conviction was strongest in those rulers who dreamt of the conquest and unification of all China.

In the south the Chinese had transformed a semicolonial area into a rich, intensive agricultural region. The "legitimate" regimes at Nanking were politically and militarily weak and had long since given up hope of a forcible reconquest of the north. But in the north the relatives of the southern aristocrats were bringing the day of unification nearer. Travel, trade, and exchange of ideas between north and south increased, and the cultural gap between the two regions was being steadily narrowed.

A further common bond between north and south was a foreign religion which had developed and spread over all China. Buddhism, first in the north and later in the south, had converted and organized the masses. It had become, in the centuries of disunion, the principal religion and the dominant intellectual interest of the ruling classes. Despite its foreign origin and institutions, which clashed with the traditions of the Chinese state and society, Buddhism had much to recommend it as an ideology for reunited China.

Confucianism was another possible ideology. It had been discredited in the fall of Han, and its thought at this time was far less rich and mature than that of Buddhism. By the sixth century it seemed to the educated classes remarkably sterile and anachronistic. But despite this and despite its lack of appeal to the common people, it remained the body of thought theoretically most suited to the reestablishment of a unified Chinese state and society. Emperor Wu of the Later Chou

(reigned 561–78), though himself a Yü-wen Turk, took up with enthusiasm his predecessor's plan to reconstitute, from the Confucian
Ritual Canon, a government patterned on that of the Chinese sage-
ruler par excellence, the duke of Chou. He hoped that such a government, with himself as its sage-king, could be extended over all China.
To assure the symmetry of his plan and to eliminate a major focus
of opposition, he attempted, in 574, to abolish the "alien" religion of
Buddhism, saying, with scant regard for the facts of his ancestry, "I am
not one of the five barbarians, whose minds are lacking in reverence.
Buddhism was contrary to the orthodox teachings [that is, Confucian
principles], and for that reason I abolished it." The measures taken
against Buddhist organizations were simultaneously taken against
those of its native rival, religious Taoism. This brings us to the third
potential ideology.[1]

Religious Taoism had as its philosophic core the writings of the
Taoist thinkers of the late Chou period. But by the sixth century A.D.
that core was barely discernible through the accretions that clung to it.
Religious Taoism had its organizational roots in the Later Han, and it
reemerged in the fifth and sixth centuries as a native rival of Buddhism. It borrowed heavily from its rival, and Taoist ritual, theology,
monastic organization, and iconography were largely pastiches of
Buddhism. It was inferior to Buddhism in philosophic range, but its
indigeneity and its absorption of a variety of native cults gained it a
numerous following. This following, however, was quantitatively inferior to that of Buddhism among the masses, just as it was qualitative-
ly inferior among the educated.[2] The literati, it should be emphasized,
continued to be interested in *philosophic* Taoism regardless of their
official or religious affiliations.

When the prime minister of the last ruler of the Later Chou decided
to overthrow his master and found a new dynasty, he had before him
the ideological problem. The Sui founder had been witness to the
Chou effort to reestablish a classical Chinese government. He had seen
that effort fail, its failure hastened by the disaffection of Buddhists and
Taoists of all ranks of society. One of his first official acts was to relax
the measures for the suppression of Buddhism and Taoism.[3] From his
subsequent decrees it is obvious that he had decided to favor the reli-

gion with the widest following both among the people and the ruling class. He saw Buddhism as a possible binding power in his efforts to weld together the north and south, which had so long been evolving along different lines. With this in mind, he ordered the building and staffing of local Buddhist temples at state expense and the assembling of Buddhist scriptures under the authority of local officials.[4] Taoism he allowed to revive, but he did not give it his active support.

The most important and powerful class in Sui China was the gentry—the educated landholding class whose support was essential for the reconstitution of a unified state and a strong central government. What was their attitude toward the Sui founder's Buddhist sympathies and his attempt to use Buddhism as an ideology of reunited China? We know that a large number of gentry families in north and south alike had been converted to Buddhism, a lesser number to religious Taoism. Yet as the gentry slowly but steadily regained their political predominance, it was obvious that they could not effectively assert or perpetuate their power through the celibate clergy of Buddhism or Taoism. Confucianism, with its roots in Chinese soil and its concept of government by a secular educated élite, was undoubtedly better suited to their purposes. But Confucian thought—as thought— was anachronistic; it had stagnated during the Period of Disunion and was now incomparably poorer and more limited than Buddhist thought. The large number of the gentry who were devout and scholarly Buddhists knew this, but they nonetheless sought to revive Confucianism as that ideology most suitable as an ideology of reunited China and as the vehicle for the perpetuation of gentry power. Their decision is reflected in the fact that Emperor Yang of the Sui, whose usurpation in 605 had wide gentry backing, immediately attempted to set up an examination system with a Confucian curriculum. At first the examinations demanded merely the repetition of ancient formulae; they were empty of intellectual content. But they did provide the sons of gentry families with a passport to public office and power. Merchants and artisans were explicitly forbidden to take them.[5]

In the early T'ang the gentry took the next step toward the revival and development of Confucianism. Schools were set up which taught a Confucian curriculum; efforts were made to reinterpret and expand

Confucian doctrine so that it might become an intellectual rival of Buddhism. But this was to take centuries and at last produce the great synthesis of neo-Confucianism. Meanwhile Buddhism flourished as never before. No outstanding intellect of the Sui and early T'ang was uninfluenced by it. New Chinese sects, of great vigor and specifically adapted to Chinese needs, grew up. Buddhist art, under the patronage of court and officialdom, reached new and brilliant heights. The Buddhist church organization, alien to China and at odds with the Confucian conception of the state, was rich and powerful. The power interests and the political ideals of the gentry were opposed to this *imperium in imperio*, yet many of the gentry were devout Buddhists, and the church was one of the three sacred essentials of the Buddhist religion.[6] Moreover, the church reached into and influenced all ranks of society. To attack it would have been political folly as much as it was sacrilege.[7] In the early T'ang, this was the gentry's dilemma: They needed the institutions of the Confucian state to assure their power. They needed Buddhism to satisfy their spiritual and intellectual needs. But the institutions of Buddhism were at odds with the Confucian state, and Confucianism remained too sterile to meet their intellectual needs.

2. THE LIFE OF FU I

It was the peculiar role of one member of the Chinese gentry, Fu I, to propose a drastic solution to this dilemma. In brief, his solution was that Buddhism be exterminated, that the Confucian state be consolidated, and that Taoism be fused with Confucian thought to provide a viable alternative to Buddhist philosophy. A biographical sketch may serve to reveal some of the motivation behind this proposal.[8]

He was born in 555 of one branch of a Chinese gentry family which had been settled in the fertile south Shensi plain since the Former Han dynasty. Among his ancestors were noted officials, frequently rewarded with enfeoffment. It seems likely that the branch to which he belonged had long been in the service of the non-Chinese rulers of the north.[9] Sometime between the ages of nineteen and twenty-three he entered the T'ung-tao kuan academy at Ch'ang-an, then the capital of the Northern Chou. This academy had been founded by Emperor Wu in 574 as part of his program for the elimination of the Buddhist and Taoist churches and the creation of a state based on the Ritual Canon of Confucianism.[10] When he struck at the churches and clergy, which he regarded as incompatible with his ideal, as drains on state resources, and threats to his autocratic rule, he sought to perpetuate through this academy not only Confucian learning but the useful knowledge of both the Buddhist and Taoist clergy. These two traditions had monopolized "scientific" knowledge, and their adepts were trained to intercede with unseen powers. The emperor decreed that 120 adepts of proven reputation should be appointed to the academy as official scholars to be supported at state expense. And, along with his enthusiasm for the Books of Ritual, he had a strong personal interest in Taoism. This was reflected in the composition of the academy, which was soon dominated by Taoist practitioners.[11] I suggest that it was probably from these academicians that Fu I acquired the technical skills for which he became noted: mathematics, with its sister science numerology; astronomy, with its applied branches, astrology and calendric calculation. It seems likely that in this organization, under the patronage of a strongly anti-Buddhist emperor, Fu I acquired many of the prejudices which appear in his writings.

We next hear of him when, in 593 at the age of thirty-eight, he requested from the Sui emperor permission to practice the profession of a Taoist doctor.[12] In 597 he secured the position of chief diviner to a provincial governor who was also a prince of the Sui royal house.[13] The story is that Fu warned the prince, at the time the gentry backed his brother's usurpation, not to revolt against the new order. The astrological warning given in the histories probably cloaks Fu's own decision, as a member of the gentry, to support the new regime. When his advice was unheeded, he fled the camp of his patron and was rewarded with the office of prefect of a county in southern Shensi, not far from the estates of his gentry ancestors.[14]

He came to the court of the newly established T'ang dynasty about 618 and was soon given the post of grand astrologer.[15] He used his specialized knowledge in giving astronomical names to the divisions of the T'ang territorial army and in devising a new method of measuring time by the clepsydra.[16]

In 621 and 624 Fu I, then in his sixties, presented two groups of proposals for the suppression of Buddhism.[17] In preparing his arguments he combed historical literature for material to be used against Buddhism. His collection of twenty-five biographies of earlier opponents of Buddhism, the *Kao-shih chuan* (Lives of Eminent Scholars), may be regarded as a by-product of his research.[18]

Fu I's personality is clearly revealed in his arguments against Buddhism and in other scattered materials which have come down to us. He was a man of choleric disposition and strong convictions. He had the two indispensable qualities of a great polemicist: emotional commitment to the case he is arguing and the capacity for trenchant and colorful discourse. There was in his behavior a certain intemperance and eccentricity which echoed the behavior of the third- and fourth-century devotees of the cult of Taoist "naturalness." We shall see that he is strong in negative attack and weak in constructive proposals. And this latter weakness reflects what I suspect was a deep-seated dissatisfaction with many aspects of the Chinese civilization of his day. It is perhaps this frustration which adds the heated—almost hysterical—note to his attacks on an alien religion.

3. FU I'S PROPOSALS FOR THE EXTIRPATION OF BUDDHISM

Fu I's proposals can most conveniently be considered in categories. An effort will be made to analyze each category of argument in terms of Fu I's origins, experience, and personality.[19]

A. Economic Arguments

Fu I's economic arguments are a veritable encyclopedia of anti-Buddhist economics, largely drawn from earlier polemics. He argues that celibacy creates parasites among the population, that these parasites not only constitute in themselves a drain on the economy; they also fail to produce children and thus deprive the empire of greatly needed labor and tax revenue. He proposes that the Buddhist clergy be forced to marry and predicts that 100,000 productive and taxable families will result.[20]

The building of tens of thousands of temples and shrines strains the resources of the country in labor and materials. He recommends that this building be stopped and available resources diverted to military and public works programs.[21]

In these arguments he reflects the economic preoccupations of his class—the landed gentry—with their unvarying concern for agricultural production and abundant cheap labor as the mainstays of the state and society. At the same time one can see him adding weight to such arguments by reference to the herculean tasks of reorganization and reconstruction which faced the new T'ang regime.

B. Political Arguments

The Buddhist church, he says, constitutes a vast *imperium in imperio*; its members are bound by a barbarian system of thought and belief.[22] He states that ten armed revolts against secular authority had been led by monks.[23] The clergy, he says, in receiving revenues and influencing the people, usurp prerogatives which belong to the emperor alone. He contrasts this disregard of secular authority with the "humility" of Confucius and Lao-tzu in paying homage to reigning princes.[24]

Buddhism, he argues, was responsible for the political and social disintegration of China following the collapse of the Han. Buddhism brought it to pass that "sovereigns were unenlightened, ministers deceitful, government tyrannical, and reigns short."[25] He here implies that the formidable tasks of reunification which the T'ang faced were gravely complicated by the presence of this religion, that a return to the unity and strength of the Han regime is impossible so long as Buddhism exists.

He deplores the influence of the Buddhist clergy at court. If unchecked, they exert a baneful influence on the ruler, and their intrigues will bring unmerited disaster upon forthright ministers.[26] In these and related arguments Fu I shows that his concern, as a member of the gentry officialdom, is the restoration of a Han-type centralized state in which that class would play the leading role. The establishment of such a regime and the predominance of that class were jeopardized by the existence of an organized clergy with a numerous popular following and great economic power.

C. Nationalistic Arguments

Closely related to Fu I's political arguments was his xenophobia. As a member of the Chinese gentry of the north, triumphant after 250 years of struggle against alien rule, he seems convinced by his own fallacious argument that Buddhism brought on the catastrophe of disunion and perpetuated the rule of "barbarians." Only the elimination of that alien faith can fully restore China to the Chinese. He argues for the superiority of Chinese thought and institutions mainly by simple assertions that they are untainted by foreignisms. He refers to Buddhism variously as "the barbarian miasma," the teachings of a "crafty wizard of the Western barbarians" or of "the seductive barbarian."[27] By such appeals he hoped to attract the support of the Chinese ruling class, which, in varying degrees, had been oppressed and humiliated under alien rule.

D. Social-Psychological Arguments

"The myriad functionaries darkly brood on the crimes of their past lives and vainly seek to make provision (through religious faith and works) for future felicity. They talk wildly of heavens and hells. They revile things Chinese."[28] Such preoccupations, he asserts, are demoralizing, unworthy of members of a Chinese government of a Chinese empire.

The Buddhist doctrines of heaven and hell and retribution beyond the grave have terrorized and deluded the masses. They are no longer contented with their lot, and in their quest for salvation, they have become contemptuous of temporal law. Imagining themselves assured of happiness beyond the grave, they are contumacious toward punishments decreed by the state.[29]

Buddhism has fostered social disintegration. The idle and improvident, the unfilial and disloyal have merely to shave their heads and put on clerical garb and they are assured of a parasitic life of ease beyond the reach of law or social sanctions.[30] The Buddhists deny the Confucian principle that the power of moral reformation belongs solely to the Son of Heaven.[31] In doing so they repudiate the moral values which emanate from that source and ensure social harmony. The consequent antinomianism and anarchy threaten the whole social structure.

In all these arguments Fu I is asserting the ancient values of the Confucian state and society. He is recommending that those in authority "honor the teaching of the Duke of Chou and Confucius and expel the Western barbarian."[32] For Fu I, member of the landed gentry and court official, the choice was clear: Restore the Han social and political order and its sanctions. To do this one must extirpate the whole complex of alien habits, ideas, and institutions which had developed since its fall.

E. Intellectual Arguments

Fu I's views on Buddhist philosophy are what we should expect from one with his background. As he expressed them they became, negatively, arguments for the extermination of a false and delusive way of thought and, positively, arguments for its replacement by an amalgam of Confucian and Taoist ideas. All Buddhism, says Fu I, is "naught but magicians' lore which mean and depraved people have ornamented by copying the profound words of Chuang-tzu and Lao-tzu."[33] The terminology of philosophic Taoism had indeed been one of the first mediums for the communication of Buddhist ideas to the Chinese, but Fu I here twists historical fact to suggest an explanation for the wide following which Buddhism had gained in China. The references to philosophic Taoism here and elsewhere in his writing suggest his notion of what should replace Buddhism as the intellectual interest of the educated class. His deathbed admonition to his sons makes this more explicit: "The Taoist writings of Lao-tzu and Chuang-tzu, the words of the Six Classics of the Duke of Chou and Confucius comprise the teachings of the sages. You should study them."[34]

This formula is strongly reminiscent of the views of the T'ung-tao kuan scholars. Fu I's own writing is full of the vocabulary and concepts of philosophic Taoism, just as his expressed social and political ideals are those of Confucianism. He himself wrote a commentary to the Lao-tzu which, unfortunately, has long been lost.[35] It is clear that it was philosophic Taoism fused with Confucianism which he advocated as the viable spiritual and intellectual alternative to Buddhism.

Despite his training in the magical and "scientific" techniques associated with religious Taoism, he seems to have had little regard for it and little hope that it could become a strong rival of Buddhism. It is said that in his whole life he had never asked for a (Taoist) physician nor taken their medicine, and his biographer goes on to say, "Though he was well versed in the writings on yin-yang and numerology, he gave neither of them credence."[36] Thus in the end he proposes that Confucian institutions be revived and that an amalgam of Confucian and *philosophic* Taoist thought become the ideology of reunited China. By this proposal he sought a solution which would serve the power interests of his class and at the same time offer attractions which would wean them away from Buddhism.

4. CONCLUSION

The reactions to Fu I's proposals for the extirpation of Buddhism reveal the prevailing attitudes of the court and gentry of the early T'ang. When his first memorial against Buddhism was presented in 621, it elicited the support of only one official in the numerous T'ang court.[37] The leading Buddhist clerics of the capital were outraged and busied themselves with lengthy rebuttals. On another occasion an official of strong Buddhist piety condemned Fu I's impious attacks on Buddhism and asked that he be dismissed from office and executed. Fu I counterattacked with vigor, and the official was moved to remark that Hell had been made for just such men as Fu I.[38] The emperor T'ai-tsung, asserting his convictions of the inherent truth of Buddhist teachings, was, in the words of the historian, "amazed" at one of Fu I's anti-Buddhist tirades.[39] Not until nearly a century later did the T'ang house take measures against the Buddhist church, and it was over two centuries before such measures were carried out effectively on a large scale. Why did Fu I's proposals receive such a cool reception?

There are a number of reasons for the rejection of Fu's proposals: (1) The Buddhist clergy fought against them with formidable resources of intellectual and political power. (2) The T'ang rulers were well aware that the Buddhist persecution of 574 had been a factor in bringing the Northern Chou dynasty to a violent end; the T'ang house, even dized its newly won hegemony by mass persecution. (3) The T'ang aspired to become the dominant power in Asia; an attack on the religion of most of the states of Eastern Asia would have been political folly. (4) Most important was the prevalence of Buddhist belief among the ruling house, the high officials, and the gentry.[40] Fu I proposed nothing which would compete with Buddhism for the religious and intellectual adherence of the upper class, no lay ethic which could replace Buddhism among the masses. When he offered a combination of Confucianism and Taoism, he was proposing that two different and often contradictory strains of Chinese thought should somehow replace the rich and varied yet homogeneous Buddhist system of thought and belief. Confucianism, as we have noted, was revived in the T'ang as the nucleus of secular education, but it had not yet been freed of the stale archaism of Han scholasticism. Philosophic Taoism had its appeal, but though its classics were full of poetic insights and its concepts greatly enriched by third- and fourth-century neo-Taoist thought, it yet lacked the comprehensiveness and subtlety of Buddhist thought. It was Fu I's tragedy that he could forcefully present the evils of a foreign religion but could find, neither for himself nor for his contemporaries, a system which could hope to replace it.

There was probably among the gentry and officialdom some measure of support for his criticism of the Buddhist church as a menace to the state and the predominance of the secular elite. But until time and the efforts of many great minds had raised Confucianism from its position of intellectual and spiritual inferiority to provide at last a competing system, the Chinese ruling class continued to give its adherence to an alien faith, despite the fact that the institutions of that faith conflicted with their power interests.

Fu I's arguments and the reactions to them challenge the easy assumption of the dominance of pragmatic considerations in Chinese thought. He showed the ruling class that the Buddhist church was a menace to the order they were attempting to establish, but he could not demonstrate the intellectual or spiritual superiority of either of the main native traditions. Thus, despite political and economic considerations, they continued for several hundred years after his death to give their allegiance to a foreign religion.

NOTES

Chapter 1 Buddhism and Chinese Culture: Phases of Interaction

1. Despite their use of modern methods, Dr. Hu Shih's studies in Chinese Buddhist history are not unmarked by this attitude. See his essay "The Indianization of China: A Case Study in Cultural Borrowing," 219–47. The last sentence of this essay reads, "With the new aids of modern science and technology, and of the new social and historical sciences, we are confident that we may yet achieve a rapid liberation from the two thousand years' cultural domination by India."

2. Robert Redfield, in his *Peasant Society and Culture*, has suggested a number of ways of looking at the relation between elite and peasant culture in a single society; see particularly the chapter "The Social Organization of Tradition," 67–104. [Although Redfield's formulations have been challenged and modified, they inspired a substantial body of research and scholarship. For critiques of Redfield's views, see, inter alia, Oscar Lewis, "Further Observations on the Folk-Urban Continuum and Urbanization with Special Reference to Mexico City," and Philip M. Hauser, "Observations on the Urban-Folk and Urban-Rural Dichotomies as Forms of Western Ethnocentrism."—Ed.]

3. The first date is conventional—that of the Buddhist observances of Ying, prince of Ch'u, brother of Han Ming-ti (r. A.D. 58–75), recorded in *Hou Han-shu* 42.1428–30. See Henri Maspero, "Le songe et l'ambassade de l'Empereur Ming," 95–130. [See also Kenneth Ch'en, *Buddhism in China*, 33.—Ed.] Wada Sei, in a recent article, "Bukkyō tōden no nendai ni tsuite," 491–501, expresses doubts—which I do not share—concerning this account written down by Fan Yeh in a much later and strongly Buddhist age. Wada believes that the first incontrovertible evidence of the presence of Buddhism in China is Chang Heng's (78–139) "Hsi-ching fu" ["Rhyme-prose on the western capital"].

4. See Etienne Balazs, "Political Philosophy and Social Crisis at the End of the Han Dynasty." Balazs, 188–90, cites the account of *Hou Han-shu* 7.305 (A.D. 159), which records that the five eunuchs who assassinated the head of one of the empress's family cliques were ennobled by the grateful monarch,

given a marquisate which entitled them to income from seventy-six thousand families and, in addition, the sum of fifty-six millions.

5. See Howard S. Levy, "Yellow Turban Religion and Rebellion at the End of Han," 214–27.

6. Balazs, "Political Philosophy and Social Crisis," 194.

7. See Etienne Balazs, "Nihilistic Revolt or Mystical Escapism: Currents of Thought in China during the Third Century A.D.," 226–54.

8. Arthur Waley, "The Fall of Loyang," 8.

9. This does not mean that there was no interest whatever. We know, for example, that the Han emperor Huan (r. A.D. 147–67), on the recommendation of the sorcerer Hsiang Chieh, paid homage to a Buddha image (*Hou Han-shu* 30B.1082) and that at the time "there were a few believers among the common people" (*Hou Han-shu* 88.2922), etc. Yet the interest that did exist seemed, on the one hand, rather idle curiosity about an exotic form of Taoism and, on the other, a desire to acquire and exploit its alleged magical power. This slowly changes toward the end of the period we are considering.

10. *PCL* 3.502c.

11. Figures from Tokiwa Daijō, *Go-Kan yori Sō-Sei ni itaru yakukyō sōro-ku*, 11–17.

12. See T'ang Yung-t'ung, *Han-Wei liang-Chin nan-pei-ch'ao Fo-chiao-shih*, 71–73. Henri Maspero suggested that this community may have been historically linked to the early Taoist-Buddhist community at P'eng-ch'eng fostered by Prince Ying of Han, who died in A.D. 71; cf. Maspero, "Les origines de la communauté bouddhiste de Lo-yang," 91–92.

13. See Paul Demiéville, "Le pénétration du Bouddhisme dans la tradition philosophique chinoise," 19–38.

14. I accept Pelliot's dating; cf. Pelliot, "Meou-tseu ou les doutes levés," 255–433.

15. Waley, "The Fall of Loyang," 10. The translation from the Sogdian is by W. B. Henning.

16. Cf. *Shih-shuo hsin-yü chiao-chien*, 71. At the end of his speech Wang Tao says, literally, "Why should we sit looking at one another like [so many] prisoners of Ch'u?" [See also Mather, *Shih-shuo hsin-yü*, 45.—Ed.] The allusion is to a prisoner from Ch'u state whom the marquis of Chin took pity on, released, and sent back to Ch'u as a peace envoy; cf. James Legge, *The Chinese Classics*, 5: 371.

17. Demiéville, "Le pénétration du Bouddhisme," 23–24, suggests that this pattern of progression from Confucianism through neo-Taoism to Buddhism was typical for educated Chinese converts from the fourth to the seventh centuries.

18. For the reflection of the vogue of Vimalakīrti in Buddhist art, see J. Leroy Davidson, "Traces of Buddhist Evangelism in Early Chinese Art," 251–

65. Vimalakīrti figures prominently in the cave-temples of north China, but the meaning of his cult in the north would be differently interpreted in relationship to a different clientele.

19. See Jacques Gernet, *Les aspects économiques du Bouddhisme dans la société chinoise du Ve au Xe siècle*, 245–69. I have reviewed this important study under the title "The Economic Role of Buddhism in China."

20. See *Nan Ch'i-shu* 53.916; also Miyakawa Hisayuki, "Rikuchō jidai jin no Bukkyō shinkō," 289–312.

21. On this ruler, see Mori Mikisaburō, *Ryō no Butei*, esp. 134–69, where his relationship to Buddhism is discussed.

22. Edict of the Later Chao ruler Shih Hu, ca. 335; see Wright, "Fo-t'u-teng: A Biography," in this volume.

23. Miyakawa, "Rikuchō jidai jin no Bukkyō shinkō," 8, cites the case of a Northern Wei general who suffered remorse for the ferocious slaughters he had perpetrated and donated his own houses for the building of temples in all the provinces in which he had held office; see *WS* 73.1633. This means of expiating mass violence was to persist in the Sui and T'ang.

24. See Gernet, *Les aspects économiques du Bouddhisme*, passim.

25. See, inter alia, Arthur E. Link, "Biography of Shih Tao-an," 1–48, and the same author's "Shyh Daw-an's Preface to Saṅgharakṣa's Yogācarabhūmi-sūtra and the Problem of Buddho-Taoist Terminology in Early Chinese Buddhism," 1–14. Ōchō Enichi has suggested the three preconditions for the development of a matured theory of translation. These preconditions, which were fulfilled by Tao-an's time, were (1) opportunities for sustained contact with foreigners, which deepened the consciousness of the differences between Chinese and foreign languages; (2) availability of multiple translations of the same texts, which made comparative study possible; (3) development of a demand, not for paraphrase and general interpretation, but for faithful and carefully modulated translations; see Ōchō, "Chūgoku Bukkyō shoki no hon'yakuron," 221–32.

26. See Gernet, *Les aspects économiques du Bouddhisme*, 245–50.

27. See Miyakawa, "Rikuchō jidai jin no Bukkyō shinkō," 8. He cites the instance (from *WS* 83A.1819) of a Northern Wei official who, besides supporting famous monks and financing sixteen copies of the Buddhist canon, built seventy-two temples. A monk criticized him for causing the death of men and oxen in his extravagant building activities. He replied—with scant piety and much cynicism—that posterity would see and admire the temples and would know nothing of the men and oxen which had perished.

28. See Arthur Wright, "Fu I and the Rejection of Buddhism," reprinted this volume; see p. 172, n. 1, for references to Tsukamoto Zenryū's three important studies of the Northern Chou suppression.

29. Some of the following is dealt with also in Arthur Wright, "The Forma-

tion of Sui Ideology, 581–604."

30. Edwin O. Reischauer, *Ennin's Travels in T'ang China*, 165.

31. On Amoghavajra, see Chou Yi-liang, "Tantrism in China," 284–307. On the powerful clerics of the Sui and T'ang, see Takao Giken, *Chūgoku Bukkyō shiron*, 51–53.

32. *HKSC* 21.610b–c. Gernet, *Les aspects économiques du Bouddhisme*, 33 and passim, points out that the Vinaya rules were favored by secular authority as a means of keeping the numbers and activities of the Buddhist clergy within strict limits.

33. Takao, *Chūgoku Bukkyō shiron*, 47.

34. Ibid.

35. The percentage is based on the figure of approximately 48,000 poems in the *Ch'üan T'ang-shih* [Complete poems of the T'ang] and on the number of titles in the index to Buddhist-related titles in that collection compiled by Kasuga Reichi, "*Zen-Tōshi* Bukkyō kankei senjutsu mokuroku."

36. See Reischauer, *Ennin's Travels in T'ang China*, 164–216.

37. The most comprehensive study of this movement is Yabuki Keiki, *Sangaikyō no kenkyū*. The sect later revived and had a huge following in the T'ang, but its fanaticism and exclusiveness brought on four further suppressions.

38. On Pure Land Buddhism in the mid-T'ang, see Tsukamoto Zenryū, *Tō chūki no Jōdokyō*.

39. See Demiéville, "La pénétration du Bouddhisme," 33–35.

40. Jacques Gernet, *Entretiens du Maître de Dhyâna Chen-Houei de Hötso (668–760)*, iv. This applies, of course, more to the "subitist" school of Ch'an than to the "gradualist." At the risk of pushing an analogy too far, one might suspect that the "gradualist" viewpoint, whether in Ch'an, Confucianism, or neo-Confucianism, reflects a strong persisting Chinese interest in heredity, status, and hierarchy which is perennially in conflict with ideas of mobility. That the Ch'an Buddhism of the T'ang struck contemporary Indian Buddhists as outlandish and heterodox is attested by the eighth-century Sino-Indian debates at Lhasa; see Paul Demiéville, *Le Concile de Lhasa*, 348–50 and passim.

41. Tsukamoto Zenryū, "Shina Bukkyōshi," 195.

42. See Gernet, *Les aspects économiques du Bouddhisme*, 298.

43. Galen Eugene Sargent, "Tchou Hi contre le Bouddhisme," 7.

44. Joseph R. Levenson, "The Amateur Ideal in Ming and Early Ch'ing Society: Evidence from Painting," 320–41.

45. Willem A. Grootaers et al., "Temples and History of Wanch'üan (Chahar)," 314. A total of 851 temples and shrines were studied.

46. Francis L. K. Hsu, *Under the Ancestors' Shadow*, 173.

47. Hu Shih, "The Concept of Immortality in Chinese Thought." It should

be pointed out that the tripartite immortality (literally, "nondecay")—of virtue, service, and wise words—was specified by an official of the state of Lu as early as 549 B.C. See Legge, *The Chinese Classics*, 5: 507.

48. Liu Shao-ch'i, "Lun Kung-ch'an-tang-yüan ti hsiu-yang," 50. Discussed by David S. Nivison in "Communist Ethics and Chinese Tradition," 60. [See also Lowell Dittmer, *Liu Shao-ch'i and the Chinese Cultural Revolution*, 17–18.—Ed.]

49. This approach has been used extensively by Nakamura Hajime in his *Tōyōjin no shii hōhō*. Nakamura's methodology was discussed at length by him and a Stanford University faculty seminar in 1951–52.

Chapter 2   Fo-t'u-teng: A Biography

1. *Pa-wang chih luan* 八王之亂. Cf. Wang Chung-ch'i, *Chin-ch'u shih-lüeh*, 44–105, and *Ajia rekishi jiten*, 7: 380–81.

2. Cf. *CS* 56.1533; Chiang T'ung died in 310.

3. Cf. Liu Shan-li, "Chin Hui-ti shih-tai Han-tsu chih ta-liu-hsi"; Wu Hsien-ch'ing, "Hsi-Chin mo ti liu-min pao-tung"; and Yang Lien-sheng, "Notes on the Economic History of the Chin Dynasty," 124–29.

4. On Liu Yüan, founder of the Former Chao dynasty (A.D. 304–29), cf. *CS* 101.2644–52. On Liu Ts'ung, cf. *BD* 1359 and *CS* 102.2657–77. See also Wolfram Eberhard, *Liu Yüan ve Liu Ts'ung, un biyographileri*, translations into Turkish and German of Liu Yüan's biography in *CS* 101.2644–52 and Liu Ts'ung's in *WS* 95.2043–46.

5. On Shih Lo, cf. *CS* 104–05.2707–52, *SLKCC* 11–13, *WS* 95.2047–50; also Franke, *Ges.*, 2: 43–62 passim, 63–66; 3: 240–41, 245; and Okazaki Fumio, *Gi-Shin nambokuchō tsūshi*, 141–52, 156, 642–44.

6. It would seem that the Chieh people spoke a Turkic language; cf. the exegesis in *KSC* 9.384b, translated in section 13 of Fo-t'u-teng's biography, below; cf. also n. 26 below. But why was it necessary for Fo-t'u-teng to interpret this language for Shih Lo if the latter was indeed of Chieh origin? Prof. Ch'en Yin-k'o, in his *T'ang-tai cheng-chih-shih shu-lun-kao*, discusses on 126–28 the racial origin of An Lu-shan and suggests that the terms *Che-chieh* 柘羯 and *Chieh-hu* 羯胡, by which An is often called, connect him with the Che-chieh who, in T'ang times, were mercenary soldiers in Samarkand and Bokhara. Cf. Thomas Watters, *On Yüan Chwang's Travels in India*, 629–645 A.D., 1: 94, and Edouard Chavannes, *Documents sur les Tou-kiue (Turcs) occidentaux*, 137. Prof. Ch'en, in a letter to this writer dated June 26, 1947, makes the further suggestion that the Chieh people to whom Shih Lo was related were possibly the mercenaries of Turkish stock who served in the Indo-Iranian kingdoms mentioned above. Prof. Ch'en points out, however, that evidence is insufficient to establish this hypothesis. Chavannes, op. cit., 313,

would equate the term *che-chieh* 柘羯 or 赭羯 to the Persian word *tchâkar*, which had in Sogdiana the special sense of "warrior." This agrees with *HTS* 221B.6244, which would give the term primarily an occupational rather than a racial connotation.

7. Cf. *CS* 105.2756.

8. Cf. *BD* 1365; *CS* 103.2683–2702; Franke, *Ges.*, 2: 41–53; 3: 239, 242, 246; and Okazaki, *Gi-Shin Nambokuchō tsūshi*, 149–52.

9. Cf. *CS* 104.2716 and 105.2748–49.

10. The incident of the Hsien-pei slave, *KSC* 9.384a, translated in section 10 of Fo-t'u-teng's biography, above, shows the evil atmosphere created by racial inequality and antagonism.

11. On Shih Hu, cf. *CS* 106.2761–107.2799; *SLKCC* 15–18; *WS* 95.2050–54; Franke, *Ges.*, 2: 65–78; 3: 245–47; Okazaki, *Gi-Shin Nambokuchō tsūshi*, 153–60, 639–44.

12. On Jan Min, cf. *CS* 107.2793–97. His rule was ended by the Mu-jung 慕容 in 352.

13. A parallel case was that of the monk Seng-she 僧涉; cf. *CS* 95.2497.

14. Both Tao-an 道安 and Kumārajīva were also regarded as military assets; cf. *KSC* 5.352c and 2.331c–332a.

15. Cf. the article "Byō" 病 in *Hōbōgirin, Dictionnaire encyclopédique du Bouddhisme d'après les sources chinoises et japonaises*, 3.224–65. One of Teng's disciples won fame (and converts) by treating eye diseases; cf. *KSC* 9.387b. Another treated female disorders; cf. *KSC* 9.387c.

16. The greatest of the monks among the Chin aristocracy was Chih-tun 支遁, also called Chih Tao-lin 支道林 (314–66); cf. *KSC* 4.348b–49c. [Chih-tun is discussed at length in E. Zürcher, *The Buddhist Conquest of China*, 116–30 and passim—Ed.] For a collection of surviving fragments of his writings, cf. Hsü Kan, comp., *Chih-tun chi*. Familiarity with the latest philosophic theory was the monk's passport into the intellectual life of the capital; cf. Zürcher, *The Buddhist Conquest of China*, 116ff.

17. For the edict, see *KSC* 9.385c, translated in section 32 of Fo-t'u-teng's biography, above, and n. 123 below. Cf. its use in the refutation of Fu I's 傅奕 (A.D. 555–639) anti-Buddhist arguments in *Kuang hung-ming chi* 6.126b–c. [Fu I's arguments are presented in Arthur Wright's essay "Fu I and the Rejection of Buddhism," reprinted this volume.—Ed.]

18. Cf. *KSC* 4.347a.

19. *Ko-i* 格義. Cf. Tsukamoto Zenryū, *Shina Bukkyōshi kenkyū: Hoku-Gi hen*, 25–34, and T'ang Yung-t'ung, *Han-Wei liang-Chin nan-pei-ch'ao Fo-chiao-shih*, 1: 235. T'ang defines *ko-i* as follows: "*Ko* means 'to measure' (*liang* 量). This was a method which took [the terms and concepts of] Chinese thought and compared and equated them to [Buddhist terms and concepts], thereby making it possible for people easily to understand Buddhist writings."

Later, new and more satisfactory translations and better exegesis rendered the system obsolete.

20. Cf. *KSC* 5.351c–54a; *Ch'u san-tsang chi-chi*, 6.43c, 44b–46b, 13.108a–09b; Paul Pelliot, "Les kuo-che ou 'maîtres du royaume' dans le Bouddhisme chinois," 675, n. 3; Bagchi, *Le canon bouddhique en Chine*, 1: 162–69. On Tao-an's catalogue, cf. Hayashiya Tomojirō, *Kyōroku kenkyū*, 333–451; Hayashiya discussed earlier fragmentary texts in ibid., 213–330. [More recently, detailed accounts of the life of Tao-an can be found in Zürcher, *The Buddhist Conquest of China*, 184–204, Arthur E. Link, "Biography of Shih Tao-an" (a translation of the *KSC* biography), and in the monograph of Ui Hakuju, *Shaku Dōan kenkyū.—Ed.*]

21. Cf. *KSC* 5.354b; *Shui-ching chu* 8.13a–b; F. S. Drake, "The Shen-t'ung Monastery and the Beginning of Buddhism in Shantung," 6–17; and Miyakawa Hisayuki, "Shin no Taizan Chiku Sōrō no jiseki." The preeminence of Chu Seng-lang's establishment was recognized by the Former Ch'in ruler Fu Chien 苻堅 (337–84) when the latter exempted it from his proposed control of monasteries; cf. *KSC* 5.354b and the essay by Miyakawa cited above.

22. Cf. *KSC* 5.354b–55a; *Ch'u san-tsang chi-chi* 12.83a–85a; [Zürcher, *The Buddhist Conquest of China*, 148–49—Ed.]. Chu Fa-t'ai was associated with Tao-an and Chu Fa-ya in the development of the *ko-i* system noted above; cf. *KSC* 4.347a and *Shih-shuo hsin-yü chiao-chien*, 361, and its commentary [translated in Mather, *Shih-shuo hsin-yü*, 238—Ed.].

23. Cf. *KSC* 5.354a; Bagchi, *Le canon bouddhique en Chine*, 1: 335–36. On his meeting with Kumārajīva, cf. *KSC* 2.332c.

24. Cf. *Pi-ch'iu-ni chuan* 1.934c–35a and Franke, *Ges.*, 3: 267–68. [On An Ling-shou, see Arthur Wright's separate study "Biography of the Nun An-ling-shou," reprinted this volume.—Ed.]

25. Cf. *KSC* 9.387b–c; *CS* 95.2491–92. He was a native of Tun-huang and was noted for his supernatural powers.

26. Cf. *KSC* 9.387c. According to one theory, Chu Fo-t'iao was of Indian origin.

27. For Hui-chiao's life, cf. the *Hsü Kao-seng chuan* of Tao-hsüan 6.471b and Seng-kuo's 僧果 biographical note appended to *KSC* 14.423a. A long study of the *KSC* is Yamanouchi Shinkyō, "*Kōsōden* no kenkyū." A commentary to the *KSC* preface by Chou Shu-chia and Su Kung-wang appeared in 1942–43. [See also Arthur Wright's fuller study of Hui-chiao and his *Kao-seng chuan*, "Biography and Hagiography: Hui-chiao's *Lives of Eminent Monks*," reprinted this volume.—Ed.]

28. Cf. *WS* 67.1501–05. He died about 525.

29. Cf. Wylie, *Notes on Chinese Literature*, 40; Pelliot, "Meou-tseu ou les doutes levés," 395–96, n. 310. There is a "reconstruction" of the original *SLKCC* by T'ang Ch'iu 湯球 (d. 1881), entitled *Shih-liu-kuo ch'un-ch'iu chi-*

pu, and chap. 22 contains a biography of Fo-t'u-teng, but this biography is simply reproduced in toto from *CS* 95, with the addition of one quotation from *TPYL* 697. The implication is that the *CS* editors simply copied the *SLKCC* account, and this, as will be shown, is mistaken. T'ang Ch'iu's "reconstructions" are in general not marked by high critical standards. [Cf. Rogers, *The Chronicle of Fu Chien*, 20–22.—Ed.]

30. For criticisms of the *CS* as a whole, cf. *Ssu-k'u ch'üan-shu tsung-mu* 45.8b–9a; *Shih-t'ung t'ung-shih* 12.349–50.

31. Cf. Maspero, "Communautés et moines bouddhistes chinoises aux IIe et IIIe siècles," 233, n. 1.

32. Cf. Pelliot, "Autour d'une traduction sanscrite du Tao tö king," 420, n. 3.

33. Cf. *CS* 94.2449–50 and 95.2490–91.

34. Cf. *KSC* 14.422c. This does not mean that no *pieh-chuan* existed; it may mean that such a work was not sufficiently comprehensive to merit listing or that Hui-chiao had not seen it.

35. Cf. *Shih-shuo hsin-yü chiao-cheng*, 82.

36. I shall treat the relation of the *KSC* to Pao-ch'ang's *Ming-seng chuan* in a later paper. [Cf. "Biography and Hagiography: Hui-chiao's *Lives of Eminent Monks*," part 4: "The Sources of the *Kao-seng chuan*," as reprinted in this volume.—Ed.] Hui-chiao made extensive use of the *Ming-seng chuan*, but his own work was more comprehensive and more critical. For the many later derivative biographies of Fo-t'u-teng, cf. *Sōden haiin*, 272–73.

37. Cf. Rémusat, *Nouveaux mélanges asiatiques*, 179–88. Cf. Maspero's translation of the memorial and edict on monasticism in "Communautés et moines bouddhistes chinoises aux IIe et IIIe siècles," 222–23; Pelliot, "Autour d'une traduction sanscrite du Tao tö king," 419–21; Bagchi, *Le canon bouddhique en Chine*, 1: xvi–xvii; Franke, *Ges.*, 3: 245–46. Cf. also T. K. Chuan, "Some Notes on the *Kao Seng Chuan*," 462.

38. Cf. T'ang Yung-t'ung, *Han-Wei liang-Chin nan-pei-ch'ao Fo-chiao-shih*, 1: 191–93, and passim; Itō Giken, *Shina Bukkyō seishi*, 111–20; Yamazaki Hiroshi, "Tō-Shin jidai no kita-Shina shokozoku Bukkyō no ichimen"; Sakaino Kōyō, *Shina Bukkyō seishi*, 281–86; Tsukamoto, *Shina Bukkyōshi kenkyū: Hoku-Gi hen*, passim; and Yamazaki Hiroshi, *Shina chūsei Bukkyō no tenkai*, 69–173, passim.

39. Cf. Pelliot, review of E. H. Parker, *China, the Avars and the Franks*, and "Autour d'une traduction sanscrite du Tao tö king," 419. The *Fo-tsu t'ung-chi* 36.339a notes, "Fo-t'u-teng in Indian means 'fully enlightened sage'" (*Fo-t'u-teng fan-yü ssu-kuo sheng-jen yeh* 佛圖澄梵語四果聖人也). The fourth fruit, in some enumerations, is arhatship; cf. Mochizuki, *Bukkyō daijiten*, 740b.

40. *Shih-shuo hsin-yü chiao-chien*, 82–83 [Mather, *Shih-shuo hsin-yü*,

52–53—Ed.]. The rest of this fragment contains no facts different from the *KSC* biography.

41. Cf. Lévi, "Le 'Tokharien B' langue de Koutcha," 332–33.

42. On the surname of the kings of Kucha, cf. Lévi, ibid., passim; also Feng Ch'eng-chün and Hsiang Chüeh-ming, "Kuan-yü Chiu-tz'u po-hsing chih t'ao-lun," 2 and passim. Hsiang, ibid., 15, points out that the correct primitive form was *po* 白 and that the later form *po* 帛 resulted from a copyist's error; thereafter both forms were interchangeably used.

43. Cf. Lionel Giles, "Dated Chinese Manuscripts in the Stein Collection," 337, no. S.1625. I was able to secure a photostatic copy of this memoir through the courtesy of Dr. E. D. Edwards.

44. Cf. Maspero, "Communautés et moines bouddhistes chinoises au IIe et IIIe siècles," 224. It is interesting that the inscription to the image of 338 has *chu* 竺 as the first character of the donor's name. Unfortunately the rest of the name is undecipherable.

45. Cf. *Feng-shih wen-chien chi chiao-cheng fu yin-te*, 8.16–18.

46. For this title, cf. *KSC* 9.384b, translated in section 15 of Fo-t'u-teng's biography, above.

47. *TCITC* 30.20a describes this stele as an "image-stele of Śakyamuni." The *Chin-shih lu* 20.12a also so identifies it.

48. Cf. the variants listed in *Feng-shih wen-chien chi*, 8.16–18.

49. Cf. *Chin-shih lu*, 20.12a.

50. This suggestion was made by Wang Kuo-wei in an annotation to a Ming MS of the *Feng-shih wen-chien chi*. It is cited by Chao Wan-li in his "Kuan-ts'ang shan-pen shu t'i-yao: *Feng-shih wen-chien chi...*," 152. I know of no example of the interchange of *sai* 塞 and *shih* 濕. While the former is primitively equated to *śaka*, the latter is not used in early Buddhist texts; it appears for the first syllable in Śiva, Śivi, etc.; cf. Mochizuki, *Bukkyō daijiten*, 462a, 1980a.

51. Cf. *WS* 114.3029 [translated in Hurvitz, "Wei Shou, Treatise on Buddhism and Taoism," 48, 49, n. 4—Ed.]; also, Ware, "Wei Shou on Buddhism," 124.

52. Cf. Watters, *On Yüan Chwang's Travels in India, 629–645 A.D.*, 1: 225. Chavannes, "Voyage de Song Yün," 399, translates Sung Yün's early sixth-century observation to the same effect.

53. In addition to the Taishō text, I have used the excellent edition of 1889 by the Chin-ling k'o-ching ch'u 金陵刻經處, which follows a Ming text. I am indebted to Achilles Fang for reading the first draft of this translation in 1941 and to Dr. Walter Fuchs for many helpful suggestions. Textual variants in the Taishō text are referred to by the following [boldface] abbreviations: P: Palace, K: Korean, S: Sung, Y: Yüan, M: Ming.

54. *Jo fu-ch'i* 若符契. Cf. Nobel, "Kumārajīva," 213, n. 4.

55. *Shen-chou* 神呪. Cf. Chou Yi-liang, "Tantrism in China," 242–45 and passim.

56. *Ma-yu* 麻油. Cf. Laufer, *Sino-Iranica*, 288–96.

57. *Yen-chih* 胭脂 K; *yen-chih* 燕脂 SYM; *yin-hui* 茵灰 P; *CS* 95.27a [T'ung-wen text] has *yen-chih* 臙脂, emended to *yen-chih* 胭脂 in Peking text, 95.2486. According to Laufer (*Sino-Iranica*, 324–28), except for P, these are all homophonous variants which were originally transcriptions of an unidentified West Asiatic word, probably meaning safflower, from which rouge was made. Chinese accounts later associated it with many plants from which a red dye was extracted.

58. See also *KSC* 9.384b, 385b, translated in sections 13 and 29 of Fo-t'u-teng's biography, above. *CS* 95.2486, derived from section 13, describes the participation of a novice in this technique. *Pi-ch'iu-ni chuan* 1.935a describes, in the biography of the nun An-ling-shou, the participation, after fasting, of a non-Buddhist layman (An-ling-shou's father) as an intermediary. [Cf. Arthur Wright's essay "Biography of the Nun An-ling-shou," reprinted this volume.—Ed.] A clue to a possible Indian origin of this method is found in Wilkie Collins, *The Moonstone*, 18–19. For its relation to the later *yüan-kuang* 圓光 divination technique, cf. *Nien-erh-shih k'ao-i* 22.13b, quoted in *Chin-shu chiao-chu* 95.27b, comm. Cf. also *Ch'ing-pai lei-ch'ao* 33.55a. The same work, 33.60a, gives the following anecdote from the life of the great Ch'ing official Liu Ming-ch'uan 劉銘傳 (1836–96; cf. Hummel, *Eminent Chinese*, 2: 526–28): "When Liu Ming-ch'uan of Ho-fei (Anhwei), whose posthumous title was Chuang-su 壯肅, was appointed provincial commander of Chih-li, [there was] a man who was proficient in the magic art of Fo-t'u-teng. Liu asked him to come to his office. The man intoned spells in a mumbling voice. In a moment, the center of his palm gave off a great bright light. The first picture [which was manifested] was a man with turbaned head and a sword worn at his side. The second picture was a man wearing the white heron insignia [of a first rank civil official]. The third picture was a man with his head severed, in a remote valley deep in the mountains. Afterward [in 1885] Chuang-su was made governor of Formosa and was concomitantly given the rank of president of a board. He subsequently pleaded illness and returned [to Ho-fei]." This nineteenth-century prophecy, in the manner of Fo-t'u-teng, is to be interpreted as follows: The first picture, that of the warrior, refers to Liu's post as commander of Chih-li. The second is that of an official of the first rank and refers to his governorship of Formosa, during which he held the rank of president of a board and was entitled to wear the white heron insignia. The third refers to his retirement, in 1891, to his native place.

59. For materials on Liu Yao, cf. n. 8 above.

60. Ko-pei 葛陂. Near the modern Ju-nan 汝南, southeast Honan.

61. A *pieh-chuan*, quoted in *Shih-shuo hsin-yü chiao-chien*, 83, gives the second character of Kuo Hei-lüeh as *mo* 默, which is a mistake. Kuo saw service under Shih Lo and Shih Hu and died sometime after 337. Cf. *CS* 104.2708 and *KSC* 9.385a, translated in section 22 of Fo-t'u-teng's biography, above.

62. A painting entitled "Shih Lo Enquiring about Buddhism" by the Yüan dynasty master Ch'ien Hsüan 錢選 (ca. 1235 to after 1301) is discussed by J. C. Ferguson, "Stories in Chinese Paintings," 89–90. Cf. also *Hsü-chai ming-hua-lu* 2.3a–4b.

63. *Ssu-ling* 四靈. The four sacred creatures are the unicorn, the phoenix, the tortoise, and the dragon. Cf. Legge, *The Li Ki*, 1: 384.

64. Fang-t'ou 枋頭; **SPK** have *fang* 坊, which is incorrect. Cf. *CS* 95.2485. Fang-t'ou was located 80 li southwest of the modern Chün 濬 county in Honan. The night raid was probably undertaken by the forces of Hsiang Ping, who was entrenched in Fang-t'ou and whom Lo later defeated; cf. *CS* 104.2717.

65. T'uan-wan ssu 團丸祠, adopting the **M** variant *ssu* 祠 for *ssu* 祀. This was a shrine to the spirit of a spring, a type very common in the period. Cf. *Shui-ching chu*, 25.2a, 26.6a, 27b–28a. On this shrine, cf. *Yüan-ho chün-hsien t'u-chih*, quoted in *Chin-shu chiao-chu* 95.26b, comm., and *Sui ch'ü-yü t'u-chih* 隋區宇圖志, quoted in *TCITC* 30.9a–b. The dragon or serpent is universally associated with springs, streams, and rainfall. Cf. Frazer, *The Magic Art and the Evolution of Kings*, 2: 156–57, and De Groot, *The Religious System of China*, 5: 521–23. [Edward Schafer has recently examined this theme in *The Divine Woman: Dragon Ladies and Rain Maidens in T'ang Literature*, 12ff. and passim.—Ed.]

66. Otherwise unknown.

67. *Sheng-ch'uang* 繩床. Cf. Watters, *On Yuan Chwang's Travels in India, 629–645 A.D.*, 1: 147, where these "corded benches" are described. On the relation of the *sheng-ch'uang* to the *hu-ch'uang* 胡床, or "barbarian benches," cf. Fujita Toyohachi, "Koshō ni tsuite," pt. 1, p. 452, and pt. 2, pp. 131–32. For Vinaya prescriptions for chairs and benches, cf. *Mo-ho seng-ch'i pi-ch'iu-ni chieh-pen* 1.561c; *Ssu-fen lu* 50.937b; *Shih-sung lü* 11.79b. Cf. also Takakusu, *A Record of the Buddhist Religion*, 22–24, and *Nan-hai chi-kuei nei-fa chuan* 1.206c–07a.

68. *An-hsi hsiang* 安息香. Cf. Pelliot, "Autour d'une traduction sanscrite du Tao tö king," 480, and Laufer, *Sino-Iranica*, 464–67.

69. Otherwise unknown.

70. Tuan Po 段波 or Tuan Mo 段末 or Tuan Mo-p'ei 段末杯 was a member of the Tuan family of Hsien-pei who held the title of duke of Liao-hsi

遼西公. The attack on Lo occurred in 312; cf. *CS* 104.2718-19. For a different version of this engagement, cf. *CS* 63.1710. Po was not, as a result of Lo's leniency, a very steadfast ally; cf. *CS* 104.2719, 2727.

71. Died in 340. He was in the service of both Lo and Hu. Cf. *CS* 104.2708, 2711, 2716, 2718.

72. A minor member of the Liu family; he probably died in the slaughter following Yao's defeat. Cf. *CS* 104.2701.

73. Shih-liang-wu 石梁塢 was east of Loyang, north of the Lo River; cf. *TCITC* 206.13a.

74. Kuan-ssu 官寺 was in Han times an official's yamen; cf. *Han-shu* 75.3171. In this case it is probably a temple erected at public expense, a forerunner of the metropolitan and provincial temples built by government order under the Northern Wei and Sui. Cf. Tsukamoto, "Kokubunji to Zui-Tō no Bukkyō seisaku narabi ni kanji," 7-8.

75. Both the Chung-ssu 中寺 Temple and the Kuan-ssu were in Hsiang-kuo. See below, n. 96.

76. Unknown outside the present text. He is mentioned also in section 39 of Fo-t'u-teng's biography, above.

77. For another account of this conference, cf. *CS* 105.2744-45.

78. *Hsiang-lun* 相輪 were wheellike finial ornaments. The form *lun-hsiang* 輪相 seems preferable. Cf. *Mo-ho seng-ch'i lü*, 33.498a, and Chavannes, "La Sūtra de la paroi occidentale de l'inscription de Kiu-yong koan," 77, n. 4.

79. *Hsiu-chih t'i-li-kang pu-ku ch'ü-t'u-tang* 秀支替戾岡僕谷劬禿當. In Karlgren's ancient transcription, this sentence would read:

si̯ə̯u' ȶ'śi̯e̯ t'iei' liei'/liet ȶkâng b'uok kuk ȶg'iu t'uk ȶtâng'.

For various unsuccessful attempts to reconstruct this sentence, cf. the references in Pelliot, "Autour d'une traduction sanscrite du Tao tö king," 420-21, n. 3; also Shiratori Kurakichi, *Über die Sprache des Hiung-nu Stammes und der Tung-hu-Stämme*, 11-13, and Bernát Munkácsi, review of K. Shiratori, 240-46. The following Turkish reconstruction by Ramstedt appeared in his "Zur frage nach der stellung des tschuwassischen," 30-31:

Hier lese ich statt t'i-li-kang oder t'ai-li-kang *tal'iqyŋ* od. *tal'iqaŋ* und stelle es mit atü. *tašyqqyŋ* 'ziehet aus' zusammen: *siu-k'i* ist wohl = atü. *sükä* (dat. zu *sü*, 'kriegsheer, krieg'); *puh-koh* ist = *bügü* 'der weise' (als titel der herrscher verwendet), mo. *böge* 'schaman' oder auch = *ügä* (eine alttürkische hohe würde); *kü* ist moglicher weise = -g, d. h. die alte endung des akkusativs, mo. -*ji*, und *t'u-t'aŋ* ist imperativ von *tut*- (atü.) 'gefangen nehmen'. Die hohische sprache, ein hunnen-idiom, stand demnach dem alttürkischen ziemlich nahe, war aber eine *l'*-sprache, und wir haben hier eine genaue zeitbestimmung.

Note that Ramstedt corrects the *KSC* transcription by placing the accusative ending on *pu-ku* and not at the beginning of the following word.

80. An official under the Later Chao, executed in 333; cf. *WCNP* 4038. His argument favoring attack is given in *CS* 105.2744.

81. He was made crown prince in 330, murdered by Shih Hu in 334; cf. his biography in *CS* 105.2752–56. His deposition is mentioned in *KSC* 9.384b, translated in section 17 of Fo-t'u-teng's biography, below.

82. Enfeoffed in 330; cf. *CS* 105.2746.

83. *Chuan* 縛, "to bind." Is this possibly a mistake for *fu* 縛, "white," resulting in a certain redundancy in the sentence? Note that *CS* 95.2486 has *po-hsi* 白晳 for *chuan* 縛. The compound there has the meaning of "light-complexioned," which is consistent with the description of Yao's appearance given in *CS* 103.2683.

84. The clairvoyancy technique here employed is described in more detail in *CS* 95.2486. Cf. also the *Yu-ming lu* 幽明錄 by Liu I-ch'ing 劉義慶 (403–44), quoted in *TPYL* 370.5a. This work is one of the acknowledged sources of the *KSC*. See *KSC* preface 14.418b. [For more detail on this work, cf. Arthur Wright's "Biography and Hagiography," reprinted this volume.—Ed.]

85. I can find no details on Shih Ts'ung or his revolt. The warning is in the form of a pun on the word *ts'ung* 葱, meaning "onion." This incident was apparently in the *Ming-seng chuan* 4, but the full text does not survive. Cf. the *Shuo-ch'u* 說處 section (a topical finding list), in *Meisoden sho*, pt. 4, p. 14b.

86. *Ta ho-shang* 大和尙. Cf. Lévi's discussion of the term and its probable origins in Chavannes, "Jinagupta," 337, n. 5.

87. I read *wei-erh* 爲兒 (foster son), following the **YM** variant, for elsewhere Pin is always referred to as Hu's son. Note that the commentary to *Chin-shu chiao-chu* 106.5a is incorrect on this point. For Pin's death, cf. *CS* 107.2787.

88. This is the appellation of Ch'in Yüeh-jen 秦越人; cf. *BD* 396. For this incident, cf. *Shih-chi* 105.2788–92.

89. *Kuan-fo* 灌佛. The eighth day of the fourth month is prescribed for this ceremony. *Chi Shen-chou san-pao kan-t'ung lu* 3.432b states that it was on this day in the year 333 that Lo performed the ceremony. Cf. *Fo-shuo kuan-hsi Fo-hsing-hsiang ching* 1.796c–97a; Takakusu, *A Record of the Buddhist Religion*, 147–52; De Visser, *Ancient Buddhism in Japan*, 1: 45–52. Note that the present instance of the ceremony is more than a century earlier than the first Chinese performance mentioned by De Visser.

90. Near the modern Lin-chang 臨漳 county, northern Honan.

91. *Ku* 顧, following the **SYM** variant.

92. *Tiao-nien* 雕輦, "sedan chair." Cf. L. C. Goodrich, *A Short History of the Chinese People*, 92–93. For another vehicle, the *pan-nien* 板輦, said to

have been used by Fo-t'u-teng, cf. *Chao-shu* 趙書, quoted in *Chin-shu chiao-chu* 95.28a, comm., and in *PWYF* 1899b. Cf. also the forged *SLKCC* 21.3a.

93. Ch'ang-shih 常侍, a military officer at the court with the same rank as the civilian shang-shu 尚書. Cf. *WHTK* 50.459a.

94. Li Nung was in high office under Shih Hu, being a Ssu-k'ung 司空 from 347 to 349. Cf. *WCNP* 4039d–40a. Li was enfeoffed by Jan Min, but was executed shortly afterward, in 350. Cf. *CS* 107.2793.

95. Following this passage, *CS* 95.2487 inserts the following incident, taken from the *Shih-shuo hsin-yü chiao-chien*, 82–83 [Mather, *Shih-shuo hsin-yü*, 52–53—Ed.]: "Chih Tao-lin [see above, n. 16] was living in the capital [i.e., Chien-k'ang, the modern Nanking]. When he heard that Teng was going about with all the Shih [family], he said, 'Mr. Teng regards Chi-lung [i.e., Shih Hu] as a seagull.'" Chih Tao-lin's remark refers to a story in the original *Chuang-tzu*, now preserved only in *Lieh-tzu* 2.12a. Cf. Waley, *Three Ways of Thought in Ancient China*, 257. [Cf. also Graham, *The Book of Lieh-tzu*, 45–46.—Ed.] The point of the story is that seagulls were thought to be capable of detecting a threat and changing their behavior accordingly. Thus Chih Tao-lin meant that Teng, in his relations with the Shih family, recognized them as wild and wary birds, not very intelligent, but well able to detect any unfaithfulness on his part, as were the gulls in the *Chuang-tzu* story.

96. See n. 75 for a temple of the same name in Hsiang-chou and *KSC* 5.351c for another reference to the present temple. *CS* 95.2488 reads *Yeh-ch'eng ssu chung* 業城寺中. The commentary to this passage, *Chin-shu chiao-chu* 95.29b, quotes the *T'ai-p'ing huan-yü-chi*; cf. Chavannes, "Les pays d'occident d'après le Wei lio," 532n): "T'ien-lo ssu 天樂寺 was built by Shih Hu for Fo-t'u-teng. In the temple there is a veined stone (*wen-shih* 文石) censer. This is what Teng used in his services." *TCITC* 197.14a locates this temple west of the modern Lin-chang county. The *KSC* text is probably correct, and I can see no reason for associating T'ien-lo ssu with this incident.

97. He appears only in this incident and in section 22 of Fo-t'u-teng's biography, above.

98. He appears only in this incident.

99. Liang-chi ch'eng 梁基城 or 梁期城, a walled city 50 li north of Yeh; cf. *Shui-ching chu* 10.12a.

100. "Pu-yüeh ching hu yu erh pu-kai, pu yüeh shen hu tu erh pu-tai" 不曰敬乎幽而不改, 不曰慎乎獨而不怠. I have been unable to locate the source of this quotation.

101. The Vinaya prescribes the same taboos in connection with Buddhist stūpas. Cf. *Ssu-fen-lü pi-ch'iu chieh-pen* 1.1021c and Wieger, *Bouddhisme chinois*, 1: 254–55.

102. He had been made crown prince in 335; cf. *CS* 106.2762. After a

career of violence and treachery, he was executed by Shih Hu; cf. *CS* 106.2766–67.

103. A Buddhist name, part of the transcription of Sanskrit Amitābha. Such names were common in this period. Cf. the lists of Buddhist personal names of the Six Dynasties period compiled by Miyakawa Hisayuki, "Riku-chō jinmei ni arawaretaru Bukkyōgo"; A-mi appears in pt. 2.

104. Otherwise unknown. *CS* 95.2488 has T'ai-i 太醫, Court Physician. Cf. *T'ung-tien* 25.148b.

105. K alone has the form *ya* 雅, which, however, is correct. His biography appears in *KSC* 4.347a, where he is said to have been a native of Ho-chien 河間, Hopei. The present text, *KSC* 9.387a (in section 41 of Fo-t'u-teng's biography, above), refers to him as Chu Fa-ya of Chung-shan 中山, the modern Ting 定 county, some one hundred miles east of Ho-chien.

106. Otherwise unknown. Many others of the same name lived in later periods.

107. Nan-t'ai 南臺 is probably the same as the Chin-hu t'ai 金虎臺 which Ts'ao Ts'ao built inside the northwest corner of the walls of Yeh in 213. Cf. *TCITC* 197.9a; Chavannes, "Pei Yuan Lou," 180, n. 1.

108. See n. 61 above.

109. He appears only in this incident and in section 19 of Fo-t'u-teng's biography, above.

110. I adopt *fa* 乏, found in **SYMP** and *CS* 95.2489 instead of *chih* 之 in **K**. Omit *chi* 際, found only in **K**.

111. See n. 87. Yu-chou 幽州 was the northernmost of the Later Chou provinces; Chi 薊, near the modern Tientsin, was its capital. The character *chi* is missing in **SYM**. Mu-chen 牧鎮 was a governor, also in charge of the defense of the area. In 343 Shih Pin neglected his duties in favor of drinking bouts and hunting. When remonstrances were ignored, Shih Hu sent a force to Yu-chou which brought Pin back; he was flogged and stripped of office, and some ten of his intimates were executed. Cf. *CS* 106.2774.

112. *Sha* 殺 before *wu-pai* 五百 and after *pu-ch'in* 不親 strikes me as a corrupt character. Emend to read *chang* 杖 "to beat" as in *CS* 106.2774. The **P** variant *chiao* 教 for the second *sha* 殺 is unacceptable.

113. The Huai 淮 River in southeast Honan, the Ssu 泗 River in southeast Shantung. Lung 隴, in western Shansi, was threatened by an uprising of Chiang 羌 in 343; cf. *Shih-liu-kuo chiang-yü-chih*, p. 4117a. Pi 比 is probably the old walled city of Pi-yang 比陽 near the modern Nan-yang, southern Ho-nan, in territory constantly disputed between the Chin and the Later Chao. Fan-ch'eng 凡城 is near the modern P'ing-ch'üan 平泉 county, southern Jehol; cf. *TCITC* 43.20b. It was taken by Mu-jung K'o 慕容恪 in 338; cf. *CS* 109.2818. A Chao attempt to retake it failed in 344; cf. *CS* 106.2775. See also n. 121.

114. This incident is drawn from T'ien Jung's *Chao-shu*, quoted in *PCL* 1.496b. There are minor variants, e.g., 6,000 arhats for 60; it lacks the phrase "knelt and gave thanks," which Hui-chiao no doubt felt would dramatize the king's submission to the monk.

115. This incident is also drawn from the *Chao-shu*, quoted in *PCL* 1.496a. There are minor variants, the most interesting of which is the attribution of the title Kuo-shih 國師 to Fo-t'u-teng. On this title, cf. Pelliot, "Les kuo-che ou 'maîtres du royaume' dans le Bouddhisme chinois," 671–76, and Pelliot, "Meou-tseu ou les doutes levés," 379, n. 318.

116. They were both given office in 319; cf. *CS* 105.2735. Chang Liang disappears from history after his appointment as Yu p'u-she 右僕射 in 349, cf. *CS* 107.2786, while Chang Li holds high office under Hu's successor, *CS* 107.2787–88, and presumably dies in the struggle for power among Hu's heirs. This incident is probably drawn from a *pieh-chuan* quoted in *TPYL* 658.3b, though the text of the latter is corrupt, e.g., *wu-ta* 無大 for *wu-yü* 無欲; *t'ien-fa* 天法 for *ta-fa* 大法; and it lacks the final sentence giving the fulfillment of Teng's prophecy.

117. The crown prince at this time was Shih Hsüan. See n. 154. Hu in this case delegated his princely rainmaking duties to the next in rank.

118. Fu-k'ou 釜口; *fu* 釜 should be 滏 as in *CS* 95.2489. *Shui-ching chu* 10.36a locates the place northwest of Yeh. Following the taboo of the emperor Huai's name, legitimist historians from 314 onward refer to Yeh as Lin-chang; cf. *TCITC* 197.2b. *Shui-ching chu* 10.36a quotes a *pieh-chuan* version of this incident. Cf. also the *pieh-chuan* versions in *TPYL* 11.5b and 64.3a. A *pieh-chuan* may be taken as the source of this incident; the only element not in the *KSC* account is a mention of *pao-lu* 暴露, exposure to the sun, as a rainmaking technique used by Fo-t'u-teng. For other examples of this technique, cf. Legge, *The Li Ki*, 1: 201; *Yen-tzu ch'un-ch'iu* 1.13a; Frazer, *The Magic Art and the Evolution of Kings*, 1: 302 and passim.

119. *Ch'eng-lu-p'an* 承露盤. Cf. Pelliot, "Meou-tseu ou les doutes levés," 381, n. 266, and Soper, "Japanese Evidence for the History of the Architecture and Iconography of Chinese Buddhism," 649.

120. Lin-tzu 臨淄. The *hsien* of that name is in central Shantung. *TCITC* 171.22a places this "discovery" on the site of the Ch'ing dynasty Hsing-kuo ssu 興國寺. For an earlier account of this "discovery," cf. Tsung Ping's 宗炳 (379–447) *Ming-fo lun* 明佛倫 or *Shen-mieh lun* 神滅論 quoted in *Hung-ming chi* 2.12c. Pelliot, "Les kuo-che ou 'maîtres du royaume' dans le Bouddhisme chinois," 421, dates the *Ming-fo lun* from the beginning of the fifth century.

121. The state attacked was the Former Yen, covering parts of Manchuria, Korea, Jehol, etc. Its rulers, the Mu-jung family, were Hsien-pei who took the title of princes of Yen 燕王 in 337. Hu's defeat here referred to occurred in

338. Cf. *CS* 109.2818, *CS* 106.2768 records Fo-t'u-teng's advice against the expedition and gives an account of the military disaster which followed. Another attack failed in 334. Cf. *CS* 106.2775 and Feng Chia-sheng, "Mu-jung shih chien-kuo shih-mo."

122. This is not the author of various works on the Later Chao. *Shih-t'ung t'ung-shih* 12.358 says that the historian Wang Tu lived under the Liu-Sung dynasty (420–78) and held the office of Pei chung-shu ts'an-chün 北中書參軍. *Chin-shu chiao-chu* 95.28b–29a, comm., attempts to reconcile the dates of the lives of the memorialist of the present text and the historian of the same name by changing the character Sung 宋 in the *Shih-t'ung* to Chin 晉, but this is quite arbitrary. The *Pu Chin-shu i-wen-chih*, 3812c, attempts to identify the memorialist, the historian, and a certain Chin general mentioned in *CS* 112.2876, but as the latter actually had the surname Liu 劉, the suggestion is absurd. A Chu-tso-lang 著作郎 is a court historian, and the fact that such an office was held by the memorialist in the present text has tempted commentators to identify him with the historian of the Chao of the same name who, however, lived at a later date.

123. If the memorialist is not guilty of polemical falsification, this would throw new light on the relation between Buddhism and the state during the Han and San-kuo periods. However, all traces of such regulations have disappeared from the records. The *Ta-Sung seng-shih lüeh* 1.237c (on this work, cf. Chou Yi-liang, "Tantrism in China," 248–51) gives the first sanctioned Chinese monk as Liu Chün, marquis of Yang-ch'eng 陽城侯劉峻, who lived in the time of Han Ming-ti (A.D. 58–75). Cf. Maspero, "Communautés et moines bouddhistes chinoises aux IIe et IIIe siècles," 222–32. *SS* 35.1097 says that the first Chinese to become monks took their vows during the Huang-ch'u 黃初 era (220–26). The "Shih-lao chih" of the *Wei-shu*, on the other hand, considers that the Chinese Prātimokṣa begins with Dharmakāla's translation in A.D. 250. Cf. Ware, "Wei Shou on Buddhism," 122. [Cf. also Hurvitz, "Wei Shou, Treatise on Buddhism and Taoism," 46–47.—Ed.] Much of the confusion rests of course on the varying conceptions of "monk," "ordination," etc., and it took many years to regularize and organize the priesthood on canonical lines. Yamanouchi Shinkyō, in his essay "Kanjin shukke kōkyo ni tsuite," by a strict definition of terms, argues that the edict translated later in this passage is the first official sanction, that Chinese had had tacit permission or private permission in earlier times to join the priesthood.

124. He was appointed by Shih Lo to take charge of the examination system about 327; cf. *CS* 105.2743. According to *WCNP*, p. 4038d–39c, he held the office of Chung-shu ling 中書令 from 334 to 338, and was then promoted to Chung-shu chien 中書監, and was executed in 344.

125. *Pai-man* 百蠻 *CS* 95.2488, in its version of the edict, has *pai-hsing* 百姓 instead of *pai-man*, which seems a somewhat more normal and inclusive

enumeration. The I 夷 would then refer to the non-Chinese, and the Chao 趙 to the Chinese people concerned. Fu I's 傅奕 summary of this edict supports this emendation. Cf. *Kuang hung-ming chi* 6.126b and *TCTC* 95.3003.

126. Cf. Maspero's translation of this memorial and the edict, "Communautés et moines bouddhistes chinoises aux IIe et IIIe siècles," 222–23. Also, Franke, *Ges.*, 3: 330.

127. Cf. *BD* 846. The brilliant strategist whose efforts greatly expanded the shrunken territory of the Eastern Chin. [On Huan Wen, cf. Rogers, *The Chronicle of Fu Chien*, passim.—Ed.] He took Loyang in 356 but was driven out; cf. *CS* 98.2572. I take the expression *ju-ho* 入河 to refer to the campaign of 369. Huan Wen dug some 300 li of canals to get his waterborne army within striking distance of the Yellow River valley. Cf. *Shui-ching chu* 8.7a. He was later defeated by the forces of the former Yen and Former Ch'in at Fang-t'ou. See n. 64. Cf. *CS* 98.2576. [See also Rogers, *The Chronicle of Fu Chien*, 60.—Ed.]

128. The character *yüan* 黿, "tortoise," is homophonous with Yüan 元 in Huan Wen's appellation.

129. Wei-hsien 魏縣 near the present Ta-ming 大名 county, southern Hopei. *CS* 95.2491 has a biography of a man called Hemp Tunic, with variants and additions which will be noted when they aid in the understanding of this text. Yamazaki, in his *Shina chūsei Bukkyō no tenkai*, 74 and passim, regards this man as a Buddhist monk, but there is insufficient evidence for that assumption.

130. T'ien-ma 天馬 meaning: (1) the fleet horses of Ferghana; (2) a star. Cf. *CS* 11.296. I have been unable to trace the connection between this incident and the accession of Yüan-ti to the Chin throne in 317, mentioned in *CS* 95.2491. The present case may be connected with a local fertility cult involving horses, such as has existed in China from antiquity. The commentary to *Chin-shu chiao-chu* 95.33b suggests that *i* 飴 ("sweet cakes") must be a mistake for *ssu* 飼 ("to nourish"), but the secondary meaning of the former is the same as 飼.

131. The name Chao-hsing 趙興 does not appear in the geographical works at my disposal. I assume it is an unrecorded variant of the Chao-kuo of the Chin, southern Hopei. *Kōsōden* [*Kokuyaku issaikyō* ed.], 213, n. 25, identifies it as Ning-hsien 寧縣, Kansu, but the latter was not established until Northern Wei times, nor was it "200 li east of the capital." Chi Pa is otherwise unknown. The *CS* variant *chuang* 壯 (95.2491) for the second character of his name is perhaps a mistake.

132. See *KSC* 9.387a for the fulfillment of this prophecy; translated in section 45 of Fo-t'u-teng's biography, above. This is also given at the end of Hemp Tunic's biography, *CS* 95.2491.

133. Hsi-jung 西戎 refers to the Later Chao rulers; cf. *CS* 104.2721. The variant *yu* 酉 in all the *CS* texts is more in keeping with the general obliquity of this discourse. The cyclical character *yu* is equated with the direction west.

134. *Chin* 金, "metal," is the element associated with the Chin dynasty. Cf. *CS* 105.2743, and the reference is, presumably, to the downfall of the Chin. All interpretations of this conversation are tentative.

135. Ling-chi 靈期 perhaps refers to the Later Chao or to Buddhism.

136. From the reply which follows, the presumption is strengthened that the discussion has been concerned with the duration of Later Chao rule.

137. *Chiu-mu shui* 九木水 is a phrase which, when made into one character, gives *jan* 染, a variant form of Jan 冉, the surname of Shih Hu's adopted son Jan Min, who in the end exterminated the Later Chao ruling house.

138. *Hsüan-che* 玄哲, literally, "profound penetration." I take it to be Teng's way of referring to himself. *Chin-shu chiao-chu* 95.34a has four characters between *pi* 必 and *t'ui* 頹 which are patently a redundancy resulting from a copyist's error; cf. also *CS* 95.2505, n. 11.

139. Ho-k'ou-ch'iao 合口橋 is mentioned in the descriptions of the suburbs of Yeh in the *Shih-liu-kuo chiang-yü-chih*, 4098c.

140. *CS* 95.2491 gives the fulfillment of the "one-pillared palace" prophecy, as found in section 45 of Fo-t'u-teng's biography, above. It then adds the following: "When Yüan-ti became emperor to the south of the Yangtze [i.e., in 318, the year following his assumption of the title of Chin wang], it was considered to be the fulfillment of the 'heavenly horse' prophecy." The *Chin-shu chiao-chu* 95.34b, comm., remarks on the chronological discrepancy, it being highly probable that Hemp Tunic's feeding of the heavenly horse occurred after the succession of Yüan-ti.

141. This monk has no biography in the *KSC*. Others of the same name lived at later times. His biography, now lost, was included in the *Ming-seng chuan*, as may be seen from the reconstructed table of contents in *Meisōden shō*, 6, no. 3. He is listed there as "Chu 竺 Tao-chin of Ch'ang-an in the time of the false Chao." The Chu was no doubt taken for a surname in honor of his master, Teng.

142. Cf. *CS* 94.2449–50. A recluse whose eccentric individualism was not subdued by offers of high office, gifts, seductive women, or brute force. What he taught is not known, but he was an exponent of the natural life, free of all restraint.

143. T'ai-kung Wang 太公望, or Lü Shang 呂尚, first ruler of the Ch'i 齊 state. Cf. *BD* 1862; Chavannes, *Les mémoires historiques de Se-ma Ts'ien*, 4: 34–40. The story is told in the *Han Fei-tzu* 13.5a–6b. [Cf. Liao, *The Complete Works of Han Fei-tzu*, 2: 94–96.—Ed.] Hua Shih and his brother presented the ruler with a comprehensive argument in favor of a completely

natural and unsocial existence. T'ai-kung put them to death and justified the sentence by giving a long list of Confucian values threatened by their ideology.

144. P'u-i 蒲衣 or P'u-i-tzu 蒲衣子. The reconstructed *Shih-tzu* 2.21b says that at the age of eight he was offered the empire by Shun. P'u-i-tzu is also mentioned in *Chuang-tzu* 3.20b. Cf. Legge, *The Texts of Taoism*, 1: 259 [also Watson, *The Complete Works of Chuang-tzu*, 92—Ed.].

145. Po-ch'eng Tzu-kao 白成子高 was one of the feudal lords under the emperor Shun. He refused to serve under the next emperor, Yü. The latter accepted his arguments for refusing and left him in peace. Cf. *Chuang-tzu* 5.5b–6a and Legge, *The Texts of Taoism*, 1: 315 [also, Watson, *The Complete Works of Chuang-tzu*, 131—Ed.].

146. Tuan Kan-mu 段干木 (or Tuan-kan Mu) was a poor but virtuous man rewarded by the marquis Wen of Wei (Warring States period) to the honor of the ruler, the delight of the people, and the benefit of the state. Cf. *Lü-shih ch'un-ch'iu* 21.6a–b and R. Wilhelm, *Frühling und Herbst des Lü Bu Wei*, 378.

147. A sage who was praised for his poverty and disinterestedness by Emperor Kuang-wu of the Han (ruled A.D. 25–57). Cf. *Hou Han-shu* 83.2761–62.

148. He lived A.D. 158–241. Cf. *BD* 1007, *San-kuo chih* 11.354–62. He steadfastly resisted the blandishments of the Wei rulers. He did not take office under the regime he disapproved of, but rather lived most of his life in voluntary exile.

149. Huang-fu Mi 皇甫謐 (215–82) and his sons were critical of the morals and policy of the Chin ruling house and, despite the latter's offers, sternly refused to serve in official positions. Cf. *BD* 854; *CS* 51.1409–19.

150. Ch'in-chou 秦州, one of the provinces of the Later Chao domain, west of the Yellow River.

151. The interpretation is based on the formation of the character *hsien* 鮮, which is composed of the element *yang* 羊 "sheep" and the element *yü* 魚 "fish." For the Mu-jung family, see n. 121. The Mu-jung overran the Chao domains after Hu's death and made their capital at Yeh in 352. [Rogers, *The Chronicle of Fu Chien*, 28–29—Ed.]

152. Chung-t'ai 中臺. I adopt the variant common to YM and *CS* 95.2489. This was probably the same as, or a reconstruction of, the T'ung-ch'iao-t'ai 銅雀臺, built in the northwest corner of Yeh by Ts'ao Ts'ao in 210. The three *t'ai* stretched north and south. See n. 107. Cf. *TCITC* 197.9a and Chavannes, "Pei Yuan Lou," 180, n. 1.

153. Yu-chou 幽州. See n. 111. This place was of course east and north of Yeh, so that the rain-bearing clouds which extinguished the fires were presumed to have been dispatched by Teng from Yeh.

154. Hsüan was crown prince from 337. Cf. *CS* 106.2767. Hsüan's plot for the murder of T'ao is recounted in *CS* 107.2783–84.

155. *Lao-hu* 老胡. The deception lies in the interpretation of *hu-tzu* 胡子 not as "the barbarian's sons" but as a humble term referring to himself, which it might plausibly do.

156. Tung-ko 東格. This may be the same as the Tung-kung 東宮, the building of which is recorded in *CS* 106.2765. The Tung-kung was the crown prince's residence. Cf. *CS* 107.2785.

157. Tu 杜 was Hsüan's mother, made empress in 337, degraded to commoner after Hsüan's death. Cf. *CS* 107.2785.

158. *Liu-ch'ing* 六情 are the *liu-ken* 六根, "six senses." The shift here is from the literal use of "rebel" in the first speech to a metaphorical use in this remark. The Buddhists regard the objects of the six senses as likely to enter through the six organs and despoil men of the truth reached through religious insight. Hence they are sometimes referred to as the six bandits or rebels. Cf. Pelliot, "Meou-tseu ou les doutes levés," 383, n. 279.

159. *CS* 107.2784–85 says three hundred people from the four ringleaders down, plus fifty eunuchs.

160. Chang-ho 漳河, the river flowing northeast of Yeh, from which the later name of the city, Lin-chang, is derived. Cf. *TCITC* 197.3a.

161. The Chung-yang 中陽 gate was the central gate in the south wall of the city of Yeh. Cf. *Shui-ching chu* 10.10b.

162. Hsien-yang 顯陽. There was a palace of this name built in the northeast quarter of the city. Cf. *TCITC* 197.6a. The gate may have taken its name from the palace and have been in that quarter of the city.

163. Tung-kung 東宮. See n. 156. The crown prince, reappearing as a horse of ill omen, tries to enter the palace in which he had lived as a man.

164. T'ai-wu ch'ien-tien 太武前殿. This palace was built in Yeh in 336; cf. *CS* 106.2765. It consisted of an eastern and a western palace built on the site of Ts'ao Ts'ao's old Wen-ch'ang Palace 文昌殿. *CS* 106.2773 recounts that, when the palace was finished, the walls were painted with pictures of Chinese worthies, but the pictures soon began to change to look like barbarians; the heads then sank into the shoulders. Hu was horrified and Teng wept. Cf. *Chin-shu chiao-chu* 106.18a–b, comm., for the *Yeh-chung chi* 鄴中記 version, one of the possible sources of this story. Cf. also *Yu-ming lu* 幽明錄 as quoted in *TPYL* 895.7b. It was also included in the original *SLKCC*. Cf. *TPYL* 369.3a–b.

165. For the fulfillment of this prophecy, see *KSC* 386c, translated in section 40 of Fo-t'u-teng's biography, above. *TPYL* 120.7a quotes a slightly different version from the original *SLKCC*.

166. See n. 76.

167. *P'in-tao* 貧道, an early translation of the term *śramaṇa*. Cf. *Ta-Sung*

seng-shih-lüeh 3.251b.

168. According to the western calendar, January 13, 349. Cf. Pelliot, "Autour d'une traduction sanscrite du Tao tö king," 421. Pelliot rightly points out, n. 1, that the statement in the *P'o-hsieh lun* 2.488a that Teng was in China twenty-five years is at variance with all other sources and must be a mistake. The original *SLKCC*, quoted in *TPYL* 120.7a and 876.10b, if we correct the two quotations against each other, has the following account: "On the hsin-ssu 辛巳 day of the twelfth month of the thirteenth year of the Chien-wu era, thunder was deafening, and rain fell in torrents. Shih Hu asked Fo-t'u-teng, 'What calamity is this?' Teng said, 'It is probably on my account,' and on the wu-tzu 戊子 day he died." The first date corresponds to February 13, 348, and the second to February 20, 348. The forged *SLKCC* 21.5a states that he died on the mou-tzu day of the fourteenth year of Chien-wu, but there was no such day in that month. Lacking other evidence, the *KSC* date seems preferable. *Kung-ssu* 宮寺, "Palace Temple," is not a usual temple name. Makita Tairyō, *Ryō Kōsōden sakuin*, 233, suggests that this may be a mistake for Kuan-ssu 官寺, on which see n. 74.

169. Tzu-mo 紫陌, originally called Chi-mo 祭陌. Cf. *TCITC* 197.7a. There is some confusion as to when the tomb was prepared. *Shui-ching chu* 10.11b says that it was built in Chien-wu 11, or 345. *TPYL* 195.7a quotes T'ien Jung's statement that Teng himself built his tomb several years before his death. This remark is quoted and criticized by Hui-chiao. Cf. *KSC* 9.387a, translated in section 46 of Fo-t'u-teng's biography, above. The *Yüan-ho chün-hsien t'u-chih*, quoted in *Chin-shu chiao-chu* 95.32b, comm., says that Teng's tomb was 17 li southwest of Fu-yang 滏陽 county, which would put it in southern Hopei, some distance northeast of Yeh. This must be ruled out as it conflicts with older texts. Another site, southwest of Tz'u-chou 磁州, in southwest Hopei, is also too far from Yeh to be reconciled to the early texts. Cf. *TCITC* 33.12b.

170. Liang Tu's revolt began in the west in 348 and was put down with difficulty; cf. *CS* 107.2786.

171. See n. 137. Jan Min had borne the surname Shih as an adopted son of Shih Hu. After exterminating the Shih family, he resumed his original surname and established his own kingdom of Wei 魏 (cf. *CS* 107.2793), which however was destroyed by the Mu-jung in 352; cf. *CS* 107.2796–97.

172. *Chi-nu* 棘奴. The first character means "thorny" or "thorn bush," the second means "slave." The thorn bushes symbolize Jan Min as he was, while the forest symbolizes Jan Min swollen with power and bent on revenge.

173. Pelliot pointed out, "Autour d'une traduction sanscrite du Tao tö king," 420, n. 3, that the story reappears in the *Sou-shen hou-chi* 2.2b–3a. This story is probably not of Chinese but of Indian origin. MacMunn, in his *The Underworld of India*, 223, expresses disbelief "in such powers as enable a

gosain to bring his long bowel from his body, air it, and put it back...," but he gives no references. I am informed by Father Rudolph Rahmann, a specialist in Indian folklore, that the ability to perform such an operation is regarded by certain peoples of northern India as proof of a shaman's invulnerability. Cf. also Ch'en Yin-k'o, "*San-kuo chih* Ts'ao Ch'ung Hua T'o chuan yü Fo-chiao ku-shih," 17–20.

174. The story of washing the intestines is traditionally associated with two springs called Hsi-ch'ang 洗腸. One is located 13 li west of Nei-hsü 內郫 county, Hopei; cf. *TCITC* 30.19a. The other is at Ta-li 大荔 eastern Shensi; cf. *TCITC* 245.33a.

175. Eight feet, if the measure was that in use under the Eastern Chin, would be 1.96 meters. Cf. J. C. Ferguson, "Chinese Foot Measure," 361.

176. See n. 26 above.

177. This is the usual transliteration of the Sanskrit name *Subhūti*. This monk is otherwise unknown.

178. See n. 20 above. Fan-mien 樊沔 is another name for Hsiang-yang 襄陽, north-central Hupei, where he lived from 364 to 379. Cf. *KSC* 5.352c.

179. See nn. 19 and 105.

180. The figure 893 is probably from a *pieh-chuan*, as quoted in *P'o-hsieh lun* 2.488a. *Fa-yüan chu-lin* 31.517c and *Chi shen-chou san-pao kan-t'ung lu* 3.432c give the figure "980-odd." Fo-t'u-teng's name is associated with various temples: (1) Pi-an ssu 彼岸寺 in northern Honan; cf. *Ching-i chi* 旌異記 of Hou Po 侯白, a Sui work quoted in *Fa-yüan chu-lin* 91.956b; (2) a Pai-ma ssu 白馬寺 in Yeh; cf. *Fo-tsu t'ung-chi* 38.358a; (3) a temple near the modern Ch'ing-ho 清河 county, southern Hopei; cf. *Shui-ching chu* 5.22a–b; (4) a temple 40 li north of T'ai-hu 太湖 county, Anhwei, attested only by the doubtful authority of the *T'ai-hu hsien-chih* 3.2a. See also the temples mentioned in nn. 74, 75, and 96.

181. This story is probably taken from the *Yeh-chung chi*; cf. *T'ai-p'ing huan-yü chi* 55.7b. The Stein MS mentioned in n. 43 states that he was seen in the desert "traveling south toward India."

182. This incident is probably taken from T'ien Jung's 田融 *Erh-shih wei-shih* 二石僞事; cf. *TPYL* 132.11b, 710.10b, 759.5b.

183. See n. 121. Cf. *BD* 1550, *CS* 110.2838.

184. The Tung-ming kuan 東明觀 was built by Shih Hu on top of the east wall of the capital; cf. *Shui-ching chu* 10.10b. The character *kuan* 館 in *KSC* is incorrect. Cf. also *Shui-ching chu* 9.36b.

185. Lived 325–75. The principal military leader of the Former Ch'in. Cf. *BD* 2204. [Cf. also Rogers, *The Chronicle of Fu Chien*, passim.—Ed.]

186. Cf. *KSC* 9.386a and section 34 of Fo-t'u-teng's biography, above.

187. Lived 337–84, ruler of the Former Ch'in. Cf. *BD* 579. [Cf. also Rogers, *The Chronicle of Fu Chien*, passim.—Ed.]

188. Lived 350–85, third son of Mu-jung Chün. Cf. *BD* 1551. Captured by Fu Chien's forces in 370. Cf. *Shih-liu-kuo nien-piao*, 4009b. [Cf. also Rogers, *The Chronicle of Fu Chien*, passim.—Ed.]

189. This may be Kuo Ch'ing 郭慶, who, according to the forged *SLKCC* 42.32b, captured Mu-jung Wei, but I can find no trace of the appellation being applied to him. *CS* 111.2858 says that Wei was captured by Chü Wu 巨武, and this agrees with the *Ch'in-shu* account (see below, n. 190). In Chü Wu's name, the second character is a substitute for *hu* 虎, tabooed under the T'ang, so that his original name would also have borne out the prophecy. [Cf. also Rogers, *The Chronicle of Fu Chien*, 227, n. 254.—Ed.]

190. This incident may be drawn from Ch'e P'in's 車頻 *Ch'in-shu* 秦書, a record of the Former Ch'in dynasty written between 432 and 441. Cf. *Shih-t'ung t'ung-shih* 12.359. [Cf. also Rogers, *The Chronicle of Fu Chien*, pp. 21–22, 96, n. 214—Ed.] The account from the *Ch'in-shu* is quoted in *TPYL* 549.2a. Mu-jung Wei, not Chün, is the one who has the dream in the *Ch'in-shu* account. The *CS* commentators, *Chin-shu chiao-chu* 110.14a, comm., regard this as a mistake and would follow the *KSC* version.

191. For T'ien Jung's *Chao-chi*, cf. Pelliot, "Autour d'une traduction du Tao tö king," 421, where he dates it as the end of the fourth or the beginning of the fifth century. A somewhat fuller version of the passage here criticized by Hui-chiao is quoted in *TPYL* 195.7a.

192. *Hsüan-chi* 懸記, a Buddhist term, used in the translated sūtras to mean prophecy. Cf. Oda, *Bukkyō daijiten*, 409b.

Chapter 3   Biography of the Nun An-ling-shou

1. The work was completed in 516 and contains the lives of sixty-five Chinese nuns. On Pao-ch'ang, cf. *Hsü Kao-seng chuan* 1.426b–28a and Pelliot, "Notes sur quelques artistes des six dynasties et des T'ang," 258, n. 1.

2. Reprinted this volume, chap. 2.

3. It is doubtful that the "ordination" described in this biography was canonical, for the first regular, recognized ordination of nuns did not take place until 434; cf. Lévi and Chavannes, "Les seize arhats protecteurs de la loi," and *Hōbōgirin*, 1: 74.

4. Cf., for example, the texts of Lung-men inscriptions dating between 495 and 516 given by Tsukamoto in Mizuno and Nagahiro, *Ryūmon sekkutsu no kenkyū*, 174–75.

5. *Pi-ch'iu-ni chuan* 1.934b.

6. Chien-hsien-ssu 建賢寺 was a temple which, according to this biography, the nun herself built. It was located in Hsiang-kuo 襄國, southwest of the modern Hsing-t'ai 邢臺 county, southern Hopei. Shih Lo made it his capital in

312; when Shih Hu moved the capital to Yeh in 335, the name was changed to Hsiang-chün 襄郡.

7. Tung-kuan 東莞 is the modern I-shui 沂水 county, southeast Shantung.

8. Hsü Chung 徐仲 is otherwise unknown. A Wai-ping-lang 外兵郎 was a subcommander of provincial troops; cf. *Li-tai chih-kuan piao*, 56. Pao-ch'ang, being a southern legitimist, regularly uses the prefix *wei* 偽, "unortho-dox," in referring to northern dynasties.

9. Legge, *The Li Ki*, 2: 441, "In her youth, she follows her father and elder brother; when married, she follows her husband; when her husband is dead, she follows her son."

10. *Li-shen hsing-tao* 立身行道 is from the *Hsiao-ching*. Legge, *The Hsiao King*, 466, translates this passage as, "When we have established our charac-ter by the practice of the (filial) course, so as to make our names famous in future ages, and thereby glorify our parents. . . ." An-ling-shou, of course, meant *tao* in the sense of Buddhism, not filial piety. Winning over her father was crucial, for the Vinaya required a would-be monk or nun to have parental permission to join the order; cf. *Ssu-fen lü* 34.810a.

11. For this technique and its paraphernalia, cf. "Fo-t'u-teng: A Biogra-phy," reprinted this volume, chap. 2, nn. 57–59.

12. *Sheng-ssu ta-k'u-hai* 生死大苦海; the sea of births and death or the sea of suffering is of enormous extent. A bodhisattva may conduct one to its further shore, which is Nirvana; cf. *Ta-sheng pen-sheng hsin-ti kuan ching* 1.294c.

13. Ching-chien 淨撿 is the first nun whose biography is given in the *Pi-ch'iu-ni chuan* 1.934c–35a; in Pao-ch'ang's opinion she was the first Chinese nun. She erected a temple before 316, but it was not until after 357 that she went through an ordination ceremony. Ching-chien was thus not, at the time she assisted in this ordination, able to lend it any canonical authority. Ching-chien died about 362, aged seventy.

14. *Chien-hua-na* 剪花納; this type of appliqué, openwork, or embroidery is unknown to me. The *na* is the outer or middle priestly robe, especially for meetings of the sangha, but is sometimes worn as an everyday gown. The commentary in the *Fo-tsu t'ung-chi* 6.180b says that in the Vinaya it is ex-plained as a garment of cast-off materials gathered (*na-shou* 納受) from dust heaps, but the commentator adds that the original meaning is lost. Takakusu, *A Record of the Buddhist Religion*, 60, n. 1, translates it as "rugged garment."

15. *Ch'i-t'iao-i* 七條衣, Skt. *uttarāsaṅga*, outer garment, worn to meetings of the *saṃgha*, services, etc. Cf. *Fan-i ming-i chi* 7.1171a–b. [Cf. also Welch, *The Practice of Chinese Buddhism*, 1900–1950, 114.—Ed.]

16. *Hsiang-pi* 象鼻; the cord or streamer used for tying the robe to the left shoulder. The end hangs loose over the breast, hence the name, which is liter-

ally "elephant trunk." Takakusu, *A Record of the Buddhist Religion*, 74, erroneously takes this to mean "forearm."

17. *Tsao-kuan* 澡罐, Skt. *kuṇḍikā*, the water pitcher which is part of the priestly equipment. Cf. Takakusu, *A Record of the Buddhist Religion*, 27–28, Pelliot, "Notes sur l'histoire de la céramique chinoise," 28–29, and *Hōbō-girin*, 3: 265–70.

18. *Huang-men shih-lang* 黃門侍郎, a court official.

19. Ch'ing-ho 清河 was located east of the modern county of that name, in southern Hopei; cf. Des Michels, *Chih lou kouh kiang yuh tchi: Histoire géographique des seize royaumes*, 166–67.

Chapter 4   Biography and Hagiography: Hui-chiao's *Lives of Eminent Monks*

BIBLIOGRAPHIC NOTE

Texts of the Kao-seng chuan   For most purposes it is desirable to use the text which appears in the *Taishō Tripitaka*, 50: 322c–423a, since this edition provides the widest range of textual variants. However, its punctuation is not reliable, and the edition of the Chin-ling k'o-ching ch'u 金陵刻經處 (1889) is the best-punctuated text available. However, it is based solely on a Ming text and contains no variants. Moreover, it follows a Ming innovation and divides the *Kao seng-chuan* into 15 chüan, an arrangement which the author's own preface does not sanction and which is an annoyance to the researcher.

On the whole, the variations among the texts used by the *Taishō* are slight. The only widely variant text of any of the biographies is that of Tao-an 道安 contained in a MS copy of the *Kao-seng chuan* dating from the period 1154–64, now in the possession of the Ishiyama-dera near Kyoto. This was published, collated with the standard texts by Iwai Tairyō, under the title "Ishi-yama-dera hon *Ryō Kōsōden* to sono Dōan den jōi." According to Iwai, the Tao-an biography is a late expansion and elaboration of the *KSC* text. The rest of the Ishiyama-dera MS contains only minor variants.

Translations from the Kao-seng chuan   The only complete translation is into Japanese, and this appears in volume 7 of the history and biography section of the *Kokuyaku issaikyō*. The late Tokiwa Daijō was in charge of this work. However, it can only be called a semitranslation since it does not resolve any serious problems of interpretation, and its notes are few and unhelpful. Cf. the scathing review by Sui Lu (1937).

Translations of portions of the *Kao-seng chuan* have appeared in Western languages for the last half-century. Cf. Chavannes, "Guṇavarman" and "Seng Hui"; Maspero, "Le songe et l'ambassade de l'Empereur Ming" (Biographies of Kāśyapa Mātaṅga and Chu Fa-lan 竺法蘭); J. Nobel, "Kumārajīva" (this includes a biography of Seng-jui 僧叡); Arthur F. Wright, "Fo-t'u-teng: A Biography" [in this volume—Ed.]; Walter Liebenthal, *The Book of Chao* (biography of Seng-chao 僧肇); Arthur Link, "Biography of Shih Tao-an." Popular, but reasonably accurate versions of some biographies by T. K. Chuan appeared in 1938 under the title "Some Notes on the *Kao Seng Chuan*."

Aids to the study of the Kao-seng chuan   The late Heinrich Hackmann compiled an "Alphabetisches Verzeichnis zum Kao sêng ch'uan" (*sic*), which appeared in 1923. This contained numerous errors and is superseded, as an aid to the study of Hui-chiao's work, by the "*Ryō Kōsōden* sakuin," jointly compiled by Tsukamoto Zenryū, Ryūchi Kiyoshi, and Iwai Tairyō (1937–39). Following each proper name is an entry for each of its occurrences; each of these entries gives the chüan, a brief quotation showing the context in which the name appears, the page and rank numbers to the Taishō edition, and the page reference to the *Shukusatsu daizōkyō* 縮刷大藏經 (Tokyo, 1880–85). All variant names are given in their syllable order, with cross-references. Further, for monks' biographies, cross-references are provided to the *Ch'u san-tsang chi-chi*, *Hung-ming chi*, *Kuang hung-ming chi*, *Li-tai san-pao chi*, and *Meisōden shō*. For secular figures, cross-references are given, chüan only, to the dynastic histories. This is the most useful single study to the *Kao-seng chuan*. [This has itself now been superseded by Makita Tairyō, *Ryō Kōsōden sakuin* (1972).—Ed.]

There is no commented edition of the *Kao-seng chuan*. Chou Shu-chia and Su Kung-wang published a commentary to the first two-thirds of the preface (1942–43). The authors' draft commentary to the remainder of the preface and their complete but unpublished commentaries to the *lun* were made available to me for copying. Lexical notes, a few to each chüan, are found in Hui-lin's *I-ch'ieh-ching yin-i*.

Studies of the Kao-seng chuan and related texts   Yamanouchi Shinkyō's "*Kōsōden* no kenkyū" (1921) remains the only comprehensive study in Japanese and has been of great help in the preparation of the present essay. In Chinese, T'ang Yung-t'ung published his reading notes on the *Kao-seng chuan* as "Tu Hui-chiao *Kao-seng chuan* cha-chi" (1930). In addition to very brief notes on some of Hui-chiao's sources, T'ang includes essays on the following topics in which he deals critically with historical problems in some of the biographies: "The Date and Place of Fa-hu's 法護 Death" (pp. 5–6); "Seng-chia-t'i-p'o's (Saṃghadeva) Abhidharma Scholarship" (p. 6); "A Chronology of Kumārajīva" (pp. 6–8); "Shih Tao-an 釋道安 and Fo-t'u-teng 佛圖澄" (pp. 8–9); "The Year of Tao-an's Escape from the Disturbances" (p. 9); "A Chronology of Tao-an" (pp. 9–10); "A Chronology of Shih Hui-yüan 釋慧遠" (pp. 10–11); "Seng-chao's 僧肇 Letter to Liu I-min 劉遺民" (p. 11); "On Chih T'an-ti 支曇諦" (p. 11); "On Fo-t'u-teng" (p. 11); "The Wei Emperor

T'ai-wu's Suppression of Buddhism" (pp. 11–12). In addition, an essay by Ch'en Yüan entitled "Kao-seng chuan lun-lüeh" [A brief discourse on the Kao-seng chuan] appeared in 1947, but I do not have access to this. The principal study devoted to the main source of the Kao-seng chuan—the Ming-seng chuan—is that of Kasuga Reichi, "Jōdokyō shiryō to shite no Meisōden . . ." (1936). Pages 53–65 discuss Pao-ch'ang and his work, the relation of the Kao-seng chuan to the Ming-seng chuan, the life and interests of the thirteenth-century monk Shūshō 宗性, especially as these affected his choice of excerpts from the Ming-seng chuan which appear in his Meisōden shō 名僧傳抄. Kasuga then reproduces (pp. 66–111) the Meisōden shō as copied by him from the MS at the Tōdaiji at Nara. In general this is less reliable than the edition in the Dainihon zoku zōkyō, which I have cited in part 4 of the present essay. On pages 111–18 Kasuga reproduces further excerpts from the Ming-seng chuan which appear in ch. 4 of Shūshō's Miryoku nyorai kannōshō 彌勒如來感應抄, also a Tōdaiji MS. These excerpts have not been published elsewhere.

1. See the bibliographic note above for references to earlier works on the Kao-seng chuan and its biographies.

2. Cf. KSC 1.325a, where Hui-chiao states that the life of K'ang Seng-hui was left out of the San-kuo chih, Wu-chih, because that monk was of foreign origin. Yamanouchi, "Kōsōden no kenkyū," 32, points out that in the dynastic histories which cover the same years as the KSC there are four biographies of monks (all in CS 95) and four subordinate biographies. This is rather striking evidence of the standard histories' neglect of a sequence of important figures in Chinese social, political, and intellectual life.

3. See below, part 3, Hui-chiao's preface, and part 4, "The Problem of the Ming-seng chuan."

4. Cf. Hui-chiao's letter to his lay disciple Wang Man-ying, in KSC 14.422c.

5. Cf., for example, J. Takakusu, trans., "The Life of Vasu-Bandhu by Paramārtha (A.D. 499–569)"; Kumārajīva's translations of the lives of Aśvaghoṣa, Nāgārjuna, and Āryadeva, Taishō Tripitaka, 50: 183–88a, excerpts in Wassiljew, Der buddhismus, 231–35.

6. Cf., for example, Nan Ch'i-shu, ch. 54–55. It is interesting to compare the relatively sober lives of Kumārajīva and Fo-t'u-teng, KSC 2.330a–33a; 9.383b–87a with their biographies in CS, 95.2499–2502; 95.2485–90. The latter, though compiled in the early T'ang, stress the miraculous incidents at the expense of the historical "facts" and the sequence of events.

7. Hui-chiao's preface states the principle that the more important biographies are placed at the beginning of the book. On variant calculations of the number of subordinate biographies, see n. 119 below.

8. Cf. Shih-chi 1.46 and KSC preface.

9. Cf. *KSC* 1.324a–b, 326b.

10. Cf., for example, *KSC* 6.357a, "A tradition says" (*hsiang-chuan yün* 相傳云); *KSC* 11.399c, "They now say in Wu-ch'ang that..." (*chin Wu-ch'ang* 今武昌).

11. Cf. *KSC* preface and *Shih-chi* 130.3299–3300. The locus classicus is of course Confucius's statement in *Lun-yü* that he had "transmitted what was taught to me without making up anything of my own"; cf. Waley, *The Analects of Confucius*, 123.

12. This does not mean that in every case the individual's biography was dropped. It was sometimes reclassified and appeared in another category.

13. Cf. *KSC* 9.386c and Wright, "Fo-t'u-teng: A Biography," reprinted this volume.

14. *KSC* 1.324a.

15. Liu Chih-chi (661–721) is, in his *Shih-t'ung*, one of the first to make the distinction. In the *SS* and *CTS*, *hsiao-shuo* are still classified in the "history" sections of the bibliographic treatises. It is not until the *HTS*, written in the first half of the eleventh century, that *hsiao-shuo* are firmly divorced from history and placed in a subsection of that great catchall, the "philosophy" section. Cf. Lu Hsün, *Chung-kuo hsiao-shuo shih-lüeh*.

16. Naitō Torajirō, *Shina shigakushi*, 158. Miyakawa Hisayuki, "Riku-chō jidai no shigaku," 415.

17. Cf. *Chin-lou tzu* 5.5b, where the prince describes the subdivisions of his biographical collection.

18. Naitō, *Shina shigakushi*, 159.

19. *Shih-t'ung t'ung-shih* 4.81.

20. Yamanouchi, "*Kōsōden* no kenkyū," 39.

21. Cf. *KSC* 1.329c and 3.346a.

22. In his letter to Wang Man-ying, Hui-chiao says, "I am now taking the *tsan* and *lun* which I have written for the ten categories and send them with this letter..."; *KSC* 14.423a. Hui-chiao indicates in his preface, however, that he regards the last two groups of biographies in his book as least important; it is possible that he did not honor them with *tsan*.

23. *Shih-t'ung t'ung-shih* 4.83.

24. *KSC* 11.403b–c. Cf. also his apt quotation from the preface to the *Book of Songs* in his critical estimate of the hymnodists. Further in that essay he juxtaposes the "four virtues" of music as laid down by the Chinese sages and the "five benefits" of Indian-style songs; *KSC* 13.414c–15a.

25. *KSC* 12.405c–06b.

26. Cf. *KSC* 1.327b; 9.384a,c; 10.392b–c, etc.

27. Cf., for example, Pao-ch'ang's preface to his *Ming-seng chuan* quoted in *HKSC* 1.427c.

28. *KSC* 6.360c–61a.

29. *SCKC* 20.310c.

30. Cf. *KSC* preface and 11.402c–03a. For Hui-chiao's indebtedness to these authors, see part 4 above.

31. *HKSC* preface, 425a.

32. Yamazaki, *Shina chūsei Bukkyō no tenkai*, 246.

33. Tao-hsüan's comment in the *HKSC* preface, 425a, was that while Hui-chiao's narratives were full for Wu and Yüeh, they were brief for Wei and Yen; this view has been echoed by all later critics.

34. Cf. *HKSC* preface, 425b. T'ang, "Tu Hui-chiao *Kao-seng-chuan* cha-chi," 11, points out the discrepancies within the *KSC* on the dating of the Northern Wei persecution of Buddhism. In the biography of T'an-shih 曇始, *KSC* 10.392b–c, Hui-chiao relates incidents following Emperor T'ai-wu's (r. 424–52) decision to persecute Buddhism that are utterly at odds with historical fact; perhaps the most absurd of these is the statement that T'ai-wu, under the influence of T'an-shih, had a change of heart and ordered the revival of Buddhism. What is of interest is not that minor facts are wrong but that Hui-chiao had a totally inadequate knowledge of the nature and significance of one of the major events in the history of the church in North China.

35. Yamazaki, *Shina chūsei Bukkyō no tenkai*, 246, shows that in contrast to the *KSC*, only 64 of the subjects with known geographical associations in the *HKSC*, out of a total of 138, are from the Central China area favored by Hui-chiao.

36. Tao-hsüan's biography of Hui-chiao, *HKSC* 6.471b, specifies that he was a native of Shang-yü 上虞, one of the *hsien* into which K'uai-chi chün was divided. The *HKSC* biography is relatively poor and consists largely of quotations from the *KSC* preface. Tao-hsüan says that he knew nothing of Hui-chiao's later years. For this we must depend on the biographical memoir by Seng-kuo 僧果 appended to Hui-chiao's work, *KSC* 14.423a.

37. Ssu-ma Hsiang 司馬相 (*chin-shih* 1521), *Yüeh-chün chih-lüeh* 越郡志略, quoted in *TCITC* 294.4b.

38. *TCITC* 295.16b–18a. Lu Hsün published an interesting collection of fragments of early accounts of personalities and sites of K'uai-chi, "K'uai-chi chün ku-shu tsa-chi."

39. *TCITC* 294.29b–30b.

40. Wang Man-ying's 王曼穎 letter to Hui-chiao is found after the author's preface in *KSC* 14.422b–c. The text of this letter and of Hui-chiao's reply also appear in *Kuang hung-ming chi* 24.275a–b. I have found no biographical data on Wang save the circumstances of his death discussed in n. 62 below. The bibliographic essay of the *HTS* 59.1540 notes that a person of this name was the author of a *Hsü Ming-hsiang chi* 續冥祥記 in 11 ch. *CTS* 46.38a [T'ung-wen ed.] gives the same title but the author's name as Wang Man

王曼; this appears to be a mistake. [The editors of the Peking ed. have corrected this to Wang Man-ying in *CTS* 46.2005.—Ed.]

41. *TCITC* 294.41a–42a.

42. Ibid. The large number of temples built or rebuilt during the Liang is striking evidence of the prosperity of Buddhism in the area. Yamazaki, *Shina chūsei Bukkyō no tenkai*, 248, remarks that the large number of monks associated with this general area in the Period of Disunion was conditioned by the economic and cultural development of the area; he adds that it also is in part a reflection of the vigorous development of Buddhism in the capital, Chien-k'ang. Of course, as Professor Yamazaki points out, we are largely dependent on Hui-chiao himself for data on the monks and their geographical distribution. Evidences of Hui-chiao's regional bias are discussed in the introduction to this paper.

43. Cf. *KSC* 5.357b. The first abbot was Chu Tao-i 竺道壹, and the builder-patron was Wang Hui 王薈; cf. *CS* 65.1759–60 for Wang Hui's biography.

44. Cf. Hui-chiao's reply to Wang Man-ying's letter, *KSC* 14.422c.

45. Cf. the section on book collecting in the *Chin-lou tzu* 3.16b. Earlier in the same chapter, 3.16a, the author remarks that among a group of books presented by Chang Wan 張縮, there was a copy of the *Kao-seng chuan*. The *Chin-lou tzu* was completed in 552. The emperor was killed and his vast library destroyed in the fall of his capital to the Western Wei conquerors in 554. Note that the emperor, early in his career, had been prefect (T'ai-shou 太守) of K'uai-chi; cf. *Liang-shu* 5.113.

46. *HKSC* 6.471b, biography of Hui-chiao.

47. Cf. Hui-chiao's letter to Wang Man-ying, *KSC* 14.422c.

48. Cf. *HKSC* 6.471b. Tao-hsüan places Hui-chiao's biography in the "Exegetes" category. Cf. also Seng-kuo's note, *KSC* 14.423a, which speaks of Hui-chiao as "well-versed in the explication of the sūtra and Vinaya." (**SYM** have *ching-yen* 精研, "a profound scholar of...") [For boldface abbreviations, see above, chap. 2, n. 53.]

49. The first work is given the title *Nieh-p'an i-shu* 涅槃義疏 in *HKSC* 6.471b and in the *LTSPC* 11.100a. Seng-kuo, in his note, abbreviates this to *Nieh-p'an shu*. The second work is described as a commentary to the *Fan-wang chieh* 梵網戒 by Seng-kuo and the *LTSPC*. Tao-hsüan's version of this title *Fan-wang ching-shu* 梵網經疏 is imprecise. A *Ni-chuan* 尼傳 (Lives of the Nuns) is attributed to "The Dharma Master Chiao" (*Chiao fa-shih* 皎法師) in *SS* 33.979, but this is an error which credits Hui-chiao with the authorship of Pao-ch'ang's *Pi-ch'iu-ni chuan*. There is no evidence in any other source for Hui-chiao's authorship of such a work. Cf. *SCKC*, 5369b–c.

50. Cf. *LTSCP* 11.100a.

51. Cf. Itō Giken, *Shina Bukkyō seishi*, 1: 618, 622.

52. Cf. the author's preface, *KSC* 14.418c and *HKSC* 6.471b.

53. *KSC* 14.422c–23a.

54. Cf. *Liang-shu* 56.853, 856.

55. This information and the following quotation are from Seng-kuo's biographical memoir, *KSC* 14.423a.

56. I have not found a biography of Hui-kung. However, he is mentioned in the preface to the Upaśūnya translation of the sixth chapter of the *Mahāprajñāpāramitā sūtra* as having participated in the work of translation which was completed in 565. Cf. *Wen-shu-shih-li so-shuo Mo-ho-po-jo p'o-lo-mi ching* 1.726a and Bagchi, *Le canon bouddhique en Chine*, 1: 265, 431.

57. A temple located at the foot of Mount Fu-chou 覆舟山, Chiang-ning fu 寧府, Kiangsu.

58. Seng-kuo later participated in the great Buddhist convocation which preceded the translation project mentioned in n. 56. In the preface to the translation he is referred to as being from K'uang-shan 匡山, i.e., Lu-shan. Cf. *Wen-shu-shih-li so-shuo Mo-ho-po-jo p'o-lo-mi ching* 1.726a.

59. Cf. Chavannes, "Seng Hui," 199, "... rédigé en 519." Pelliot, "Meou-tseu ou les doutes levés," 395, "... qui date de 519." Cf. also Kasuga, "Jōdokyō shiryō," 57, and Mochizuki, *Bukkyō dainempyō*, 125, etc.

60. One can give little weight to this discrepancy because of the peculiar significance of the five-hundred-year period, it being, according to Mencius, the interval between the appearance of two sages. Do Hui-chiao and Wang Man-ying, who also uses the expression, wish vaguely to suggest that Han Ming-ti and Liang Wu-ti, two imperial patrons of Buddhism separated by approximately such an interval, were "sages"? Yet if Hui-chiao had such a notion he would probably have included in his preface some salute to the pious Wu-ti, and this he did not do.

61. Cf. *Liang-shu* 22.348 and *Nan-shih* 52.1292. Chiang Ko himself died in 535. Cf. *Liang-shu* 36.526. There is a problem in the incident following the death of Wang Man-ying which is difficult to resolve. In both the *Liang-shu* and *Nan-shih* versions the prince is referred to as "Prince of Chien-an" 建安王, a title he relinquished in 518 when he was made prince of Nan-p'ing; cf. *Liang-shu* 22.347. I can only suppose that the anachronistic use of his former title in this exemplary story reflects the popular renown his charities had gained him in his seventeen years as prince of Chien-an, 502–18. Yao Chen-tsung, *SCKC*, 5382a, assumes that the title was not anachronistically used and thus places the death of Wang before 518; this cannot be, since the year 519 is mentioned in the preface on which we have Wang's letter of comment. Yao hazards the guess that Wang Man-ying was a learned recluse of the early Liang.

62. Cf. *Liang-shu* 3.77.

63. *KSC* 13.412b.

64. *LTSPC* 3.45a; *HKSC* 1.427b–c. Pao-ch'ang took a vow to write such a work in 510, completed the organization of it in 514, the writing in 519. Further support for this date for the completion of the work is found in the fact that it contained a biography of Seng-yu, who did not die until 518. See part 4 of this paper, "The Problem of the *Ming-seng chuan*," above.

65. *T'i-ch'üan* 蹄筌, "rabbit snares" and "fish nets," representing the provisional media, such as words, for the apprehension of reality; they are to be discarded when direct apprehension is achieved through Taoist discipline. Cf. *Chuang-tzu* 9.8a–b (*p'ien* 26); Legge, *The Texts of Taoism*, 2: 141. [Cf. also Watson, *The Complete Works of Chuang-tzu*, 302.—Ed.]

66. *Shih-pao* 師保, literally "tutors and guardians." Cf. Legge, *The Chinese Classics*, 5: 556a, and ibid., 3: 538.

67. *Chün-fu* 君父. I here adopt the reading of the SYP texts. In this passage Hui-chiao is probably referring to collections of biographies of individuals who exemplified these virtues, e.g., *Chung-ch'en chuan* 忠臣傳 (Biographies of loyal ministers), *Lieh-shih chuan* 列士傳 (Biographies of virtuous knights), *Hsiao-tzu chuan* 孝子傳 (Biographies of filial sons). In this and the following sentence he is speaking of writers in the Confucian tradition.

68. *Shang hsü-ch'ung* 尚虛沖. Hui-chiao is here probably referring to the philosophical Taoists and to the neo-Taoist tradition which was still vigorous in his own day. [Cf. the studies in Holmes Welch and Anna Seidel, eds., *Facets of Taoism.*—Ed.].

69. *Ta-ming* 達命. This recalls the passage from *Chuang-tzu* 10.16a (*p'ien* 32) (*ta ta-ming-che sui, ta hsiao-ming-che tsao* 達大命者隨, 達小命者遭) which Legge, *The Texts of Taoism*, 2: 211, translates, ". . . understanding the great condition appointed for him and following it, and the smaller conditions, and meeting them as they occur." [Cf. Watson, *The Complete Works of Chuang-tzu*, 360.—Ed.] Chou-Su (5) cites *Chuang-tzu, p'ien* 19, ("Mastering Life," *Ta-sheng* 達生) and interprets the term used here to mean *ch'ang-sheng* 長生, "prolonging life." It seems to me possible that Hui-chiao, in speaking of the two strains of the Taoist tradition, may again have had in mind the biographical collections which represented them, e.g., for philosophic Taoism the *Chu-lin ming-shih chuan* 竹林名士傳 and for magical-longevity Taoism the *Lieh-hsien chuan* 列仙傳.

70. *Chien-jan chih fang* 漸染之方. I am uncertain of the translation of this phrase. *Chien-jan* is used in a different context, and clearly with a different sense, in Hui-chiao's letter to his disciple, *KSC* 14.422c. There it clearly means the gradual penetration of Buddhism into China.

71. *Neng-jen* 能仁. A translation of the name Śākyamuni based on a false etymology. Cf. James R. Ware, "Wei Shou on Buddhism," 116.

72. *Yeh-kuo* 業果, literally Karma, acts, and their effects.

73. *Shih-ti* 十地. Skt. *daśa bhūmayaḥ*, the ten stages through which the Buddhist saint passes on the way to complete enlightenment. The Hinayāna and Mahāyāna each has its series. Cf. Nalinaksha Dutt, *Aspects of Mahāyāna Buddhism and Its Relation to Hinayāna*, 268–69.

74. *Hui-tsung* 慧宗. Skt. *prajñā-siddhānta* (?).

75. *Erh-ti* 二帝, the two truths: common truth (*su-ti* 俗諦), Skt. *saṁvṛti-satya* or the truth obtained through observation and knowledge, and absolute truth (*chen-ti* 眞諦), Skt. *paramārtha-satya*, attained through *prajñā*, transcendental wisdom. Hui-chiao wrote a commentary to the *Mahāparinirvāna sūtra*, and in Dharmarakṣa's fifth-century translation of this work there is an elaborate statement of the two truths; cf. *Ta-po nieh-p'an ching* 12.443.

76. *Chih-fu* 智府. *Chih* is the usual translation for Skt. *jñāna*, "knowledge," the means of obtaining the "common truth" mentioned in the preceding note.

77. M here has *yü fang i* 餘方亦, *yü chiao fang chih* 餘教之方, common to SYPK, is preferable.

78. *Kung* 共, found only in K, is unacceptable. The simile is from *Analects* 2. Cf. Legge's translation in *The Chinese Classics*, 1: 145. [Also, Waley, *The Analects of Confucius*, 88.—Ed.]

79. *San-ch'ien* 三千, abbreviation of *san-ch'ien ta-ch'ien shih-chieh* 三千大千世界, Skt. *tri-sāhasra-mahā-sāhasra-lokadhātu*, one great chiliocosm or one Buddha-world.

80. *Liu-tao* 六道, Skt. *gati*, the six states of being: devas, men, asuras, beings in hell, pretas, and animals.

81. *Ch'iu-fang* 秋方, literally the autumn quarter. In the Chinese equations of seasons and directions, autumn is paired with the west. Here it means specifically India.

82. For parallelism adopt YMP *feng* 奉 instead of SK *pen* 本.

83. *Yün-lung feng-hu* 雲龍風虎. Cf. *Chou-i* 1.3b. Legge, *Yi King*, 411, translates the passage containing this sentence as follows: "What is the meaning of the words under the fifth line, 'The dragon is on the wing in the sky;—it will be advantageous to see the great man?' The Master said, 'Notes of the same key respond to one another; creatures of the same nature seek one another; . . . clouds follow the dragon, and winds follow the tiger:—[so] the sage makes his appearance, and all men look to him." Buddhist apologists have searched early Chinese sources for favorable omens coincident with Buddha's birth in India. Hui-chiao, in his critical estimate of the translators, *KSC* 3.346a, indicates that he believed the phenomenon recorded in the *Ch'un-ch'iu*, Seventh year of Duke Chuang, or 687 B.C., to have been the sign of Buddha's birth: "In summer, in the fourth month, on Sin-mao, at night, the regular stars were not visible. At midnight there was a fall of stars like rain." Legge's translation, *The Chinese Classics*, 5: 80. This is the reference of

"cloud dragon." The "wind tiger" here refers to the dream of the emperor Ming of the Han, which, in legend, was the first introduction of Buddhism into China. Cf. *KSC* 3.346a and Chou-Su (3).

84. Hui-chiao was a legitimist, and he thus refers to the Han, San-kuo Wei, Sung, Ch'i, and Liang.

85. I here adopt the variant Sung 宋 common to all but **M**, which has *tsung* 宗. The **T** editors punctuate after Sung, which makes the sentence meaningless. This word specifies the dynasty of which the author at the opening of the following sentence was a prince.

86. References to verbosity and unreliability are thought to be aimed at Pao-ch'ang's *Ming-seng chuan*. T'ang Yung-t'ung, "Tu Hui-chiao *Kao-seng chuan* cha-chi," 3, suggests that only the phrase *k'ung-yin tz'u-fei* 空引辭費 was directed at the *Ming-seng chuan*, but admits that the passage is by no means clear. Neither the work nor the author could be mentioned by name because the work was written by a high metropolitan cleric under imperial patronage. Cf. Chou-Su (5) and see part 4 of this paper.

87. This last critical comment may be directed at the *Chung-seng chuan* 衆僧傳 of P'ei Tzu-yeh 裴子野 (467–528), another biographical compendium written under imperial orders by a Liang official who was Hui-chiao's contemporary. Here again it would have been impolitic to mention author or title. Cf. Chou-Su (5) and part 4 above.

88. *Kao-tao* 高蹈. The expression seems first to appear in the *Tso-chuan*, twenty-first year of Duke Ai. Cf. Legge, *The Chinese Classics*, 5: 853. While it there meant "to travel far," it is here used in its later sense of those who lived withdrawn from and above the common herd.

89. Chou-Su (5) cites a passage from the *Huai-nan tzu* 淮南子 which shows the way Hui-chiao, like other Buddhist authors, drew on the traditions of Taoist asceticism to explain and justify Buddhist monasticism: *li-chieh k'ang-kao i chüeh shih-su* 勵節亢高以絕世俗, "To encourage chaste behavior and to exalt nobility set one apart from the worldly commonalty."

90. I add the adversative "yet." All but the **M** text have *hsün* 尋 here, which does not make sense. I follow the **M** editors in omitting it. For my interpretation of this passage, see the introduction to this chapter, "Attitudes."

91. The traditional date for the introduction of Buddhism into China. On its adventitious nature, cf. Pelliot, "Meou-tseu ou les doutes levés," 385, n. 293.

92. At the beginning of this group of biographies, *KSC* 12.403c, the heading is, according to **Y** and **M** *chih-shen* 志身, according to **SPK** *wang-shen* 亡身. Hui-chiao, in his critical estimate of this group of biographies, *KSC* 12.405c–06a, discusses at some length the propriety of self-immolation in the light of his own (Chinese) values and in the light of Buddhist doctrine.

93. In this term, *hsing* 興 has the usual meaning of "to foster." *Fu* 福 is an abbreviation of *fu-yeh* 福業, Skt. *puṇya-kriyā*, meaning acts of moral or religious merit. Here the compound refers to those who sponsored or worked at the making of images, the copying of sūtras, the building of temples, reliquaries etc.

94. This category includes the monks who dealt with the difficult problems of translating Indian Buddhist hymns, of finding or developing appropriate Chinese musical forms for such hymns, or of finding Chinese words and music adaptable to the expression of Buddhist ideas. The earliest surviving Chinese Buddhist stanzas in the Indian style are attributed to Ts'ao Chih (A.D. 192–232). Cf. *Hōbōgirin*, 1: 93–96; 2: 97–113. For a summary of Hui-chiao's *lun* on this group, cf. esp. 1: 95–96.

95. Hui-chiao, in his *lun* on this group of biographies, *KSC* 13.417c, says, "*Ch'ang-tao* 唱導 means to speak [*hsüan* 宣] and intone [*ch'ang* 唱] the principles of the Dharma in order to open a way to the hearts of men. Formerly, when the Buddhist Dharma was first brought to China, at the time of an Uposatha meeting [*chai-chi* 齋集], they would simply recite aloud the names of the Buddha and pay him worship according to the texts. By midnight [the congregation's] fatigue was very great. Something was needed to wake them up. So they would specially ask an eminent monk to take the chair and speak on the Dharma. Sometimes he would give a miscellaneous narrative of birth stories [*yin-yüan* 因緣]; sometimes, in passing, he would introduce an allegory." This is the beginning of the popular method of religious instruction which employed allegories, rhymed narratives, and edifying anecdotes to hold or revive a congregation's interest. These popular presentations were first transmitted orally and were often improvised by the monks. During the Sung they began to be written down as *pao-chüan* 寶卷. Cf. Jaroslav Průšek, "Narrators of Buddhist Scriptures and Religious Tales in the Sung Period." [Cf. also Daniel L. Overmyer, *Folk Buddhist Religion*, 179–86.—Ed.]

96. *Chen-tan* 震旦 Skt. *Cīna-sthāna* (?). Thought to be a transliteration into Chinese of the Indian transliteration of the name Ch'in 秦, referring to China. Cf., inter alia, Pelliot, "Autour d'une traduction sanscrite du Tao tö king."

97. *Ssu-i* 四依, Skt. *catvāri pratisaraṇāni*. The four classes of beings to whom Buddha entrusted the propagation of his teaching and the salvation of all creatures: (1) *Fan-nao-hsing jen* 煩惱性人, deluded transmigrating humans; (2) *hsü-t'o-huan* 須陀洹 Srotāpanna and *ssu-t'o-han* 斯陀含 Sakṛdāgāmin—the two lower classes of saints; (3) *A-na-han* 阿那含, Anāgāmin, the next higher class of saints who will not be born again as men; (4) *A-lo-han* 阿羅漢, Arhat, the fully enlightened.

98. *San-yeh* 三業, Skt. *trīṇikarmāṇi*. The term has many sets of meanings. I take it that Hui-chiao here means to suggest the following meritorious ac-

tions: (1) *Shen-yeh* 身業, *kāya-karma*, making the physical body perform acts of worship and emulate the Buddhas and Bodhisattvas; (2) *k'ou-yeh* 口業, *vāk-karma*, making the mouth praise the saints and teach the Dharma; (3) *i-yeh* 意業, *manas-karma*, making the mind think correctly and, concentrating on the saints, devise means of spreading the Dharma.

99. *Tsan-lun* 贊論. I have discussed these traditional Chinese forms of historical estimates and Hui-chiao's use of them in the introduction to this chapter.

100. *Chuan-tu* 轉讀. Hui-chiao, in his *lun* on the Hymnodists, *KSC* 13.415b, says, "But it is the Indian custom that whenever they sing Buddhist words they call this *pai* 唄. In this country, when we sing [the words of] the scriptures, we call it *chuan-tu*; when we sing the hymns of praise we call them *fan-yin* 梵音." On this last, cf. *Hōbōgirin*, 2: 102.

101. *Hsüan-ch'ang* 宣唱. See n. 95 above.

102. *Shu er pu-tso* 述而不作. The locus classicus is *Lun-yü* 11. See introduction to this chapter, and n. 11 above.

103. *Ming-seng* 名僧. As is seen in the review of sources in part 4 above, the word *ming* was not at all common in earlier book titles. This is of course another veiled criticism of Pao-ch'ang's *Ming-seng chuan*. See part 4 above.

104. *Ming-che pen-shih chih pin yeh* 名者本實之賓也. Cf. *Chuang-tzu* 1.7b (*p'ien* 1) and Legge, *The Texts of Taoism*, 1: 170. [Cf. also Watson, *The Complete Works of Chuang-tzu*, p. 32.—Ed.] The distinction that Hui-chiao draws is based on the ambivalent meaning of the word *ming*, either "name" or "fame." The sincerity of this passage is brought into question when one contemplates the indebtedness of Hui-chiao to the *Ming-seng chuan*. See part 4 above.

105. *Yin-kua* 隱括. The locus classicus is Ho Hsiu's 何休 (A.D. 129–82) commented edition of the *Ch'un-ch'iu Kung-yang chuan Ho-shih chieh-ku*, preface, 1b. The expression was originally drawn from carpentry, where it meant "to straighten and square" or the tools used to do this.

106. *HKSC* 6.471b. The expression *k'ai-li ch'eng-kuang* 開例成廣 is also used in Wang Man-ying's letter to describe Hui-chiao's writing; cf. *KSC* 14.422c.

107. Yamanouchi, "*Kōsōden* no kenkyū," 28, takes the whole series of criticisms introduced by "Down to the present day . . ." and ending, after the discussion of the independence of the clergy, ". . . what is there to record?" to be of Pao-ch'ang. However, in the preface generally *huo* 或 is used to introduce coordinate statements, and I doubt that it would have been used here in a continuous criticism of Pao-ch'ang. Nor is it likely that Hui-chiao would have criticized Pao-ch'ang for *both* prolixity and brevity. As was pointed out in n. 87 above, the strictures on overbrevity were probably directed at P'ei Tzu-yeh's *Chung-seng chuan*. Chou-Su (5) supports this interpretation.

There is no doubt that Hui-chiao had the *Ming-seng chuan* in mind when he wrote, later in his preface, about his grounds for preferring the word *kao* to the word *ming*. See nn. 103, 104 above.

Both the passage I have quoted and the *ming* vs. *kao* discussion were directed at Pao-ch'ang. The reasons for Hui-ch'ang's failure to mention author or title were suggested in the introduction section of this chapter. Pao-ch'ang was a protégé of the devout emperor Wu, and the *Ming-seng chuan* was compiled under imperial patronage and contained in its preface the most fulsome praise of the Liang dynasty; cf. *HKSC* 1.427a. It would have been impolitic, to say the least, for a younger provincial monk to criticize openly a work by a great metropolitan prelate who enjoyed the emperor's favor and patronage, a work which was written for and presented to the reigning monarch. Hui-chiao mentions Pao-ch'ang only once in the *KSC*, 3.345b, and there only as one of the participants in a translation project at the capital early in the Liang dynasty.

108. *KSC* 14.422c.

109. The first two dates appear in Pao-ch'ang's biography, *HKSC* 1.427b. The third is given in *LTSPC* 3.45a. This last date of 519 is supported by the fact that Seng-yu, who died in 518, was given a biography in the *Ming-seng chuan*. Cf. *Meisōden shō* 3b, 14. Kasuga, "Jōdokyō shiryō," 57, doubts the *Li-tai san-pao-chi* date on the grounds that it places the completion of the *Ming-seng chuan* too soon before that of the *KSC*. But, as we pointed out at the end of part 2, the *KSC* was completed not in 519 but probably around 530. Pelliot, "Notes sur quelques artistes des six dynasties et des T'ang," 258, n. 1, gives the date 514 for the completion of the *Ming-seng chuan*, but this is at variance with the facts noted above.

110. In the preface to his *Pi-ch'iu-ni chuan* Pao-ch'ang says, "I began by making a catholic collection of stone inscriptions and eulogies and collecting on a wide scale records and collectanea [all concerned with nuns]. I have questioned those with broad knowledge about them and queried old people concerning them. Having selected and classified [these materials] from beginning to end, I wrote biographies of them." Cf. *Pi-ch'iu-ni chuan*, preface, 934b, and "Biography of the Nun An-ling-shou," reprinted this volume. This is strikingly similar to Hui-chiao's account of his methods in his *KSC* preface.

111. *HKSC* 1.427c.

112. The *K'ai-yüan shih-chiao lu*, completed in 730, remarks that while the *Ming-seng chuan* was mentioned in the *LTSPC* (of early Sui date) it had not meanwhile been accorded canonical status and was therefore not discussed. Cf. 6.538a.

113. It was consulted, after the middle of the eighth century, by the author of the *Feng-shih wen-chien chi*. Cf. "Fo-t'u-teng: A Biography," reprinted this volume, chap. 2.

114. Cf. the *Meisōden shō* of Shūshō. These excerpts were copied, between the fifteenth and eighteenth days of the fifth moon of the second year of Bunryaku 文曆 (1235), from a MS *Ming-seng chuan* then in the possession of the Tōdaiji at Nara. Shūshō was strongly interested in evidences of the working of the grace of the Bodhisattvas, particularly Maitreya, and his selection of excerpts reflects this interest. He copied out the table of contents, portions of thirty-six biographies (including one biography—that of Fa-yü—which was probably complete), and added a topical finding list *shuo-ch'u* 說處 of the items that interested him chüan by chüan. And, in compiling another collection of excerpts, the *Miroku nyorai kannōshō* 彌勒如來感應抄, he copied portions of sixteen biographies, all incidents involving Maitreya. Cf. Kasuga, "Jōdokyō shiryō," 111–18. On Shūshō's life and activities, cf. ibid., 59–60. Shūshō's MS copies of the two works are still in the Tōdaiji library.

115. Yamanouchi, "*Kōsōden* no kenkyū," 37, cautions that Shūshō's copy of the table of contents may not be fully reliable for these category headings. He goes on to say that these headings may well represent six major categories and twelve subcategories. Yet even if this is correct, the breakdown is clearly characterized by overlapping categories. And the separation of "foreign" from "Chinese" monks impaired the consistency of a breakdown in terms of activity. The lack of a category for "exegetes" shows a failure to abstract and use for classificatory purposes a major activity of the monks of the period covered.

116. Cf. *KSC* 14.419b–22b and *Meisōden shō*, 1a–5b. The two schemes are given a comparative table in Yamanouchi, "*Kōsōden* no kenkyū," 36–37.

117. Cf. *Meisōden shō*, 9b, and *KSC* 11.403a–c. From its location in Shūshō's excerpts there is an indication, necessarily inconclusive, that Pao-ch'ang's critical estimates, like Hui-chiao's, followed a group of biographies. The discourse in the *Meisōden shō*, 8b, headed "The *lun* says" appears to be a doctrinal discussion with no clear relation to any group of biographies.

118. This is, of course, an old and recurrent theme in Buddhist apologetics. Cf. Pelliot, "Meou-tseu ou les doutes levés," 291.

119. Cf. Yamanouchi, "*Kōsōden* no kenkyū," 17–27, for comparative tables of contents of the two works. There are divergent figures of the number of subordinate biographies arising from differing judgments as to what constituted a subordinate biography; Hui-chiao did not label these and simply noted in his preface that there were "more than 200" of them. The Chin-ling k'o-ching ch'u editors, in their annotated table of contents, list 259. The copyist of the Ishiyama-dera MS substituted the figure "239" for Hui-chiao's "more than 200" in the preface. Cf. Iwai Tairyō, "Ishiyama-dera hon *Ryō Kōsōden* to sono Dōan den jōi," 74, and see the bibliographical note above.

120. Cf. *KSC* 5.356a–b and *Meisōden shō*, 8a. Fa-yü's biography was

no. 6 in ch. 11 of the *Ming-seng chuan.*

121. *SS* 33.19a [T'ung-wen ed.]. [*SS* 33.978 and 33.995, n. 24, corrects this to Hui-chiao.—Ed.]

122. The fact that no such attribution is made in any Buddhist catalogue would make its existence very doubtful. The most indisputable evidence is Pao-ch'ang's preface to his *Ming-seng chuan*, in which he remarks that while other biographical compendia exist, ". . . yet of the pure conduct of the śramaṇas alone do we lack a record"; cf. *HKSC* 1.427c. He certainly would not have made this remark if his own revered master had written a *Kao-seng chuan.* Wang Man-ying, in his letter, remarks that Seng-yu's work shares the criticism given to that of Fa-chi, i.e., that he dealt with only one category of monks. Cf. *KSC* 14.422c. Hui-chiao, in his preface, deplores the fact that Seng-yu's *Ch'u san-tsang chi-chi* dealt only with the lives of thirty-odd monks. These criticisms would be beside the point if Seng-yu had written a major biographical compendium.

123. Yamanouchi, "*Kōsōden* no kenkyū," 4. The story appears in *Shih-shih chi-ku-lüeh* 3.818a. Cf. also *Ta-Sung kao-seng chuan* 14.790b.

124. *Ssu-k'u ch'üan-shu tsung-mu* 145.7a–b.

125. *SS* 33.975, 34.1010; *CTS* 46.2003; *HTS* 59.1525.

126. *Fa-yüan chu-lin* 100.1021c. The prince of Hsiang-t'ung, later the emperor Yüan, was a contemporary of Hui-chiao. See part 2 of this chapter above.

127. It is the only earlier source known to me which mentions the two categories. Moreover the character *min* 敏, found in Ch'ao's work and later in the *Ssu-k'u* catalogue, is probably an error of Ch'ao's; *SCKC*, 5350a, supports this. For Ch'ao's notice, cf. *Chün-chai tu-shu chih* 9.12b. As Yao Chen-tsung remarks, *SCKC*, 5350a, Ch'ao's work is full of errors.

128. *Wen-hsüan* 60.7a.

129. Cf. *SCKC*, 5349b, 5350a. The quotation in the *Wen-hsüan* commentary, only nine characters long, is too slight to support any hypothesis about the content or scope of Yü Hsiao-ching's work as a whole.

130. That is, the date of its citation by Li Shan in his commentary; cf. n. 128 above.

131. *HKSC* 6.471b.

132. Cf. P'ei's biography in *Liang-shu* 30.444. *SS* 33.978 and 34.1010 cites it twice as a work in 20 ch. *CTS* 46.2005 and *HTS* 59.1525 both list it as a *Ming-seng lu* 名僧錄 in 15 ch. The T'ang histories are probably citing it incorrectly. Cf. also *SCKC*, 5368c.

133. See *KSC* preface 14.418c and n. 87 above.

134. The work and its supplement are listed in the *Ta-T'ang nei-tien lu* 10.331c, a catalogue completed in 664. It is there listed as a *Sha-men chuan* 沙門傳 and not under its correct title. Liu Ch'iu was a Wai-ping-lang 外兵郎

under the Liang and compiled, under imperial commission, an account of the temples of Yang-chou called *Yang-tu ssu-chi* 楊都寺記; cf. ibid.

135. Cf. *KSC* preface 14.418b, 422c.

136. *KSC* 4.348b.

137. *LTSPC* 8.74a.

138. *Shih-shuo hsin-yü chiao-chien*, 85, 96, 176, 178, 179, 284, 359, 601 [Mather, *Shih-shuo hsin-yü*, 54, 113, 114, 115, 191, 237–38, 413—Ed.].

139. Compare *Shih-shuo hsin-yü chiao-chien*, 96, and *KSC* 4.349c.

140. See *KSC* preface and *KSC* 14.422c.

141. *KSC* 8.380a. This note was probably taken from the *Ming-seng chuan*. Cf. *Meisōden shō, sessho* 說處 section, pt. 17, p. 15b.

142. Yamanouchi, "*Kōsōden* no kenkyū," 10. T'ang, "Tu Hui-chiao *Kao-seng-chuan* cha-chi," 1, agrees with Y and suggests that the work may have been included in ch. 6 of Seng-yu's lost compendium, *Fa-yüan chi* 法苑集. Cf. *Ch'u san-tsang chi-chi* 12.92b.

143. *KSC* 8.380a.

144. See *KSC* 14.422c; cf. also Chou-Su (4). On the accounts by pilgrims see n. 225 below.

145. Cf. *KSC* 8.375c, 379c, 382a. The last of these is probably the Seng-pao who had a biography in the *Ming-seng chuan*. Cf. *Meisōden shō, sessho* 說處 section, item 17, p. 15b. Yamanouchi, "*Kōsōden* no kenkyū," 10, associates the first reference given above with the Seng-pao who wrote these biographies, but there is no evidence to establish this.

146. See *KSC* 14.422c.

147. *SS* 33.978.

148. T'ang, "Tu Hui-chiao *Kao-seng-chuan* cha-chi," 1.

149. *SCKC*, 5368a–b. Sun Ch'o (ca. 301–ca. 380; cf. *Chin-shu* 56.1544–47) was a prolific writer of eulogies of eminent monks, and these are quoted again and again by Hui-chiao; cf. n. 243 below. Sun's favorite device was to compare a monk with a neo-Taoist philosopher or wit.

150. Cf. *KSC* 10.392c, 393a; 12.404a–b.

151. This prince of the Sung ruling house was also author of work no. VI discussed in Hui-chiao's preface (part 3 above), the *Shih-shuo hsin-yü*, and of a collection of biographies of optimi of his family's seat; cf. *Sung-shu* 51.1470–80, passim, and *SCKC* 20.303c.

152. See above.

153. *KSC* 1.324a, in the discussion of the date of An Shih-kao's death.

154. *SS* 33.980.

155. Cf. Lu Hsün, *Ku hsiao-shuo kou-ch'en*, 549–59.

156. Compare, for example, the miraculous feats of K'ang Seng-hui as found in Lu Hsün's reconstruction, ibid., 366–68, and in K'ang's biography, *KSC* 1.325a–26b.

157. Cf. *KSC* 14.422c.

158. *SS* 30.980; *HTS* 59.1540 gives 30 ch., which is incorrect.

159. This is contained in the *Lin-lang pi-shih ts'ung-shu*, pt. 3, under the title *Yu-ming lu fu chiao-e* 幽明錄附校譌. [Postface to Hu's text dated Hsien-feng 3 (1853).]

160. Lu Hsün, *Ku hsiao-shuo kou-ch'en*, 353–436.

161. Compare the unnatural events befalling An Shih-kao in his biography *KSC* 1.323a–24b and the prodigies recounted in Hu T'ing's reconstructed text *Yu-ming lu fu chiao-o*, 35b–36a. I have noted in "Fo-t'u-teng: A Biography" two instances of Fo-t'u-teng's clairvoyance recounted in the *KSC* which may have been drawn from the *Yu-ming lu*; cf. chap. 2, nn. 84, 164 above. Compare *KSC* 9.384b and *TPYL* 370.5a; *KSC* 9.386b and *TPYL* 895.7b.

162. *HTS* 59.1540; *SS* 33.980 gives the title as *Pu-hsü ming-hsiang chi* 補續冥祥記, in 1 ch. Cf. *SCKC*, 5382a–b.

163. *SS* 33.980 and *SCKC*, 5378b–c.

164. Lu Hsün, *Ku hsiao-shuo kou-ch'en*, 563–648.

165. Cf. Maspero, "Le songe et l'ambassade de l'Empereur Ming," 112–13; also, Pelliot, "Meou-tseu ou les doutes levés," 388, n. 297.

166. Compare, for example, the life of Shan Tao-k'ai 單道開 in *KSC* 9.387b–c with the *Ming-hsiang chi* account in Lu Hsün's reconstruction, *Ku hsiao-shuo kou-ch'en*, 605; also, the life of Chu Fo-t'iao 竺佛調, *KSC* 9.387c–88a with the *Ming-hsiang chi* account in Lu Hsün's text, op. cit., 573–74; and the life of Ch'i-yü 耆域, *KSC* 9.388a–c with the *Ming-hsiang chi* version in Lu Hsün, op. cit., 571–73. T'ang, "Tu Hui-chiao *Kao-seng-chuan* cha-chi," 2, points out that the *Ming-hsiang chi* was extensively used for the biography of T'an-huo 曇霍, *KSC* 10.389c–90a.

167. Maspero, "Le songe et l'ambassade de l'Empereur Ming," 112–13.

168. Cf. his biography in *Nan Ch'i-shu* 37.649–54 and *Ch'i fang-chen nien-piao*, 4320.

169. *KSC* 13.416b.

170. *KSC* 1.324a–b.

171. Cf. *SS* 33.985. [The error has been corrected in this edition of *SS*; cf. *SS* 33.995, n. 33.—Ed.] Cf. *SCKC*, 5404b.

172. Cf. *SCKC*, 5403c.

173. *KSC* 14.422c.

174. *SS* 33.980; 34.1010. The second entry is incorrect in identifying Wang as a Shang-shu lang 尚信郎 under the Chin. [The error has been corrected in this edition of *SS*; cf. *SS* 34.1052, n. 19.—Ed.] See also nn. 175, 176 below.

175. *Sung-shu* 66.1734, biography of Ho Shang-chih 何尚之.

176. Yen K'o-chün's 嚴可均 *Ch'üan Sung-wen* 全宋文, quoted in *SCKC*, 5379a.

177. *KSC* 14.422c.

178. *CTS* 46.2005; *HTS* 59.1540.

179. The suggestion is made in Chou-Su (5).

180. Cf. the *P'o-hsieh lun* of A.D. 622, 2.485c.

181. *SS* 33.980.

182. Cf. *SCKC*, 5380c–81; Pelliot, "Autour d'une traduction sanscrite du Tao tö king," 420, n. 1.

183. Cf. Pelliot, ibid., and Wright, "Fo-t'u-teng: A Biography," chap. 2, n. 173 above. Also, *Sou-shen hou-chi* 2.2b–3a for the account in that work.

184. Cf. *KSC* 10.390b. The incident referred to does not appear in the present edition of the *Sou-shen hou-chi*.

185. See above.

186. Cf. his biography in *Nan Ch'i-shu* 40.692–701.

187. Cf. *LTSPC* 11.96c. *Nan Ch'i-shu* 40.701 remarks that his writings lacked literary polish.

188. *Ta-T'ang nei-tien lu* 4.263b; 10.331a.

189. See above.

190. *SS* 33.978; *LTSCP* 11.96c. Cf. also *SCKC*, 5368b–c.

191. A short biography is quoted from the *Hsing-shih ying-hsien lu* 姓氏英賢錄 in the commentary to *Wen-hsüan* 59.1a. Wang Chin's inscription for the T'ou-t'o ssu 頭陀寺, north of the modern Nanking, appears in *Wen-hsüan* 59.1a–9a.

192. Ibid., and *LTSPC* 11.96c.

193. Yen Chen-tsung says categorically that Wang Chin used the prince of Ching-ling's book as the basis of his own; *SCKC*, 5368c. Wang Chin's book was apparently used by Pao-ch'ang for his *Ming-seng chuan*. He cites "Wang Chin" on a variant geographical origin of the monk T'an-pin 曇斌; cf. the excerpt in *Miroku nyorai kannōshō*, quoted in Kasuga, "Jōdokyō shiryō," p. 113.

194. See above. [See also Arthur E. Link, "Remarks on Shih Seng-yu's *Ch'u san-tsang chi-chi* as a Source for Hui-chiao's *Kao-seng chuan*."—Ed.]

195. *KSC* 14.422c. This comment seems somewhat inaccurate since Seng-yu's work included two broad groups of biographies, those of translators and of exegetes, though he did not use these rubrics. Many of these comments seem to me early examples of an apparently universal failing of book critics: condemning an author for not writing another kind of book from the one he set out, with good reasons, to write.

196. See the text of *Ch'u san-tsang chi-chi* in *Taishō Tripitaka*, vol. 55. Also, Seng-yu's biography, *KSC* 11.402c. In this biography Hui-chiao suggests that the *Ch'u san-tsang chi-chi* and certain other works of Seng-yu were the by-products of the collection of a massive Tripiṭaka, a project in which Seng-yu was long engaged. Hui-chiao did not regard Seng-yu as, in the full sense, "author" of these works, for he says, "He had the important items copied and

compiled to produce the *san-tsang-chi...*" ("shih-jen ch'ao chuan yao-shih wei san-tsang-chi" 使人抄撰要事爲三藏集).

197. The last date mentioned in the work is T'ien-chien 天監 9, or A.D. 510. Cf. *Ch'u san-tsang chi-chi* 5.40b. Seng-yu died in 518.

198. Cf. *HKSC* 1.427c, quotation from the preface of the *Ming-seng chuan*.

199. Chou-Su (6) simply states that in the vast majority of cases the *KSC* biographies of these thirty-two individuals were based on Seng-yu's accounts.

200. For Chu Shih-hsing, compare *KSC* 4.346b–c and *Ch'u san-tsang chi-chi* 13.97a–b; for T'an-wu-ch'en, compare *KSC* 2.335c–337b and *Ch'u san-tsang chi-chi* 14.102c–03b (note the *KSC*'s fuller account of secular events and the added data at the end of the biography); for Kumārajīva, compare *KSC* 2.330a–33a and *Ch'u san-tsang chi-chi* 14.100a–02a. Nobel, "Kumārajīva," 208, states that the two biographies "[werden] auf dieselbe Quelle zurückgehen" ["...derive from the same source"]. This fails to take account of the different relation between the two works outlined above.

201. For Po Yüan's biography compare *KSC* 1.327a–c and *Ch'u san-tsang chi-chi* 15.107a–c.

202. Hui-chiao's heavy reliance on Seng-yu's work led him, in at least one case, to perpetuate an error in the earlier work which he might have corrected from other sources available to him. Cf. T'ang, "Tu Hui-chiao *Kao-seng-chuan* cha-chi," 5–6 ("The date and place of Fa-hu's 法護 death").

203. See above.

204. *KSC* 14.422c.

205. Cf. his biography, *Chin-shu* 67.1802–06. His *ch'ing-t'an* colloquies with Chih Tun are extensively reported in the *Shih-shuo hsin-yü*. Of Hsi Ch'ao's Buddhist writings apparently only the *Feng-fa yao* 奉法要 has survived; cf. *Hung-ming chi* 13.86a–89b.

206. Cf. Chou-Su (6) and the *Yen-lu* 剡錄 by the Sung writer Kao Ssu-sun 高似孫, 8.3b–12b. T'ang, "Tu Hui-chiao *Kao-seng-chuan* cha-chi," 2, suggests that Hsi Ch'ao's "Biography with a Preface of Chih Tun" mentioned in the latter's biography, *KSC* 4.349c, may have been included in the *Tung-shan seng-chuan*. According to one theory, Chin Tun died in Yen-hsien; cf. *KSC* 4.349c.

207. *KSC* 14.422c.

208. Cf. *Liang-shu* 51.752–53; *Nan-shih* 76.1905–06.

209. The work is listed as *Chi Lu-shan seng-chuan* 集盧山僧傳 in the bibliography of works on Lu-shan in the *Lu-shan chih* of 1933, 10.1b.

210. Cf. *Liang-shu* 26.398–99; *Nan-shih* 48.1204–05.

211. *Liang-shu* 26.399.

212. *KSC* 8.382b.

213. Cf. the *Wu-ti chi* by the T'ang author Lu Kuang-wei, 17b.

214. *Liang-shu* 26.399; *Nan-shih* 48.1205.

215. I am indebted to Professor Tsukamoto for calling my attention to this work and for permitting me to study his photographs of the MS.

216. Cf., for example, *KSC* 1.327a, biography of Po Yüan, where direct and indirect quotations are taken over verbatim from Seng-yu's earlier biography.

217. Cf. Chou-Su (7).

218. *KSC* 1.325a. Hui-chiao points out that despite the rank and favor accorded him by Sun Ch'üan 孫權, K'ang was omitted from the *Wu-chih* because of his foreign birth.

219. *KSC* 7.368c. Hui-chiao notes that a miracle which he has described is also attested by the *Sung shih* 宋史. There is the possibility in this case that Hui-chiao is not speaking of a title but of "Sung histories" in a general sense.

220. *KSC* 13.414a. The emperor instructs Hsü Yüan 徐爰 not to omit the monk T'an-ch'ien 曇遷 from the *Sung-shu* 宋書 he is writing. On this lost history, cf. *SCKC*, 5249c–50a.

221. *KSC* 9.387a. This is a direct quotation, followed by a critique of T'ien Jung's account. Cf. "Fo-t'u-teng: A Biography," chap. 2, n. 191 above.

222. On the *Yeh-chung chi* 鄴中記, cf. "Fo-t'u-teng: A Biography," chap. 2, n. 164 above; on T'ien Jung's *Erh-shih wei-shih* 二石僞事, ibid., n. 192; on Ch'e P'in's 車頻 *Ch'in-shu* 秦書, cf. ibid., n. 190.

223. Cf. *KSC* 5.355c for the identification of a mountain.

224. *KSC* 1.324a. This work is briefly noted in Wen T'ing-shih's *Pu Chin-shu i-wen-chih*, 3739a. Although the other work of the same name is sometimes quoted with its author specified, Yü's name is apparently never mentioned. In most cases the work is quoted by title only, and there is no way to determine which author's work is cited; cf. *SCKC*, 5391b.

225. For Pao Yün's 寶雲 account of foreign countries, cf. *KSC* 3.340a; for Tao P'u's 道普, cf. *KSC* 2.337b; for Fa-sheng's 法盛, cf. *KSC* 2.337b and *SCKC*, 5405a; for T'an-wu-chieh's 曇無竭, cf. *KSC* 3.339a and *SCKC*, 5405a; for Fa-hsien's 法顯—the only one to survive—cf. *KSC* 3.338b. T'ang, "Tu Hui-chiao *Kao-seng-chuan* cha-chi," 3, suggests that this last reference may be to the *Yu-li T'ien-chu-chi* 遊歷天竺記, which T'ang, unlike many modern scholars, believes to be a lost work distinct from the well-known *Fo-kuo chi* 佛國記. That Hui-chiao was well acquainted with this literature is attested by his remark on the discrepancies among various monks' accounts of foreign lands; cf. *KSC* 3.343c.

226. For a challenging statement on the nature and significance of the *pieh-chuan* in the history of Chinese biographical writing, cf. Ch'en Shih-hsiang, "An Innovation in Chinese Biographical Writing," 51–52.

227. Cf., for example, "Fo-t'u-teng: A Biography."

228. Cf., for example, *KSC* 2.337a; 5.354a; 1.324b.

229. Cf., for example, *KSC* 1.328a; 7.370a; 9.387c.

230. Cf. *KSC* 14.422c. Wang has no comment beyond the obvious fact that they were about single individuals.

231. On Shan Tao-k'ai, cf. "Fo-t'u-teng: A Biography," chap. 2, n. 25. *SS* 33.978 lists the work as *Tao-jen Shan Tao-k'ai chuan* 道人單道開傳 by K'ang Hung 康泓 in 1 ch.; cf. *SCKC*, 5367a–b. K'ang Hung's admiration for Shan Tao-k'ai is described at the end of the latter's biography, *KSC* 9.387c, where it states that K'ang wrote a biography with a eulogy of his master; the eulogy alone is there quoted. It is possible that this is the same work that is quoted in *Fa-yüan chu-lin* 27.485 simply as "a *pieh-chuan*."

232. Wang Man-ying speaks of the author of this memoir as Wang Hsiu 王秀 (or, according to **SYMP**, Wang Chi 季). Kao-tso is a courtesy name of Śrīmitra 尸梨密多羅, who died between 335 and 342. [Cf. Mather, *Shih-shuo hsin-yü*, 541.—Ed.] In Śrīmitra's biography, *KSC* 1.328a, it mentions and quotes a memoir (*hsü* 序) of Śrīmitra by a lay disciple named Wang Mien of Lang Ya 瑯琊王眠. But, as Yamanouchi, "*Kōsōden* no kenkyū," 14–15, pointed out, the Wang Mien, *tzu* Chi-yen 季琰, who appears in *Chin-shu* 65.1758 was not born until after Śrīmitra's death. Thus, three questions remain unresolved: Who was the person mentioned as the author of a memoir in Śrīmitra's biography? Is this the same work on Śrīmitra that is mentioned in Wang's letter?; if so, what is the correct name of the author? And what is the relation between this work or works and the *Kao-tso pieh-chuan* or *Kao-tso chuan* quoted in the commentary of the *Shih-shuo hsin-yü chiao-chien*? Cf. *Shih-shuo hsin-yü chiao-chien*, 78, 338, 580. None of the biographical facts in these quotations are at odds with those in the *KSC* biography, and it seems likely that Hui-chiao drew on one or more such works for his biography of Śrīmitra.

233. This is mentioned in *KSC* 12.405a as a *Seng-yü chuan-tsan* 僧瑜傳讚 by Chang Pien 張辯, a lesser Sung official whose biography appears in *Sung-shu* 53.1515. The eulogy is directly quoted at the end of Seng-yü's biography. Seng-yü, who lived from 412 to 455, settled in Lu-shan in 438 and ended his life in a spectacular self-immolation. The same Chang Pien is credited with another biography and eulogy (*chuan-tsan* 傳讚) of the monk T'an-chien 曇鑒, and the eulogy is quoted in his biography, *KSC* 7.370a.

234. Wang uses the term *ku-lu* 孤錄 with reference to this biography, and I am dubious about the suggestion in Yamanouchi, "*Kōsōden* no kenkyū," 15, that this refers to the memorial inscription to Hsüan-ch'ang written by Chou Yung 周顒 (d. 485; cf. *Nan Ch'i-shu* 41.730–34; *Nan-shih* 34.894–95; Giles, *Chinese Biographical Dictionary*, no. 429) which is mentioned at the end of Hsüan-ch'ang's biography, *KSC* 8.377c. Hsüan-ch'ang (416–84) enjoyed the respect of the Sung rulers at their capital. In the first year of the Ch'i dynasty he built a temple in Szechwan and called it Ch'i-hsing 齊興. It comes as no

surprise that he was later able to get an imperial grant for its support. It seems likely that the work mentioned in Wang's letter was a *pieh-chuan* and that it was known to and used by Hui-chiao.

235. Cf., for example, *KSC* 8.377c; Chou Yung's memorial inscription to Hsüan-ch'ang mentioned in n. 234 above; memorial inscriptions by the great critic Liu Hsieh 劉勰, *KSC* 8.378c, 11.402c, 12.408b. The historian Shen Yüeh 沈約 wrote such a memorial inscription for Fa-hsien; cf. *KSC* 14.411c. The biography of Seng-ch'üan 僧詮, *KSC* 7.369c, specifies the donor of the monument, the writer of the principal text, and the composer of the funerary ode (*lei* 誄) which was also inscribed upon it.

236. Funerary odes, which were often graven on monuments, were highly conventionalized.

237. Cf., for example, Wang Chin's stele inscription for the T'ou-t'o ssu in *Wen-hsüan* 59.1a–9a; cf. n. 191 above. For some of the details on the history of the T'an-ch'i ssu 檀溪寺 at Hsiang-chou 襄州 (the modern Hsiang-yang, Hupei) which he gives in Tao-an's biography, *KSC* 5.352b, Hui-chiao may well have relied on the stele erected there in T'ien-chien 天監 11 (512). On this inscription, cf. *Pao-k'o ts'ung-pien* by the Sung author Ch'en Ssu, ch. 3, 5b.

238. Those materials included, for example, the Fo-t'u-teng stele of 322 (?), which was still to be seen in the period 766–80; cf. "Fo-t'u-teng: A Biography."

239. Cf., for example, *KSC* 5.356b; 7.367c, 369a; 8.379b.

240. Cf., for example, *KSC* 4.346c, 347b, 349c, 350; 6.360a.

241. Cf. *KSC* 1.324a for a quotation from the preface to the *An-pan shou-i-ching* 安般守意經 with a commentary by K'ang Seng-hui. Cf. *KSC* 8.381c for a quotation from Pao-liang's 寶亮 preface to his commentary on the *Nirvāṇa sūtra*. T'ang, "Tu Hui-chiao *Kao-seng chuan* cha-chi," 6, 9, discusses two instances where Hui-chiao might have avoided mistakes by the use of available prefaces.

242. Cf., for example, *KSC* 6.359b–c, 361b; 8.377b, 381c.

243. For Sun Ch'o see n. 149 above. The surviving fragments of his writings were brought together in Yen K'o-chün's *Ch'üan shang-ku san-tai Ch'in-Han San-kuo liu-ch'ao wen*, Chin 晉 section, 2: 1806–15. Sun's *Tao-hsien lun* 道賢論, written as a Buddhist counterpart to Tai K'uei's 戴逵 *Chu-lin ch'i-hsien lun* 竹林七賢論 (cf. *KSC* 1.326c and *SCKC*, p. 5354a), is quoted five times by title, giving his comparisons between eminent monks and great *ch'ing-t'an* adepts. Two similar comparisons, probably from the same work, are mentioned in *KSC* 4.348a, 350b. In addition, seven of his eulogies, outside the comparative framework of the *Tao-hsien lun*, are quoted. His work entitled *Ming-te sha-men lun-mu* 名德沙門論目 is quoted in the biography of Tao-an, *KSC* 5.354a. (Emend all *KSC* texts to read, after *Ch'u san-tsang chi-*

chi 15.109a, *lun-mu yün* 論目云 instead of *lun-tzu yün* 論自云.) T'ang, "Tu Hui-chiao *Kao-seng-chuan* cha-chi," 3, takes the view that this is the same work as the *Ming-te sha-men t'i-mu* 名德沙門題目 quoted in the *Shih-shuo hsin-yü chiao-cheng* commentary, 116, 179, 361 [Mather, *Shih-shuo hsin-yü*, 93, 115, 238—Ed.].

244. Cf., for example, *KSC* 3.341b–42b, a poetical translation of Guṇa-varman's 求那跋摩 testament (*i-wen* 遺文); *KSC* 1.328c, two songs (*ko* 歌) and an ode (*sung* 頌) by Chao Cheng 趙正, the last celebrating his entrance into the priesthood; *KSC* 8.377b, a poem in praise of Ch'i-shan 齊山 which elicited imperial patronage for the temple there—see n. 234 above.

Chapter 5   Fu I and the Rejection of Buddhism

1. Tsukamoto Zenryū has brought together a wealth of material on the Northern Chou experiment and has written three articles of great importance: "Hoku-Shū no haibutsu ni tsuite," pts. 1 and 2; and "Hoku-Shū no shūkyō haiki seisaku no hōkai." The quotation is from *Kuang hung-ming chi* 10.154b.

2. The *Liang-ching hsin-chi*, 203, states that in the early Sui Buddhist monasteries at Ch'ang-an numbered 64, nunneries 27, Taoist abbeys 10, Taoist nunneries 6. It further states that at the beginning of the Ta-yeh period (605–17) the total of Buddhist temples in the city was 120, Taoist temples 10; cf. also Tsukamoto, "Hoku-Shū no shūkyō haiki seisaku no hōkai," 30.

3. This was begun in 580 while the Sui founder was still chief minister of the Northern Chou; cf. *Chou-shu* 8.132 and Tsukamoto, "Hoku-Shū no shūkyō haiki seisaku no hōkai," 16–26. Cf. also Peter A. Boodberg, "Marginalia to the Histories of the Northern Dynasties," 331, and, for a characterization of the Sui founder, 332–34.

4. Cf. *SS* 2.45–46. For a full account of Sui Wen-ti's policies on Buddhism, cf. Yamazaki Hiroshi, *Zui no Kōso Buntei no Bukkyō chikokusaku*, 64, and his "Zuichō no Bukkyō fukkō ni tsuite," 50–58. The extent of the revival of Buddhism is reflected in the following figures from *PCL* 3.509b (they are for the years 581–604): clergy ordained, 230,000; temples throughout the country, 3,792; Sūtra and Śāstra copied, 46 collections in 132,086 rolls; old copies of the sacred books repaired, 3,853 works; images, large and small, of various materials, 16,580; images repaired, 1,508,940 "odd." A Confucian lament, dating from after the edict of 581 ordering Buddhist works to be copied at state expense, states, "Among the people Buddhist scriptures are more numerous than the Six Classics [of Confucianism] several thousand fold"; *SS* 35.1099.

5. Cf. *T'ung-tien* 14.81a. In the T'ang merchants, artisans, those whose families had been prosecuted, and those attempting to enter officialdom by

fraud were debarred from the "Placement Examination" (*wen-hsüan*); cf. R. des Rotours, *Le traité des examens*, 215. For a scathing comment on the content and conduct of the examinations, delivered in 681, cf. ibid., 166–67.

6. Buddha, Dharma, and Saṅgha; or the Buddha, the Teaching, and the Community of Believers.

7. Tsukamoto, "Hoku-Shū no haibutsu ni tsuite," pt. 2, p. 102, analyzes the groups disaffected by the Northern Chou persecution. Anti-Buddhist measures by the T'ang government would have created opposition from comparable groups. Tsukamoto's breakdown is as follows: (1) secularized clergy whose way of life had been abruptly changed; (2) lay adherents of all classes who had supported clergy, temples, the copying of scriptures, etc., in the hope of salvation; (3) military and civil officials whose loyalty to the throne was shaken by oppressive measures against their personal religion; (4) the vast numbers of artists, artisans, copyists, provisioners, etc. who depended for their livelihood on serving Buddhist establishments. One might add those who profited directly or indirectly from the tax-free, corvée-free status of temple lands.

8. Sources for the life of Fu I are: *CTS* 79.1714–17; *HTS* 107.4059–62; *Kuang hung-ming chi* 7.134a–35b. The latter is the last biography in the *Kao-shih chuan*, a work compiled by Fu I himself. It seems likely, however, that Tao-hsüan (596–667), the compiler of the *Kuang hung-ming chi*, himself wrote the biography of Fu I, probably making use of T'ang Lin's (ca. 601–60) *Ming-pao chi*. For clarification on this point I am indebted to Professor Tsukamoto. De Groot, in *Sectarianism and Religious Persecution in China*, 36–43, translated a portion of *CTS* 79. The translation is in need of revision. I have found, here as elsewhere, that the use of parallel Buddhist and official historical accounts gives a fuller and clearer picture than the use of either alone.

9. The Fu family genealogy is found in *HTS* 74A.3154. There is a lacuna of ten generations between the last notable Fu, a San-kuo Wei official, and Fu I. *Kuang hung-ming chi* 7.134a would suggest that at least Fu I's own branch of his family served under successive non-Chinese regimes in the north. This would account for the fact that both *T'ang-shu* biographies give his birthplace as Yeh, in northern Honan, then the Northern Ch'i capital, while both *HTS* genealogy and the *Kuang hung-ming chi* associate him with Ni-yang county, the old seat of the Fu family in southern Shensi. The T'ang gave him, in his later years, the title of Ni-yang hsien-nan, baron of Ni-yang county.

10. Cf. Tsukamoto, "Hoku-Shū no haibutsu ni tsuite," pt. 1, pp. 37–44; pt. 2, pp. 101–08. The edict setting up the T'ung-tao kuan is found in *Chou-shu* 5.85.

11. Tsukamoto, from an investigation of Taoist, Buddhist, and Confucian official writings, has been able to identify only two Buddhists, appointed in their twenties, and one monk of some distinction, appointed just before

Emperor Wu's death. The Taoists were represented by ten adepts of some note. Cf. Tsukamoto, "Hoku-Shū no haibutsu ni tsuite," pt. 2, pp. 106–08. Fu I was of course a youth at the time of his appointment. See n. 26 below.

12. *Kuang hung-ming chi* 7.134a.

13. Ibid.

14. *CTS* 79.2714–15. The *CTS* biography of Fu I is in some ways a fuller and more coherent account than that in *HTS* 107, where this incident occurs on p. 4059.

15. *CTS* 79.2715; *HTS* 107.4059.

16. For a discussion of the naming of the divisions, cf. R. des Rotours, *Traité des fonctionnaires et traité de l'armée*, 757–60, wherein is translated the portion of *HTS* 50 dealing with this subject. Des Rotours dates the reform as of 619. The territorial armies were abolished in 623. According to *CTS* 79.2715, his new system of measuring time by the water clock was proposed in 620. It was about this time that he urged the T'ang to cease following Sui precedents and introduce new official names, new laws, a new color for clothing, etc.; cf. *HTS* 107.4059–60.

17. According to *Kuang hung-ming chi* 7.134a, it was in 621 that he presented his "Eleven articles for the reduction of Buddhist establishments and clergy to the advantage of the state and to the benefit of the people." These are not given in full in the histories, and the *Kuang hung-ming chi* text of them is often cryptic and garbled. For the memorial of 624, cf. *CTS* 79.2715–16; *HTS* 107.4060–61.

18. This work is preserved in *Kuang hung-ming chi* 6.123b–7.135b. As the editing was in the hands of the great Buddhist controversialist Tao-hsüan, Fu I's compilation suffered abridgment and some distortion. Tao-hsüan appends a rebuttal to each biography. There are fourteen biographies of those who sought to control Buddhism and eleven of those who attempted to destroy it. The last in the second category is Fu I, but see n. 8 above.

19. In grouping topically the main points of the two sets of proposals, I cite in the notes the texts of the proposals of 621 in *Kuang hung-ming chi* 7 and that of the proposal of 624 in *CTS* 79.

20. *Kuang hung-ming chi* 7.134a and 134b, article 1. The Buddhist editors accuse him of gross exaggeration in the number of clergy, which, they claim, was—including Taoists—less than 70,000, not 200,000. Their figure is probably too low. See n. 4 above. Cf. also *CTS* 79.2716, where Fu I's own figure is 100,000!

21. *Kuang hung-ming chi* 7.134b, articles 2 and 3; *CTS* 79.2716.

22. *Kuang hung-ming chi* 7.134b, article 1.

23. *Kuang hung-ming chi* 7.134c, article 3. Fu I was not doing violence to historical fact in this instance. Buddhist messianism and apocalypticism readily provided the psychological and ideological basis for armed insurrec-

tion. Cf. the article by T'ang Ch'ang-ju, "Po-i t'ien-tzu shih-shih," which identifies the Maitreya cult as the nexus of revolutionary groups.

24. *Kuang hung-ming chi* 7.134a–b; *CTS* 79.2715.

25. *Kuang hung-ming chi* 7.134c; *CTS* 79.2716. The quotation is from the latter. That disunion and social chaos had been brought on *by* Buddhism recalls the pagan argument that the disasters culminating in the fall of Rome had been caused *by* Christianity. And just as Augustine answered these arguments in the *City of God*, Tao-hsüan and other great clerics of Ch'ang-an made every effort to refute Fu I's assertion.

26. *CTS* 79.2716. He cites the case of Chang-ch'ou Tzu-t'o, a minister of the Northern Ch'i, who was put to death after remonstrating against wasteful expenditures on Buddhism. This man's life is biography 16 of Fu's *Kao-shih chuan, Kuang hung-ming chi* 7.131c. If, as the *CTS* text seems to indicate, Fu I was himself a witness to these events in Northern Ch'i, his entrance into the T'ang-tao kuan should be placed after 577, when the Northern Chou conquered the Northern Ch'i and appointed several Ch'i scholars to the academy.

27. *Kuang hung-ming chi* 7.134c, article 3; *HTS* 107.4061; *CTS* 79.2717.

28. *Kuang hung-ming chi* 7.134b, article 2.

29. *CTS* 79.2715.

30. Ibid.

31. Ibid. and *Kuang hung-ming chi* 7.134a. The Buddhists, in leading "unnatural" lives and in turning their backs on the natural forces—yin-yang and heaven and earth—impair the natural harmony, just as their disrespect for the emperor's moral power destroys the moral harmony emanating from that source.

32. *Kuang hung-ming chi* 7.134c, article 7.

33. *CTS* 79.2717.

34. Ibid. *HTS* 107.4061 omits the reference to the Taoists, thus making the deathbed admonition at odds with what is known of Fu I's life and interests.

35. *CTS* 79.2717, where it also states that he compiled a phonology to go with it. The *Lao-tzu pen-i* of Wei Yüan (1794–1856) contains numerous variants cited from a "Fu I text," but there are not sufficient passages from the commentary to reveal Fu's own ideas.

36. *CTS* 79.2717. *HTS* 107.4061 states that Fu I himself always said that his learning (and I presume this to be the Taoist "science" in which he specialized) was not worth transmitting to posterity. This strengthens the impression one gains from his life and writings that he was a rationalist to whom none of the existing ways of thought could offer satisfaction.

37. *CTS* 79.2716.

38. Ibid.

39. *HTS* 107.4061. *CTS* 79.2717 states that Emperor T'ai-tsung "inclined to agree with this," i.e., this extreme anti-Buddhist view. But such a reaction is

completely at odds with the emperor's own statement which elicited Fu's remarks. We find here, as in most cases where the Standard Histories deal with Buddhism, that the historian's standard of accuracy is in conflict with his strong Confucian bias; the result is often contradiction and confusion.

40. Arthur Waley, *The Life and Times of Po Chü-i*, 23, describes the situation in the T'ang as follows: "Buddhism had now so strong a hold over all classes of society that any system of belief that did not incorporate the fundamental ideas of Buddhist metaphysics had no chance of general acceptance in China, and one party of reformers was already attempting to make the synthesis between Confucianism and Buddhist philosophy which culminated later in what we know as neo-Confucianism." A valuable index to the prevalence of Buddhism among the gentry could be derived from an analysis of Kasuga Reichi's indices to those prose and poetic compositions relating to Buddhism contained in the *Ch'üan T'ang-wen* (Complete Prose of the T'ang Dynasty) and the *Ch'üan T'ang-shih* (Complete Poetry of the T'ang Dynasty); cf. Kasuga, "*Zen-Tōbun* Bukkyō kankei senjutsu mokuroku," and *Zen-Tōshi* Bukkyō kankei senjutsu mokuroku."

BIBLIOGRAPHY

Traditional and Standard Chinese and Japanese Works

Ch'ang-an chih 長安志 [Gazetteer of Ch'ang-an]. Comp. by Pi Yüan 畢沅 (1729–97). Facsimile edition in Hiraoka Takeo 平岡武夫, ed., *Chōan to Rakuyō: Shiryō* 長安と洛陽：資料 [Ch'ang-an and Loyang: Texts]. T'ang Civilization Reference Series, vol. 6. Kyoto: Jimbun kagaku kenkyūjo 人文科學研究所, 1956.

Chen-kuan cheng-yao 貞觀政要 [Essentials of government of the Chen-kuan era, 627–50]. Comp. ca. 707–09 by Wu Ching 吳兢. *Ssu-pu pei-yao* 四部備要 ed. Shanghai: Chung-hua shu-chü 中華書局, 1936.

Chi Shen-chou san-pao kan-t'ung lu 集神州三寶感通錄 [Collection of miraculous tales concerning Buddhism in China]. Comp. ca. 644 by Tao-hsüan 道宣 (596–667). In *Taishō Tripitaka*, vol. 52.

Ch'i fang-chen nien-piao 齊方鎮年表 [Chronological tables of regional commands under the Ch'i dynasty, A.D. 479–502]. Comp. by Wan Ssu-t'ung 萬斯同 (1638–1702). In *Erh-shih-wu shih pu-pien* 二十五史補編 [Supplements to the twenty-five dynastic histories, vol. 3, pp. 4317–22. Shanghai: K'ai-ming shu-tien 開明書店, 1937. Reprint. Taipei: K'ai-ming shu-tien, 1959.

Chih-tun chi 支遁集 [Writings of Chih-tun (314–66)]. Comp. by Hsü Kan 徐幹 (d. 1888). 2 chüan. In Hsü Kan, comp., *Shao-wu Hsü-shih ts'ung-shu* 邵武徐氏叢書, 1884, case 4, ts'e 16.

Chin-lou tzu 金樓子 [Book of the Golden Hall Master]. Completed 552 by Hsiao I 蕭繹 (508–55) [Emperor Yuan of the Liang dynasty 梁元帝, r. 549–55]. *Lung-ch'i ching-she ts'ung-shu* 龍谿精舍叢書 ed., 1917, ts'e 91–92.

Chin-shih lu 金石錄 [Collection of inscriptions]. Comp. by Chao Ming-ch'eng 趙明誠 (1081–1129). In *Hsing-su ts'ao-t'ang chin-shih ts'ung-shu* 行素草堂金石叢書. Soochow: Wu-hsien Chu-shih k'an 吳縣朱氏刊, 1887.

Chin-shih ts'ui-pien 金石萃編 [Collected inscriptions]. Comp. by Wang Ch'ang 王昶 (1725–1806). Shanghai: Sao-yeh shan-fang 掃葉善房, 1919. Facsimile reproduction of Ch'ing-p'u Wang-shih ching-hsün t'ang 青浦 王氏經訓堂 ed. of 1805. Reprint. Taipei: Kuo-feng ch'u-pan she 國風出版社, 1964.

177

Chin-shu 晉書 [History of the Chin dynasty]. Comp. by Fang Hsüan-ling 房玄齡 (578–648) et al. Peking: Chung-hua shu-chü 中華書局, 1974.

Chin-shu chiao-chu 晉書斠注 [Annotated history of the Chin dynasty]. Comp. by Fang Hsüan-ling 房玄齡 (578–648) et al. With commentary by Wu Shih-chien 吳士鑑 (1868–1933) and Liu Ch'eng-kan 劉承幹. Peking: Liu-shih Chia-yeh t'ang 劉氏嘉業堂, 1928.

Ch'ing-pai lei-ch'ao 清稗類鈔 [A Ch'ing miscellany]. Comp. by Hsü K'o 徐珂 (1869–1928). Shanghai: Commercial Press, 1917, 1920.

Chiu T'ang-shu 舊唐書 [Old T'ang history]. Comp. by Liu Hsü 劉昫 (887–946), et al. Peking: Chung-hua shu-chü 中華書局, 1975. Also, T'ung-wen 同文 ed., Shanghai: T'ung-wen shu-chü 同文書局, 1884 (specifically noted when cited).

Chou-i 周易 [Book of changes]. Commentary by Wang Pi 王弼 (226–49) and Han K'ang-po 韓康伯 (fl. 371–85). In *Ssu-pu ts'ung-k'an* 四部叢刊. Shanghai: Commercial Press, 1919.

Chou shu 周書 [History of the Chou dynasty]. Comp. by Ling-hu Te-fen 令狐德棻 (583–661). Peking: Chung-hua shu-chü 中華書局, 1971.

Ch'u san-tsang chi-chi 出三藏記集 [Collection of notes concerning the translation of the *Tripitaka*]. Comp. by Seng-yu 僧祐 (445–518). In *Taishō Tripitaka*, vol. 55.

Ch'üan shang-ku san-tai Ch'in-Han San-kuo liu-ch'ao wen 全上古三代秦漢三國六朝文 [Complete prose of ancient and medieval China]. Comp. by Yen K'o-chün 嚴可均 (1762–1843). Peking: Chung-hua shu-chü 中華書局, 1965.

Ch'üan T'ang-wen 全唐文 [Complete prose of the T'ang]. Comp. by Tung Kao 董誥 (1740–1818) et al. Taipei: Hua-wen shu-chü 華文書局, 1965. Facsimile reproduction of Imperial edition of 1814.

Chuang-tzu 莊子 [Writings of Chuang-tzu]. Chuang Chou 莊周 (4th century B.C.). Commentary by Kuo Hsiang 郭象 (d. 312) and Lu Te-ming 陸德明 (556–627). *Erh-shih-erh tzu* 二十二子 ed. Che-chiang shu-chü 浙江書局, 1876. 2d printing, 1901.

Chün-chai tu-shu chih 郡齋讀書志 [Memoirs of my reading in the Chün studio]. Ch'ao Kung-wu 晁公武 (d. 1171). Ch'ang-sha: Wang-shih k'an-pen 王氏刊本, 1884–85.

Ch'un-ch'iu Kung-yang chuan Ho-shih chieh-ku 春秋公羊傳何氏解詁 [Ho Hsiu's interpretations of the *Kung-yang Commentary* to the *Spring and Autumn Annals*]. Comp. by Ho Hsiu 何休 (129–82). *Ssu-pu pei-yao* 四部備要 ed. Shanghai: Chung-hua shu-chü 中華書局, 1936.

CS. See *Chin-shu*.

CTS. See *Chiu T'ang-shu*.

Fa-yüan chu-lin 法苑珠林 [The forest of jewels in the garden of the Dharma (i.e., collection of Buddhist tales)]. Completed in 668 by Tao-shih 道世. In *Taishō Tripitaka*, vol. 53.

Fan-i ming-i chi 翻譯名義集 [A glossary of Sanskrit terms translated into Chinese]. Comp. by Fa-yün 法雲 (1088–1158). In *Taishō Tripitaka*, vol. 54.

Feng-shih wen-chien chi chiao-cheng fu yin-te 封氏聞見記校證附引得 [Miscellaneous notes to Feng Yen: a critical edition, with index]. Comp. by Feng Yen 封寅 (fl. 763–80). Ed. by Chao Chen-hsin 趙貞信. Harvard-Yenching Sinological Index Series, supplement 7. 2 vols. Peiping: Harvard-Yenching Institute, 1933. Reprint. Taipei: Chinese Materials and Research Aids Service Center, 1966.

Fo ch'ui po-nieh-p'an lüeh-shuo chiao-chieh-ching 佛垂舶涅槃略說教誡經 [Sutra of the precepts uttered by the Buddha in abridged form before his Parinirvāṇa]. Trans. by Kumarajiva (350–409). In *Taishō Tripitaka*, vol. 12.

Fo-shuo kuan-hsi Fo-hsing-hsiang ching 佛說灌洗佛形像經 [Sutra on the bathing of the Buddha's image]. Trans. by Fa-chü 法炬 (fl. 290–306). In *Taishō Tripitaka*, vol. 16.

Fo-tsu t'ung-chi 佛祖統紀 [Record of the lineage of the Buddha and the Patriarchs]. Comp. by Chih-p'an 志盤 (fl. 1258–69). In *Taishō Tripitaka*, vol. 49.

Han Fei-tzu 韓非子 [Works of Han Fei]. Han Fei 韓非 (d. 233 B.C.). Textual emendations by Ku Huang-ch'i 顧黃圻 (1766–1835). *Erh-shih-erh tzu* 二十二子 ed. Che-chiang shu-chü 浙江書局, 1875. 2d printing, 1901.

Han-shu 漢書 [History of the Former Han dynasty]. Comp. by Pan Ku 班固 (A.D. 32–92). Peking: Chung-hua shu-chü 中華書局, 1962.

HKSC. See *Hsü Kao-seng chuan.*

Hou Han-shu 後漢書 [History of the Later Han dynasty]. Comp. by Fan Yeh 范曄 (398–445). Peking: Chung-hua shu-chü 中華書局, 1963.

Hsin T'ang-shu 新唐書 [New T'ang history]. Comp. by Sung Ch'i 宋祁 (998–1061) et al. Peking: Chung-hua shu-chü 中華書局, 1975.

Hsü-chai ming-hua-lu 虛齋名畫錄 [Famous paintings from Hsü studio]. Comp. by P'ang Yüan-chi 龐元濟 (b. 1864). Wu-ch'eng P'ang-shih Shen-chiang 烏程龐氏申江 ed., 1908.

Hsü Kao-seng chuan 續高僧傳 [Continuation of the *Lives of Eminent Monks*]. Also called *T'ang Kao-seng chuan* 唐高僧傳. Comp. ca. 645 by Tao-hsüan 道宣 (596–667). In *Taishō Tripitaka*, vol. 50.

HTS. See *Hsin T'ang-shu.*

Hung-ming chi 弘明集 [Collection for propagating the Dharma and enlightening people]. Comp. ca. 510–518 by Seng-yu 僧祐 (445–518). In *Taishō Tripitaka*, vol. 52.

I-ch'ieh-ching yin-i 一切經音義 [Glossary of the Tripiṭaka]. Comp. by Hui-lin 慧琳 (ca. 783–807). In *Taishō Tripitaka*, vol. 54.

K'ai-yüan shih-chiao lu 開元釋教錄 [A catalogue of Buddhist sutras compiled during the K'ai-yüan era (713–25). Comp. 730 by Chih-sheng 智昇. In *Taishō Tripitaka*, vol. 55.

Kao-seng chuan 高僧傳 [Lives of eminent monks]. Also called *Liang Kao-seng chuan* 梁高僧傳. Probably compiled in 519 by Hui-chiao 慧皎 (d. 554). In *Taishō Tripitaka*, vol. 50, and edition of Chin-ling k'o-ching ch'u 金陵刻經處, 4 ts'e, 1889. Translated into Japanese in *Kokuyaku issaikyō* 國譯一切經 [The Chinese Buddhist scriptures translated into Japanese]. Tokyo: Daitō shuppansha 大東出版社, 1936. Vol. 75 (Shidenbu 史傳部, vol. 7), pp. 1–347. Reprint. Tokyo: Daitō shuppansha, 1961.

Kōsōden. See *Kao-seng chuan*.

KSC. See *Kao-seng chuan*.

Kuang hung-ming chi 廣弘明集 [Second collection of documents for propagating the Dharma and enlightening the people]. Comp. by Tao-hsüan 道宣 (596–667). In *Taishō Tripitaka*, vol. 52.

Lao-tzu pen-i 老子本義 [Fundamental meaning of Lao-tzu]. Comp. by Wei Yüan 魏原 (1794–1856). In *Ts'ung-shu chi-ch'eng* 叢書集成, ts'e 542. Shanghai: Commercial Press, 1937.

Li-tai chih-kuan piao 歷代職官表 [Tables of official posts from the earliest times to the nineteenth century]. Comp. by Huang Pen-chi 黃本驥 (*chü-jen* of 1821). With a new introduction and glossary by Ch'ü T'ui-yuan 瞿蛻園. Shanghai: Chung-hua shu-chü 中華書局, 1965.

Li-tai san-pao chi 歷代三寶記 [Buddhism's Three Treasures through the ages]. Comp. by Fei Ch'ang-fang 費長房, ca. 597. In *Taishō Tripitaka*, vol. 49.

Liang-ching hsin-chi 兩京新記 [New account of two capitals]. Comp. by Wei Shu 韋述 (d. 757). Hiraoka Takeo 平岡武夫 includes several facsimile editions (Tsun-ching-ko wen-k'u 尊經閣文庫 ed., pp. 181–96; Nan-ching cha-chi 南菁札記 ed., pp. 197–210) in *Chōan to Rakuyō: Shiryō* 長安と洛陽：資料 [Ch'ang-an and Loyang: Texts], T'ang Civilization Reference Series, vol. 6. Kyoto: Jimbun kagaku kenkyūjo 人文科學研究所, 1956.

Liang shu 梁書 [History of the Liang dynasty]. Comp. by Yao Ch'a 姚察 (533–606) and Yao Ssu-lien 姚思廉 (d. 637). Peking: Chung-hua shu-chü 中華書局, 1973.

Lieh-tzu 列子. Post-Han work attributed to pre-Ch'in philosopher Lieh Yü-k'ou 列禦寇. Commentary by Chang Chan 張湛 (A.D. 4th century) and Yin Ching-shun 殷敬順 (fl. 827). *Erh-shih-erh tzu* 二十二子 ed. Che-chiang shu-chü 浙江書局, 1876. 2d printing, 1901.

LTSPC. See *Li-tai san-pao chi*.

Lu-shan chih 廬山志 [Gazetteer of Lu-shan, Kiangsi]. Comp. 1933 by Wu Tsung-tz'u 吳宗慈 (b. 1879). Reprinted in 4 vols. as item 22 in *Chung-kuo ming-shan sheng-chi-chih ts'ung-shu* 中國名山勝蹟志叢書. Taipei: Wenhai ch'u-pan-she 文海出版社, 1971.

Lü-shih ch'un-ch'iu 呂氏春秋 [Spring and autumn annals of Mr. Lü]. Comp. under sponsorship of Lü Pu-wei 呂不韋 (d. A.D. 237). Commentary by Kao Yu 高誘 (fl. 205–12) and Pi Yüan 畢沅 (1729–97). *Erh-shih-erh tzu* 二十二子 ed. Che-chiang shu-chü 浙江書局, 1875. 2d printing, 1901.

Meisōden shō 名僧傳抄 [Extracts from the *Ming-seng chuan*]. Based on MS of Shūshō 宗性 (13th century), from original text completed in 519 by Pao-ch'ang 寶唱 (fl. early 6th century). In *Dai Nihon zoku zōkyō* 大日本續藏經. 1st collection 第壹輯, pt. 2B 第貳編乙, case 7 第七套, ts'e 冊 1. Kyoto: Zōkyō shoin 藏經書院, 1905–12.

Mo-ho seng-ch'i lü 摩訶僧祇律 [*Vinaya* of the Mahāsaṃghika school]. Trans. 416–18 by Buddhabhadra (359–429). In *Taishō Tripitaka*, vol. 22.

Mo-ho seng-ch'i pi-ch'iu-ni chieh-pen 摩訶僧祇比丘尼戒本 [Nun's precepts extracted from the *Vinaya* of the Mahāsaṃghika school. Trans. by Fa-hsien 法顯 (d. before 429) and Buddhabhadra (359–429). In *Taishō Tripitaka*, vol. 22.

Nan Ch'i-shu 南齊書 [History of the Southern Ch'i dynasty]. Comp. by Hsiao Tzu-hsien 蕭子顯 (489–537). Peking: Chung-hua shu-chü 中華書局, 1971.

Nan-hai chi-kuei nei-fa chuan 南海寄歸內法傳 [Biographies of monks who traveled to the Southern Sea]. By I-ching 義淨 (613–713). In *Taishō Tripitaka*, vol. 54.

Nan-shih 南史 [History of the southern dynasties]. Comp. by Li Yen-shou 李延壽 (d. 629). Peking: Chung-hua shu-chü 中華書局, 1975.

Nien-erh-shih cha-chi 廿二史劄記 [Notes on the twenty-two standard histories]. Chao I 趙翼 (1727–84). Shanghai: Shih-chieh shu-chü 世界書局, 1939. Reprint. Taipei: Shih-chieh shu-chü, 1958.

Nien-erh-shih k'ao-i 廿二史考異 [Critical notes on the twenty-two standard histories]. Ch'ien Ta-hsin 錢大昕 (1728–1804). In *Kuang-ya shu-chü ts'ung-shu* 廣雅書局叢書, 1894.

Pao-k'o ts'ung-pien 寶刻叢編 [General edition of precious engravings]. Comp. in 1229 by Ch'en Ssu 陳思 (ca. 1200–after 1259). Ed. of Wu Shih-fen 吳式芬 (1796–1856). In *Shih-wan-chüan lou ts'ung-shu* 十萬卷樓叢書, 1888.

PCL. See Pien-cheng lun.

P'ei-wen yün-fu 佩文韻府. Comp. ca. 1711 by Chang Yü-shu 張玉書 et al. Shanghai: Commercial Press, 1937.

Pi-ch'iu-ni chuan 比丘尼傳 [Lives of the nuns]. Comp. by Pao-ch'ang 寶昌 (fl. 505). In *Taishō Tripitaka*, vol. 50.

Pien-cheng lun 辯正論 [Treatise on discerning correct doctrine]. Fa-lin

法琳 (572–640). In *Taishō Tripitaka*, vol. 52.

P'o-hsieh-lun 破邪論 [Discussions on destroying heterodoxy]. Comp. by Fa-lin 法琳 (572–640). In *Taishō Tripitaka*, vol. 52.

Pu Chin-shu i-wen-chih 補晉書藝文志 [Supplement to the bibliographical treatise of the *History of the Chin Dynasty*]. Comp. by Wen T'ing-shih 文廷式 (1856–1904). In *Erh-shih-wu shih pu-pien* 二十五史補編 [Supplements to the twenty-five dynastic histories], vol. 3, pp. 3703–95. Shanghai: K'ai-ming shu-tien 開明書店, 1937. Reprint. Taipei: K'ai-ming shu-tien, 1959, 1967.

PWYF. See *P'ei-wen yün-fu*.

San-kuo chih 三國志 [History of the Three Kingdoms]. Comp. by Ch'en Shou 陳壽, (233–97). Peking: Chung-hua shu-chü 中華書局, 1962.

SCKC. See *Sui-shu ching-chi-chih k'ao-cheng*.

Shih-chi 史記 [Records of the Grand Historian]. Comp. by Ssu-ma T'an 司馬談 (180–110? B.C.) and Ssu-ma Ch'ien 司馬遷 (145–86? B.C.). Peking: Chung-hua shu-chü 中華書局, 1962.

Shih-liu-kuo chiang-yü-chih 十六國疆域志 [Gazetteer of the Sixteen Kingdoms]. Comp. by Hung Liang-chi 洪亮吉 (1746–1809). In *Erh-shih-wu shih pu-pien* 二十五史補編 [Supplements to the twenty-five dynastic histories], vol. 3, pp. 4083–4209. Shanghai: K'ai-ming shu-tien 開明書店, 1937. Reprint. Taipei: K'ai-ming shu-tien, 1959, 1967.

Shih-liu-kuo ch'un-ch'iu 十六國春秋 [Chronicle of the Sixteen Kingdoms]. Comp. by Ts'ui Hung 崔鴻 (d. 525). Ed. of Jen-ho Wang Jih-kuei chiao-k'an-pen 仁和汪日桂校刊本. Hsin-t'o-shan fang 欣託山房, 1774. Reprint. Hu-pei kuan-shu-ch'u 湖北官書處, 1896.

Shih-liu-kuo ch'un-ch'iu chi-pu 十六國春秋輯補 [Reconstructed text of the Chronicle of the Sixteen Kingdoms]. Comp. by Ts'ui Hung 崔鴻 (d. 525). Reconstructed text by T'ang Ch'iu 湯球 (d. 1881). In *Ts'ung-shu chi-ch'eng ch'u-pien* 叢書集成初編, ts'e 3816–19. Shanghai: Commercial Press, 1936.

Shih-liu-kuo ch'un-ch'iu tsuan-lu chiao-pen 十六國春秋纂錄校本 [Reconstructed text of the Chronicle of the Sixteen Kingdoms]. Comp. by Ts'ui Hung 崔鴻 (d. 525). Reconstructed text by T'ang Ch'iu 湯球 (d. 1881). In *Ts'ung-shu chi-ch'eng ch'u-pien* 叢書集成初編, ts'e 3820. Shanghai: Commercial Press, 1936.

Shih-liu-kuo nien-piao 十六國年表 [Chronological tables of the Sixteen Kingdoms]. Comp. by Chang Yü-tseng 張愉曾 (1753–1818). In *Erh-shih-wu shih pu-pien* 二十五史補編 [Supplements to the twenty-five dynastic histories], vol. 3, pp. 4007–11. Shanghai: K'ai-ming shu-tien 開明書店, 1937. Reprint. Taipei: K'ai-ming shu-tien, 1959, 1967.

Shih-shih chi-ku lüeh 釋氏稽古略 [Abridged history of the Buddhist church]. Completed in 1354 by Chüeh-an 覺岸. In *Taishō Tripitaka*, vol. 49.

Shih-shuo hsin-yü chiao-chien 世說新語校牋 [Annotated text of the *Shih-shuo hsin-yü*]. Liu I-ch'ing 劉義慶 (403–44). Annotations edited by Yang Yung 楊勇. Hong Kong: Ta-chung shu-chü 大衆書局, 1969.

Shih-sung lü 十誦律 [The *Vinaya* in ten sections]. Trans. 404–06 by Kumāra-jīva, Puṇyatara, and Vimalākṣa. In *Taishō Tripiṭaka*, vol. 23.

Shih-t'ung t'ung-shih 史通通釋 [Conspectus of history, with comprehensive commentary]. Liu Chih-chi 劉知幾 (661–721). Commentary by P'u Ch'i-lung 浦起龍 (1679–post-1761). Shanghai: Ku-chi ch'u-pan-she 古籍出版社, 1978.

Shih-tzu 尸子 [Works of Shih Chiao]. Shih Chiao 尸佼 [校] (4th century B.C.). Comp. by Wang Chi-p'ei 汪繼培 (b. 1775). *Erh-shih-erh tzu* 二十二子 ed. Che-chiang shu-chü 浙江書局, 1877. 2d printing, 1901.

Shui-ching chu 水經注 [Commentary on the *Waterways Classic*]. Comp. by Li Tao-yüan 酈道元 (d. 527). Wang Hsien-ch'ien's 王先謙 (1842–1918) commented edition. Ch'ang-sha: Wang-shih Ssu-hsien chiang-she k'an-pen 王氏思賢講舍刊本, 1892.

SLKCC. See *Shih-liu-kuo ch'un-ch'iu.*

Sōden haiin 僧傳排韻 [Monks' biographies arranged by rhyme]. 2 vols. In *Dai Nihon Bukkyō zensho* 大日本佛教全書, vols. 99–100. Tokyo: Bussho kankōkai 佛書刊行會, 1912.

Sou-shen hou-chi 搜神後集 [Further investigations into the supernatural]. Trad. attrib. to T'ao Ch'ien 陶潛 (365–427). In *Hsüeh-chin t'ao-yüan ts'ung-shu* 學津討原叢書, sec. 16. Shanghai: Commercial Press, 1922. Facsimile reproduction of Yü-shan Chang-shih K'uang-chao-ko 虞山張氏曠照閣 ed. of 1805.

SS. See *Sui-shu.*

Ssu-fen lü 四分律 [The *Vinaya* in four sections]. Trans. 408 by Buddhayaśas, Chu Fo-nien 竺佛念 et al. In *Taishō Tripiṭaka*, vol. 22.

Ssu-fen-lü pi-ch'iu chieh-pen 四分律比丘戒本 [A manual for monks' precepts extracted from the *Vinaya* in four sections]. Comp. by Huai-su 懷素 (624–97). In *Taishō Tripiṭaka*, vol. 22.

Ssu-k'u ch'üan-shu tsung-mu 四庫全書總目 [Catalogue of the imperial library]. Compiled under imperial auspices by Chi Yün 紀昀 (1724–1805) et al. Completed 1782. Shanghai: Ta-tung shu-chü 大東書局, 1926.

Sui-shu 隋書 [History of the Sui dynasty]. Comp. by Wei Cheng 魏徵 (580-643) et al. Peking: Chung-hua shu-chü 中華書局, 1973. Also, T'ung-wen 同文 ed., Shanghai: T'ung-wen shu-chü 同文書局, 1884 (specifically noted when cited).

Sui-shu ching-chi-chih k'ao-cheng 隋書經籍志考證 [A critical study of the *Sui History*'s Bibliographical Treatise]. Comp. by Chang Tsung-yüan 章宗源 (1752?–1800). In *Erh-shih-wu shih pu-pien* 二十五史補編 [Supplements to the twenty-five dynastic histories], vol. 4, pp. 4943–5904. Shanghai: K'ai-ming shu-tien 開明書店, 1937. Reprint. Taipei: K'ai-ming shu-tien, 1959, 1967.

Sung shu 宋書 [History of the Sung dynasty]. Comp. by Shen Yüeh 沈約 (441–513). Peking: Chung-hua shu-chü 中華書局, 1974.

Ta-Ch'ing i-t'ung-chih 大清一統志 [Comprehensive gazetteer of the Ch'ing]. Comp. by Mu-chang-a 穆彰阿 (1782–1856) et al. In *Ssu-pu ts'ung-k'an hsü-pien* 四部叢刊續編 Shanghai: Commercial Press, 1935. Facsimile reproduction of *Chia-ch'ing ch'ung-hsiu i-t'ung-chih* 嘉慶重修一統志 ed. of 1820.

Ta po-nieh-p'an ching 大舶涅槃經 [The Mahāparinirvāṇa sutra]. Trans. by Dharmarakṣa (385–433). In *Taishō Tripitaka*, vol. 12.

Ta-sheng pen-sheng hsin-ti kuan ching 大乘本生心地觀經. Trans. by Po-jo 舶若 (arrived in China in 781) in 811. In *Taishō Tripitaka*, vol. 3.

Ta-Sung kao-seng chuan 大宋高僧傳 [Lives of eminent monks, compiled under the Sung dynasty]. Comp. by Tsan-ning 贊寧 (919–1001). In *Taishō Tripitaka*, vol. 50.

Ta-Sung seng-shih lüeh 大宋僧史略 [History of the saṃgha in China, compiled under the Sung dynasty]. Comp. by Tsan-ning 贊寧 (919–1001). In *Taishō Tripitaka*, vol. 54.

Ta-T'ang nei-tien lu 大唐內典錄 [The Great T'ang catalogue of the Buddhist Scripture]. Comp. 664 by Tao-hsüan 道宣 (596–667). In *Taishō Tripitaka*, vol. 55.

Ta-T'ang Ta tz'u-en ssu San-tsang fa-shih chuan 大唐大慈恩寺三藏法師傳 [Biography of the Tripitaka Master (i.e., the monk Hsüan-tsang) of the Ta tz'u-en temple of the Great T'ang]. Comp. by Hui-li 慧立 (7th century) and Yen-tsung 彥悰 (7th century). In *Taishō Tripitaka*, vol. 50.

Taishō shinshū daizōkyō 大正新修大藏經 [Taishō Tripitaka]. Ed. Takakusu Junjirō 高楠順次郎 (1866–1945) and Watanabe Kaigyoku 渡邊海旭 (1872–1933). 55 vols. Tokyo: Taishō shinshū daizōkyō kankōkai 大正新修大藏經刊行會, 1924–29.

Taishō Tripitaka. See *Taishō shinshū daizōkyō*.

T'ai-hu hsien-chih 太湖縣志 [Gazetteer of T'ai-hu county, Anhwei]. Comp. by Li Ying 李英 and Kao Shou-heng 高壽恒, 1922.

T'ai-p'ing huan-yü chi 太平寰宇記 [Gazetteer of the world during the T'ai-p'ing era, 976–983]. Comp. by Yüeh Shih 樂史 (930–1007). Nanking: Chin-ling shu-chü 金陵書局, 1882.

T'ai-p'ing yü-lan 太平御覽 [Imperially reviewed encyclopedia of the T'ai-p'ing era, 976–83]. Comp. 983 by Li Fang 李昉 (925–96) et al. She-hsien Pao-shih 歙縣鮑氏 ed. of 1807.

T'ang hu-fa sha-men Fa-lin pieh-chuan 唐護法沙門法琳別傳 [The indepen-

dent biography of the monk Fa-lin, who is a defender of the *dharma*].
Comp. between 640 and 649 Yen-tsung 彥琮. In *Taishō Tripitaka*, vol. 50.

T'ang hui-yao 唐會要 [Institutes of T'ang]. Comp. by Wang Pu 王溥 (923–
82). Peking: Chung-hua shu-chü 中華書局, 1955.

T'ang liang-ching ch'eng-fang k'ao 唐兩京城坊考 [A study of the wards of the
two T'ang capitals]. Comp. by Hsü Sung 徐松 (1781–1848). Facsimile reproduction in Hiraoka Takeo 平岡武夫, ed., *Chōan to Rakuyō: Shiryō*
長安と洛陽:資料 [Ch'ang-an and Loyang: Texts]. T'ang Civilization Reference Series, vol. 6. Kyoto: Jimbun kagaku kenkyūjo 人文科學研究所.

TCITC. See *Ta-Ch'ing i-t'ung-chih.*

TCTC. See *Tzu-chih t'ung-chien.*

TFYK. See *Ts'e-fu yüan-kuei.*

TPYL. See *T'ai-p'ing yü-lan.*

T'ung-tien 通典 [Conspectus of documents]. Comp. ca. 801 by Tu Yu 杜佑
(735–812). *Shih-t'ung* 十通 ed. Shanghai: Commercial Press, 1935.

Tzu-chih t'ung-chien 資治通鑑 [Comprehensive mirror for aid in govern-
ment]. Comp. by Ssu-ma Kuang 司馬光 (1019–86) Peking: Chung-hua shu-
chü 中華書局, 1956.

WCNP. See *Wei-Chao chiang-hsiang ta-ch'en nien-piao.*

Wei-Chao chiang-hsiang ta-ch'en nien-piao 僞趙將相大臣年表 [Chronologi-
cal tables of high military and civil officials of the Later Chao dynasty
(A.D. 319–50)]. Comp. by Wan Ssu-t'ung 萬期同 (1638–1702). In *Erh-
shih-wu shih pu-pien* 二十五史補編 [Supplements to the twenty-five
dynastic histories], vol. 3, pp. 4037–40. Shanghai: K'ai-ming shu-tien
開明書店, 1937. Reprint. Taipei: K'ai-ming shu-tien, 1959, 1967.

Wei-shu 魏書 [History of the Wei dynasty]. Comp. by Wei Shou 魏收 (506–
72). Peking: Chung-hua shu-chü 中華書局, 1974.

Wen-hsien t'ung-k'ao 文獻通考 [General history of institutions and critical
examination of documents]. Comp. by Ma Tuan-lin 馬端臨 (1254–1325).
Shih-t'ung 十通 ed. Shanghai: Commercial Press, 1935.

Wen-hsüan 文選 [Literary anthology]. Comp. by Hsiao T'ung 蕭統 (Prince
Chao-ming 昭明太子, A.D. 501–31). With commentary by Li Shan 李善
(d. 689) et al. Taipei: I-wen yin-shu-kuan 藝文印書館, n.d. Facsimile reproduction of P'o-yang Hu-shih 鄱陽胡氏 1809 reprint of Sung ed. of the
period 1174–89.

Wen-shu-shih-li so-shuo Mo-ho-po-jo p'o-lo-mi ching 文殊師利所說摩訶般
若波羅密經 [The Mahāprajñāpāramitā Sūtra spoken by Mañjuśrī]. Trans.
by Mandrasena (?) (arrived in China in 503). In *Taishō Tripitaka*, vol. 8.

WHTK. See *Wen-hsien t'ung-k'ao.*

WS. See *Wei-shu.*

Wu-ti chi 吳地記 [A record of the region of Wu]. Lu Kuang-wei 陸廣微

(T'ang). In *Hsüeh-chin t'ao-yüan ts'ung-shu* 學津討原叢書, sec. 7. Shanghai: Commercial Press, 1922. Facsimile reproduction of Yü-shan Changshih K'uang-chao-ko 虞山張氏曠照閣 ed. of 1805.

Yen-lu 剡錄 [Records of Yen-hsien, Che-chiang]. Comp. by Kao Ssu-sun 高似孫 (ca. 1160–1220). In Hsü Kan 徐幹 (d. 1888), comp., *Shao-wu Hsü-shih ts'ung-shu* 邵武徐氏叢書, 1884.

Yen-tzu ch'un-ch'iu 晏子春秋. Traditionally attributed to Yen Ying 晏嬰 (6th century B.C.). Commentary by Sun Hsing-yen 孫星衍 (1753–1818) and Huang I-chou 黃以周 (1828–99). *Erh-shih-erh tzu* 二十二子 ed. Chechiang shu-chü 浙江書局, 1875. 2d printing, 1901.

Yu-ming lu fu chiao-e 幽明錄附校譌 [The *Yu-ming lu*, with collations and emendations]. By Liu I-ch'ing 劉義慶 (403–44). Collations by Hu T'ing 胡珽. In *Lin-lang mi-shih ts'ung-shu* 琳瑯秘室叢書, 1853.

Modern Chinese and Japanese Secondary Works

Ajia rekishi jiten アシア歴史辭典 [Historical encyclopedia of Asia]. Edited by Kaizuka Shigeki 貝塚茂樹, et al. 10 vols. Tokyo: Heibonsha 平凡社, 1962.

Chao Wan-li 趙萬里 (b. 1905). "Kuan-ts'ang shan-pen shu t'i-yao: *Feng-shih wen-chien chi, Ch'ung-kuang hui-shih, Ts'e-fu yüan-kuei* ts'an-pen" 館藏善本書提要：封氏聞見記, 重廣會史, 冊府元龜殘本 [An introduction to some of the rare editions in the Peking Library: *Feng-shih wen-chien-chi, Ch'ung-kuang hui-shih* and *Ts'e-fu yüan-kuei*]. *Pei-ching t'u-shu-kuan yüeh-k'an* 北京圖書館月刊, vol. 1, no. 3 (1928): 143–63.

Ch'en Yin-k'o 陳寅恪 (1890–1969). "*San-kuo chih* Ts'ao Chung Hua T'o chuan yü Fo-chiao ku-shih" 三國志曹沖華佗傳與佛教故事 [The biographies of Ts'ao Chung and Hua T'o in the *San-kuo chih* and Buddhist tales]. *Ch'ing-hua hsüeh-pao* 清華學報, vol. 6, no. 1 (1930): 17–20. In author's collection *Ch'en Yin-k'o hsien-sheng lun-wen-chi*, 2: 417–20.

———. *T'ang-tai cheng-chih-shih shu-lun-kao* 唐代政治史述論稿 [Preliminary discourse on T'ang political history]. In author's collection *Ch'en Yin-k'o hsien-sheng lun-chi*, 105–209. Republished in author's collection *Ch'en Yin-k'o hsien sheng lun-wen-chi*, 1: 151–304.

———. *Ch'en Yin-k'o hsien-sheng lun-chi* 陳寅恪先生論集 [The collected writings of Prof. Ch'en Yin-k'o]. Taipei: Chung-yang yen-chiu-yüan li-shih yü-yen yen-chiu-so 中央研究歷史語言研究所, 1971.

———. *Ch'en Yin-k'o hsien-sheng lun-wen chi* 陳寅恪先生論文集 [The collected writings of Prof. Ch'en Yin-k'o]. 2 vols. Taipei: San-jen-hsing ch'u-pan-she 三人行出版社, 1974.

Ch'en Yüan 陳垣 (1880–1971). "*Kao-seng chuan* lun-lüeh" 高僧傳論略 [A brief discourse on the *Kao-seng chuan*]. *Ta-kung pao* 大公報 (Tientsin), Jan. 1, 1947.

Chou Shu-chia 周叔迦 (1899–1970) and Su Kung-wang 蘇公望. Commentary on *KSC* preface. *T'ung-yüan* 同員 (Peking, 1942–43). (1) Vol. 3, no. 10, p. 27; (2) Vol. 3, no. 11, p. 7; (3) vol. 3, no. 12, p. 11; (4) vol. 4, no. 1, p. 11; (5) vol. 4, no. 2, p. 9; (6) vol. 4, no. 3, p. 13; (7) vol. 4, no. 5, p. 12.

Chou-Su. See Chou Shu-chia and Su Kung-wang, Commentary on *KSC* preface.

Feng Ch'eng-chün 馮承鈞 and Hsiang Chüeh-ming 向覺明. "Kuan-yü Kuei-tzu po-hsing chih t'ao-lun" 關於龜茲白姓之討論 [A discussion of Kucha surnames]. *Nü-shih-ta hsüeh-shu chi-k'an* 女師大學術季刊, vol. 2, no. 2 (1931): 1–17.

Feng Chia-sheng 馮家昇 (b. 1904). "Mu-jung shih chien-kuo shih-mo" 慕容氏建國始末 [The establishment of the Mu-jung state]. *Yü-kung* 禹貢, vol. 3, no. 11 (1935): 9–20.

Fujita Toyohachi 藤田豐八 (1870–1929). "Koshō ni tsuite" 胡床について [Concerning "barbarian benches"]. *Tōyō gakuhō* 東洋學報, vol. 12, no. 4 (Dec. 1922): 429–56; vol. 14, no. 1 (July 1924): 131–32.

Hayashiya Tomojirō 林屋友次郎 (1886–1953). *Kyōroku kenkyū* 經錄研究 [Studies of catalogues of Buddhist texts]. Tokyo: Iwanami shoten 岩波書店, 1941.

Itō Giken 伊藤義賢 (1889–1969) *Shina Bukkyō seishi* 支那佛教正史 [A standard history of Chinese Buddhism]. Fukui: Takeshita gakuryō shuppanbu 竹下學寮出版部, 1923.

Iwai (now Makita) Tairyō 岩井(牧田)諦亮 (b. 1912). "Ishiyama-dera hon *Ryō Kōsōden* to sono Dōan den kōi" 石山寺本梁高僧傳と其の道安傳校異 [A critical study of the variants in the biography of Tao An in the text of Hui Chiao's *Kao-seng chuan* in the Ishiyama temple]. *Shina Bukkyō shigaku* 支那佛教史學, vol. 2, no. 2 (1938): 69–82.

Kasuga Reichi 春日禮智. "Jōdokyō shiryō to shite no *Meisōden* shijishō *Meisōden* yōmonshō narabi ni Miroku nyorai kannōshō daishi shoin no *Meisōden* ni tsuite" 淨土教史料としての名僧傳指示抄名僧傳要文抄并に彌勒如來感應抄第四所引の名僧傳について [Extant sections of the *Ming-seng-chuan* as materials on Pure Land Buddhism]. *Shūgaku kenkyū* 宗學研究, vol. 12 (1935): 53–118.

———. "*Zen-Tōbun* Bukkyō kankei senjutsu mokuroku" 全唐文佛教關係撰述目錄 [A listing of Buddhist-related works in the *Complete Prose of the T'ang Dynasty*]. *Nikka Bukkyō kenkyūkai nempō* 日華佛教研究會年報 [Annual of the Sino-Buddhist Research Society], vol. 1 (Kyoto, 1936): 20–55.

———. "*Zen-Tōshi* Bukkyō kankei senjutsu mokuroku" 全唐詩佛教關係撰述目錄 [A listing of Buddhist-related works in the *Complete Poems of the T'ang Dynasty*]. *Nikka Bukkyō kenkyūkai nempō* 日華佛教研究會年報 [Annual of the Sino-Buddhist Research Society], vol. 2 (Kyoto,

1937), separately paginated appendix, pp. 1–68.

Li Shu-t'ung 李樹桐. *T'ang-shih k'ao-pien* 唐史考辯 [Critical studies in T'ang history]. Taipei: Chung-hua shu-chü 中華書局, 1965.

Liu Shan-li 劉掞藜. "Chin Hui-ti shih-tai Han-tsu chih ta-liu-hsi" 晉惠帝時代漢族之大流徙 [The great Chinese migrations during the reign of Chin Hui-ti (290–307 A.D.)]. *Yü-kung* 禹貢, vol. 4, no. 11 (1936): 11–23.

Liu Shao-ch'i 劉少奇 (1898–1973?). "Lun Kung-ch'an-tang-yüan ti hsiu-yang" 論公產黨員的修養 [The training of a Communist Party member]. Peking and Tientsin: Chung-hua shu-chü 中華書局, 1949.

Lu Hsün 魯迅 [Chou Shu-jen 周樹人 (1881–1936), pseud.]. *Lu Hsün ch'üan-chi* 魯迅全集 [The complete works of Lu Hsün]. Shanghai: Lu Hsün ch'üan-chi ch'u-pan-she 魯迅全集出版社, 1938. Reprint 1948 by same publisher.

———. "K'uai-chi chün ku-shu tsa-chi" 會稽郡故書雜集 [A historical miscellany from K'uai-chi county, Chekiang]. In *Lu Hsün ch'üan-chi*, 8: 7–117.

———. *Ku hsiao-shuo kou-ch'en* 古小說鈎沈 [Retrieving submerged passages in old stories]. In *Lu Hsün ch'üan-chi*, 8: 123–657.

———. *Chung-kuo hsiao-shuo shih-lüeh* 中國小說史略 [A short history of Chinese fiction]. In *Lu Hsün ch'üan-chi*, 9: 145–450.

Makita Tairyō 牧田諦亮. *Ryō Kōsōden sakuin* 梁高僧傳索引 [Index to the *Liang Kao-seng-chuan*]. Vol. 1 of *Chūgoku Kōsōden sakuin* 中國高僧傳索引. Kyoto: Heirakuji shoten 平樂寺書店, 1972. An earlier version was published under the same title of Tsukamoto Zenryū 塚本善隆, Ryūchi Kiyoshi 龍池清, and Iwai (Makita) Tairyō in *Shina Bukkyō shigaku* 支那佛教史學, vols. 1–3 (1937–39), 8 parts.

Miyakawa Hisayuki 宮川尚志 (b. 1913). "Shin no Taizan Chiku Sōrō no jise-ki" 晉の泰山竺僧朗の事蹟 [The career of the Chin dynasty monk Chu Seng-lang of T'ai-shan]. *Tōyōshi kenkyū* 東洋史研究, vol. 3 (1938): 184–209. Reprinted with slight revisions as chap. 10 (pp. 255–78) of author's collection *Rikuchōshi kenkyū: Shūkyōhen* 六朝史研究:宗教篇 [Studies in the history of the Six Dynasties: Religion]. Kyoto: Heirakuji shoten 平樂寺書店, 1964.

———. "Rikuchō jinmei ni arawaretaru Bukkyōgo" 六朝人名に現はれたる佛教語 [Buddhist personal names in the Six Dynasties period]. *Tōyōshi kenkyū* 東洋史研究, vol. 3, no. 6 (1938), p. 41 [pt. 1]; vol. 4, no. 1 (1938), p. 71 [pt. 2]; vol. 4, no. 2 (1938), p. 94 [pt. 3]; vol. 4, no. 6 (1939), pp. 78–79 [pt. 4].

———. "Rikuchō jidai no shigaku" 六朝時代の史學 [Historiography in the Six Dynasties period]. *Tōyōshi kenkyū* 東洋史研究, vol. 5, no. 6 (1940): 1–25.

———. "Rikuchō jidai jin no Bukkyō shinkō" 六朝時代人の佛教信仰 [The Buddhist faith of the people of the Six Dynasties period]. *Bukkyō shigaku* 佛教史學, vol. 4, no. 2 (1955): 1–17. Reprinted with slight revisions as chap. 11 (pp. 289–312) of author's collection *Rikuchōshi kenkyū: Shūkyō hen* 六朝史研究：宗教篇 [Studies in the history of the Six Dynasties: Religion]. Kyoto: Heirakuji shoten 平樂寺書店, 1964.

Mizuno Seiichi 水野清一 (1905–71) and Nagahiro Toshio 長広敏雄 (b. 1905). *Ryūmon sekkutsu no kenkyū* 龍門石窟の研究 [A study of the Buddhist cave-temples at Lung-men, Honan]. Tokyo: Tōhō bunka kenkyūjo 東方文化研究所, 1941.

Mochizuki Shinkō 望月信亨 (1869–1948). *Bukkyō daijiten* 佛教大辭典 [A comprehensive dictionary of Buddhism]. 7 vols. Tokyo: Bukkyō daijiten hakkōjo 佛教大辭典發行所, 1931–36.

———. *Bukkyō dainempyō* 佛教大年表 [A comprehensive chronological table of Buddhism]. 4th rev. ed., ed. Tsukamoto Zenryū 塚本善隆. Vol. 6 of *Bukkyō daijiten* 佛教大辭典. Kyoto: Sekai seiten kankō kyōkai 世界聖典刊行協會, 1955. First published as supplementary volume to Mochizuki, *Bukkyō daijiten*. Tokyo: Buyōdō shoten 武揚堂書店, 1909.

Mori Mikisaburō 森三樹三郎 (b. 1909). *Ryō no Butei* 梁の武帝 [Emperor Wu of the Liang]. Kyoto: Heirakuji shoten 平樂寺書店, 1956.

Naitō Torajirō 內藤虎次郎 (1866–1934). *Shina shigakushi* 支那史學史 [A history of Chinese historiography]. In *Naitō Konan zenshū* 內藤湖南全集 [Collected writings of Naitō Torajirō (Konan)], vol. 11. Tokyo: Chikuma shobō 筑摩書房, 1969.

Ōchō Enichi 橫超慧日 (b. 1906). "Chūgoku Bukkyō shoki no hon'yakuron" 中國佛教初期の飜譯論 [Discussion concerning the method of translation in early Chinese Buddhism]. In *Yamaguchi hakushi kanreki kinen Indogaku Bukkyōgaku ronsō* 山口博士還曆記念印度學佛教學論叢 [Studies in Indology and Buddhology presented in honour of Prof. Susumu Yamaguchi on the occasion of his sixtieth birthday], 221–32. Kyoto: Hōzōkan 法藏館, 1955. A revised and expanded version appears in author's collection *Chūgoku Bukkyo no kenkyū* 中國佛教の研究 [Studies in Chinese Buddhism], 219–55. Kyoto: Hōzōkan, 1958.

Oda Tokunō 織田得能 (1860–1911). *Bukkyō daijiten* 佛教大辭典 [Comprehensive Buddhist dictionary]. Rev. ed. Tokyo: Ōkura shoten 大倉書店, 1931.

Okazaki Fumio 岡崎文夫 (b. 1888). *Gi-Shin nambokuchō tsūshi* 魏晉南北朝通史 [A history of the Period of Disunion]. Tokyo: Kōbundō 弘文堂, 1935. Reprint. Tokyo: Kōbundō, 1954.

Sakaino Kōyō 境野黃洋 (1871–1933). *Shina Bukkyō seishi* 支那佛教精史 [A comprehensive history of Chinese Buddhism]. Tokyo: Sakaino Kōyō hakase ikō kankōkai 境野黃洋博士遺稿刊行會, 1935.

Sui Lu 遂盧. Review of *Kokuyaku issaikyō* translation of Hui Chiao's *Kaoseng chuan* into Japanese. *Wei-miao sheng yüeh-k'an* 微妙聲月刊, vol. 1, no. 8 (Shanghai: 1937): 26–28.

Takao Giken 高雄義堅 (b. 1888). *Chūgoku Bukkyō shiron* 中國佛教史論 [Essays in the history of Chinese Buddhism]. Kyoto: Heirakuji shoten 平樂寺書店, 1952.

T'ang Ch'ang-ju 唐長孺. "Po-i t'ien-tzu shih-shih" 白衣天子試釋 [A tentative discussion of the "Emperor in white robes"]. *Yen-ching hsüeh-pao* 燕京學報, vol. 35 (1948): 227–38.

T'ang Yung-t'ung 湯用彤 (1892–1964). "Tu Hui-chiao *Kao-seng chuan* cha-chi" 讀慧皎高僧札記 [Notes on Hui Chiao's *Kao-seng chuan*]. *Shih-hsüeh tsa-chih* 史學雜誌 (Nan-ching Chung-kuo shih-hsüeh-hui 南京中國史學會), vol. 2, nos. 3–4 (Sept. 1930): 1–12.

———. "T'ang T'ai-tsung yü Fo-chiao" 唐太宗與佛教 [T'ang T'ai-tsung and Buddhism]. *Hsüeh-heng* 學衡, vol. 75 (1931): 1–7.

———. *Han-Wei liang-Chin nan-pei-ch'ao Fo-chiao-shih* 漢魏兩晉南北朝佛教史 [A history of Buddhism from the Han to the end of the Period of Disunion]. 2 vols. Ch'ang-sha: Commercial Press, 1938. Reprint. Peking: Chung-hua shu-chü 中華書局, 1955, 1963; Taipei: Commercial Press, 1965; Kuo-shih yen-chiu-shih 國史研究室, 1973.

Tokiwa Daijō 常盤大定 (1870–1945). *Go-Kan yori Sō-Sei ni itaru yakukyō sōroku* 後漢より宋齊に至る譯經總錄 [General list of translated scriptures from the later Han through the Liu-Sung and Ch'i dynasties]. Tokyo: Tōhō bunka gakuin Tōkyō kenkyūjo 東方文化學院東京研究所, 1938.

Ts'en Chung-mien 岑仲勉. *Sui-shu ch'iu-shih* 隋書求是 [Investigations in the *Sui History*]. Peking: Commercial Press, 1958.

Tsukamoto Zenryū 塚本善隆 (b. 1898). *Tō chūki no Jōdokyō* 唐中期の淨土教 [The Pure Land sect in mid-T'ang times]. Kyoto: Tōhō bunka gakuin Kyoto kenkyūjo 東方文化學院京都研究所, 1933. Republished with revisions in *Tsukamoto Zenryū chosakushū*, 4: 209–510.

———. "Shina Bukkyōshi" 支那佛教史 [History of Chinese Buddhism]. In *Shina shūkyōshi* 支那宗教史 [History of Chinese religions], vol. 11 of the *Shina chiri rekishi taikei* 支那地理歷史大系 [Compendium on Chinese geography and history], 45–196. Tokyo: Shina chiri rekishi kankōkai 支那地理歷史刊行會, 1942.

———. *Shina Bukkyōshi kenkyū: Hoku-Gi hen* 支那佛教史研究：北魏篇 [A history of Chinese Buddhism: The Northern Wei]. Tokyo: Kōbundō 弘文堂, 1942. Substantially reprinted as *Tsukamoto Zenryū chosakushū*, vol. 2.

———. "Kokubunji to Zui-Tō no Bukkyō seisaku narabi ni kanji" 國分寺と隋唐の佛教政策並びに官寺 [Sui-T'ang policy toward official temples and the *kokubunji*]. In idem, *Nisshi Bukkyō kōshōshi kenkyū* 日支佛教交涉史研究 [Studies in relations between Chinese and Japanese Buddhism], 1–47. Tokyo: Kōbundō 弘文堂, 1944.

———. "Hoku-Shū no shukyō haiki seisaku no hōkai" 北周の宗教廢毀政策の崩壞 [The failure of the Northern Chou policy for the suppression of religion]. *Bukkyō shigaku* 佛教史學, vol. 1 (1949): 3–31. Reprinted in *Tsukamoto Zenryū chosakushū*, 2: 641–71.

———. Hoku-Shū no haibutsu ni tsuite" 北周の廢佛に就いて [On the Northern Chou suppression of Buddhism]. *Tōhō gakuhō* 東方學報, vol. 16 (1948): 29–101 [pt. 1]; *Tōhō gakuhō*, vol. 18 (1950): 78–111 [pt. 2]. Reprinted in *Tsukamoto Zenryū chosakushū*, 2: 463–640.

———. *Tsukamoto Zenryū chosakushū* 塚本善隆著作集 [The collected writings of Tsukamoto Zenryū]. 7 vols. Tokyo: Daitō shuppansha 大東出版社, 1974–76.

——— et al. "*Ryō Kōsōden* sakuin." See under Makita Tairyō, *Ryō Kōsōden sakuin.*

Ui Hakuju 宇井伯壽 (1882–1963). *Shaku Dōan kenkyū* 釋道安研究 [A study of the monk Tao-an]. Tokyo: Iwanami shoten 岩波書店, 1956.

Wada Sei 和田清 (1890–1963). "Bukkyō tōzen no nendai ni tsuite" 佛教東漸の年代について [Concerning the date of the eastward transmission of Buddhism]. *Nihon daigaku bungakubu kenkyū nempō* 日本大學文學部研究年報, vol. 6 (1955): 491–501.

Wang Chung-ch'i 王鍾麒 (b. 1897). *Chin-ch'u shih-lüeh* 晉初史略 [A brief history of the early Chin]. Shanghai, 1934.

Wu Hsien-ch'ing 武仙卿. "Hsi-Chin mo ti liu-min pao-tung" 西晉末的流民暴動 [Refugee violence at the end of the Western Chin]. *Shih-huo* 食貨, vol. 1, no. 6 (1935): 3–7.

Yabuki Keiki 矢吹慶輝 (1879–1939). *Sangaikyō no kenkyū* 三階教之研究 [Studies of the Three Stages sect]. Tokyo: Iwanami shoten 岩波書店, 1947.

Yamanouchi Shinkyō 山內晉卿. "Kanjin shukke kōkyo ni tsuite" 漢人出家公許に就て [Concerning official sanction of entrance of Chinese into the Buddhist priesthood]. In author's collection *Shina Bukkyōshi no kenkyū* 支那佛教史之研究 [Studies in the history of Chinese Buddhism], 167–84. Kyoto: Bukkyō daigaku shuppanbu 佛教大學出版部, 1921.

———. "*Kōsōden* no kenkyū" 高僧傳の研究 [A study of Hui Chiao's *Lives of Eminent Monks*]. In author's collection *Shina Bukkyōshi no kenkyū* 支那佛教史之研究 [Studies in the history of Chinese Buddhism]. 1–41. Kyoto: Bukkyo daigaku shuppanbu 佛教大學出版部, 1921.

Yamazaki Hiroshi 山崎宏 (b. 1903). "Tō-Shin jidai no kita-Shina shokozoku Bukkyō no ichimen" 東晉時代の北支那諸胡族佛教の一面 [An aspect of Buddhism under the foreign peoples of North China during the Eastern China]. *Shichō* 史潮, vol. 4 (1934): 40–77.

———. *Zui no Kōso Buntei no Bukkyō chikokusaku* 隋の高祖文帝の佛教治國策 [Sui Kao-tsu Wen-ti's governmental policy toward Buddhism].

Monograph no. 8 of the Society for the Study of Buddhist Law, Government, and Economics. Tokyo: Bukkyō hōsei keizai kenkyūjo 佛教法政經濟研究所, 1934.

——. *Shina chūsei Bukkyō no tenkai* 支那中世佛教の展開 [The development of medieval Chinese Buddhism]. Kyoto: Hōzōkan 法藏館, 1942. Reprint. Tokyo: Hōzōkan, 1971.

——. "Zuichō no Bukkyō fukkō ni tsuite" 隋朝の佛教復興について [Concerning the revival of Buddhism in the Sui dynasty]. *Bukkyō shigaku* 佛教史學, vol. 1 (1949): 50–58.

Yūki Reimon 結城令聞 (b. 1902). "Sho-Tō Bukkyō no shisōshiteki mujun to kokka kenryoku no kōsatsu" 初唐佛教の思想史的矛盾と國家權力の考察 [Doctrinal contradictions in early T'ang Buddhist thought and state power]. *Tōyō bunka kenkyūjo kiyō* 東洋文化研究所紀要, vol. 25 (1961): 1–28.

Works in Western Languages

Bagchi, Prabodh Chandra (1898–1956). *Le canon bouddhique en Chine: Les traducteurs et les traductions.* 2 vols. Paris: P. Guethner, 1927, 1938.

Balazs, Etienne (1905–63). "Nihilistic Revolt or Mystical Escapism: Currents of Thought in China during the Third Century A.D." In Balazs, *Chinese Civilization and Bureaucracy: Variations on a Theme,* 226–54. Originally published as "Entre révolte nihiliste et évasion mystique: Les courants intellectuels en Chine au IIIe siècle de notre ère." *Etudes asiatiques* 2 (1948): 27–55.

——. "Political Philosophy and Social Crisis at the End of the Han Dynasty." In Balazs, *Chinese Civilization and Bureaucracy: Variations on a Theme,* 187–225. Originally published as "La crise sociale et la philosophie politique à la fin des Han." *T'oung pao* 39 (1949): 83–131.

——. *Chinese Civilization and Bureaucracy: Variations on a Theme.* Edited by Arthur F. Wright. New Haven: Yale University Press, 1964.

BD. See Herbert A. Giles, *A Chinese Biographical Dictionary.*

Bingham, Woodbridge. "Wen Ta-ya: The First Recorder of T'ang History." *Journal of the American Oriental Society* 57 (1937): 368–74.

——. *The Founding of the T'ang Dynasty: The Fall of Sui and the Rise of T'ang.* 1941. Reprint. New York: Octagon Books, 1975.

Boodberg, Peter A. (1903–72). "Marginalia to the Histories of the Northern Dynasties." In Alvin P. Cohen, ed., *Selected Works of Peter A. Boodberg,* 265–349. Berkeley: University of California Press, 1979. Originally published in the *Harvard Journal of Asiatic Studies* 3 (1938): 223–53; 4 (1939): 230–83.

Chavannes, Edouard (1865–1918). *Mémoire composé à l'époque de la grande dynastie T'ang sur les réligieux éminents qui allèrent chercher la loi dans les pays d'occident*. Paris: E. Leroux, 1894.

———. *Les mémoires historiques de Se-ma Ts'ien*. 5 vols. Paris: E. Leroux, 1895–1905. Republished with a sixth, posthumous volume, Paris: Adrian Maisonneuve, 1967–69.

———. "La Sūtra de la paroi occidentale de l'inscription de Kiu-yong koan." In *Mélanges Charles de Harlez*, 60–81. Leiden: E. J. Brill, 1896.

———. *Documents sur les Tou-kiue (Turcs) Occidentaux*. St. Petersburg: Commissionaires de l'Académie impériale des Sciences, 1903. Reprint. Taipei: Ch'eng-wen Publishing Co., 1969.

———, trans. "Voyage de Song Yün dans l'Udyāna et le Gandhāra (518–522 p. C.)" *Bulletin de l'Ecole Française d'Extrême-Orient* 3 (1903): 379–441.

———. "Pei Yuan Lou 北轅錄: Récit d'un voyage dans le Nord." *T'oung pao* 5 (1904): 163–92.

———. "Guṇavarman (367–431 p. C.)" *T'oung pao* 5 (1904): 193–206.

———. "Jinagupta (528–605 après J.-C.)" *T'oung pao* 6 (1905): 332–56.

———. "Les pays d'occident d'après le Wei lio." *T'oung pao* 6 (1905): 519–71.

———. "Seng Hui." *T'oung pao* 10 (1909): 199–212.

———. *Le T'ai Chan: Essai de monographie d'un culte chinois*. Paris: E. Leroux, 1910. Reprint. Taipei: Ch'eng-wen Publishing Co., 1970.

Ch'en Kenneth K. S. *Buddhism in China: A Historical Survey*. Princeton: Princeton University Press, 1964.

Ch'en Shih-hsiang (1912–71). "An Innovation in Chinese Biographical Writing." *Far Eastern Quarterly* 13, no. 1 (1953): 49–62.

Chou Yi-liang. "Tantrism in China." *Harvard Journal of Asiatic Studies* 8 (1944–45): 241–332.

Chuan, T. K. "Some Notes on the *Kao Seng Chuan*." *T'ien Hsia Monthly* 7, no. 5 (Dec. 1938): 452–68.

Collins, Wilkie (1824–89). *The Moonstone*. Garden City, N.Y.: Doubleday, 1944.

Davidson, J. Leroy. "Traces of Buddhist Evangelism in Early Chinese Art." *Artibus Asiae* 11 (1948): 251–65.

De Groot, Jan J. M. (1854–1921). *The Religious System of China*. 6 vols. Leiden: E. J. Brill, 1892–1910.

———. *Sectarianism and Religious Persecution in China*. 2 vols. Amsterdam: Johannes Miller, 1903–04.

De Visser, Marinus Willem (1876–1930). *Ancient Buddhism in Japan: Sūtras and Ceremonies in Use in the Seventh and Eighth Centuries* A.D. *and Their History in Later Times*. Leiden: E. J. Brill, 1935.

Demiéville, Paul (b. 1894). *Le Councile de Lhasa: Une controverse sur les quiétisme Bouddhistes de l'Inde et de la Chine au VIIIe siècle de l'ère Chrétienne.* Paris: Presses Universitaires de France, 1952.

———. "La pénétration du Bouddhisme dans la tradition philosophique chinoise." *Cahiers d'histoire mondiale* 3 (1956): 19–38.

———. "Le Bouddhisme et la guerre." In *Mélanges*, published by l'Institut des Hautes Etudes Chinoises. Tome Ier. Bibliothèque de l'Institut des Hautes Etudes Chinoises, 11: 347–85. Paris: Presses Universitaires de France, 1957.

Des Michels, Abel (1833–1910), trans. *Chih lou kouh kiang yuh tchi: Histoire géographique des Seize royaumes.* Publications de l'Ecole des Langues Orientales Vivantes, 3d ser., vol. 9. Paris: E. Leroux, 1891–92.

des Rotours, Robert. *See* Rotours, Robert des.

Dittmer, Lowell. *Liu Shao-ch'i and the Chinese Cultural Revolution: The Politics of Mass Criticism.* Berkeley: University of California Press, 1974.

Drake, F. S. "The Shen-t'ung Monastery and the Beginning of Buddhism in Shantung." *Monumenta Serica* 4 (1939): 1–39, Pls. 1–3 and 2 maps.

Dubs, Homer H. (1892–1969). *The History of the Former Han Dynasty.* 3 vols. Baltimore: Waverly Press, 1938–55.

Dutt, Nalinaksha. *Aspects of Mahāyāna Buddhism and Its Relation to Hinayāna.* London: Luzac, 1930.

Eberhard, Wolfram (b. 1909). *Liu Yüan ve Liu Ts'ung, un biyographileri* [The biographies of Liu Yüan and Liu Ts'ung]. Ankara: Sinoloji Enstitüsü neşriyatî, no. 4, 1942.

Eidmann, Philipp. *The Last Word.* Kyoto, 1952.

Ferguson, John C. (1866–1945). "Stories in Chinese Paintings, III." *Journal of the North China Branch of the Royal Asiatic Society* 63 (1932): 81–99.

———. "Chinese Foot Measure." *Monumenta Serica* 6 (1941): 357–82, 8 pls.

Franke, Otto (1863–1946). *Geschichte des Chinesichen Reiches, Eine Darstellung seiner Enstehung, seins Wesens und seiner Entwicklung bis zur Neuesten Zeit.* 5 vols. Berlin: W. de Gruyter, 1930–52.

Frazer, James G. (1854–1941). *The Magic Art and the Evolution of Kings.* 2 vols. London: Macmillan, 1911.

Gernet, Jacques. *Entretiens du Maître de Dhyâna Chen-Houei de Hö-tso (668–760).* Hanoi: Ecole française d'Extrême-Orient, 1946.

———. *Les aspects économiques du Bouddhisme dans la société chinoise du Ve au Xe siècle.* Saigon: Ecole Française d'Extrême Orient, 1956.

Ges. See Franke, Otto, *Geschichte des chinesischen Reiches.*

Gibbon, Edward (1737–94). *The Decline and Fall of the Roman Empire.* Edited by J. B. Burry. 3 vols. New York: Heritage Press, 1946.

Giles Herbert A. (1845–1935). *A Chinese Biographical Dictionary*. Shanghai: Kelly and Walsh, 1898. Reprint. Taipei: Literature House, 1962.

Giles, Lionel (1875–1958). "Dated Chinese Manuscripts in the Stein Collection, V: Tenth Century A.D. (to the end of the Later Chin Dynasty)." *Bulletin of the School of Oriental Studies* 10 (1940): 317–44.

Gombrich, Richard. "The Consecration of a Buddhist Image." *Journal of Asian Studies* 26 (1966): 23–36.

Goodrich, L. C. (b. 1894). *A Short History of the Chinese People*. 4th ed. New York: Harper and Row, 1969.

Graham, A. C., trans. *The Book of Lieh-tzu*. London: John Murray, 1960.

Grootaers, Willem A. (b. 1911), Li Shih-yu, and Chang Chi-wen. "Temples and History of Wanch'üan (Chahar): The Geographical Method Applied to Folklore." *Monumenta Serica* 13 (1948): 209–316.

Hackmann, Heinrich (1864–1935). "Alphabetisches Verzeichnis zum Kao sêng ch'uan." *Acta Orientalia* (Copenhagen) 2 (1923): 81–112.

Hauser, Philip M. "Observations on the Urban-Folk and Urban-Rural Dichotomies as Forms of Western Ethnocentrism." In Philip M. Hauser and Leo F. Schnore, eds., *The Study of Urbanization*, 503–17. New York: Wiley, 1965.

Hōbōgirin, Dictionnaire encyclopédique du Bouddhisme d'après les sources chinoises et japonaises. Edited by Paul Demiéville et al. Tokyo: Maison franco-japonaise, 1929–.

Hsü, Francis L. K. *Under the Ancestors' Shadow: Chinese Culture and Personality*. New York: Columbia University Press, 1948. A revised version was published as *Under the Ancestors' Shadow: Kinship, Personality and Social Mobility in China*. New York: Anchor Books, 1967. Reissue. Stanford: Stanford University Press, 1971.

Hu Shih (1891–1962). "The Indianization of China: A Case Study in Cultural Borrowing." In *Independence, Convergence and Borrowing in Institutions, Thought and Art*, 219–47. Harvard Tercentenary Publications. Cambridge: Harvard University Press, 1937.

———. "The Concept of Immortality in Chinese Thought." *Peiping Chronicle*, Feb. 12, 1947.

Hummel, Arthur W. (1884–1975), ed. *Eminent Chinese of the Ch'ing Period (1644–1912)*. 2 vols. Washington: United States Government Printing Office, 1943–44.

Hurvitz, Leon, trans. "Wei Shou, Treatise on Buddhism and Taoism, An English Translation of the Original Chinese Text of Wei-shu CXIV and the Japanese Annotation of Tsukamoto Zenryū." In Mizuno Seiichi 水野清一 and Nagahiro Toshio 長広敏雄, *Unkō sekkutsu no kenkyū* 雲岡石窟の研究 [A study of the Buddhist cave-temples at Yün-kang], 16: 23–103.

Kyoto: Kyoto University Research Institute for the Humanistic Sciences, 1951–56.

Jordan, David P. "Gibbon's 'Age of Constantine' and the Fall of Rome." *History and Theory* 8 (1969): 71–96.

Laufer, Berthold (1874–1934). *Sino-Iranica: Chinese Contributions to the History of Civilization in Ancient Iran, with Special Reference to the History of Cultivated Plants and Products*. Publication 201, Anthropology Series, vol. 15, no. 3. Chicago: Field Museum of Natural History, 1919.

Legge, James (1815–97), trans. *The Chinese Classics, Vol. 1: Confucian Analects, The Great Learning, The Doctrine of the Mean*. 2d ed., rev. Oxford: Clarendon Press, 1893. Reprint. Hong Kong: Hong Kong University Press, 1960.

———. *The Chinese Classics, Vol. 3: The Shoo King, or The Book of Historical Documents*. London: Henry Frowde, 1865. Reprint. Hong Kong: Hong Kong University Press, 1960.

———. *The Chinese Classics, Vol. 5: The Ch'un Ts'ew with the Tso Chuen*. London: Henry Frowde, 1872. Reprint. Hong Kong: Hong Kong University Press, 1960.

———. *The Hsiao King*. In Max Müller, ed., *Sacred Books of the East*, vol. 3. Oxford: Clarendon Press, 1879.

———. *The Yi King*. In Max Müller, ed., *Sacred Books of the East*, vol. 16. Oxford: Clarendon Press, 1882.

———. *The Li Ki*. 2 vols. In Max Müller, ed., *Sacred Books of the East*, vols. 27–28. Oxford: Clarendon Press, 1885.

———. *The Texts of Taoism: The Tao Teh King and the Writings of Kwang-Sze*. 2 vols. In Max Müller, ed., *Sacred Books of the East*, vols. 39–40. Oxford: Clarendon Press, 1891.

Levenson, Joseph (1920–69). "The Amateur Ideal in Ming and Early Ch'ing Society: Evidence from Painting." In John K. Fairbank, ed., *Chinese Thought and Institutions*, 320–41. Chicago: University of Chicago Press, 1957.

Lévi, Sylvain (1863–1935). "Le 'Tokharien B' langue de Koutcha." *Journal asiatique*, 11th ser., vol. 2 (1913): 311–80.

———, and Edouard Chavannes. "Les seize arhats protecteurs de la loi." *Journal asiatique*, 11th ser., vol. 8 (1916), pt. 1, pp. 5–50; pt. 2, pp. 189–304.

Levy, Howard S. "Yellow Turban Religion and Rebellion at the End of Han." *Journal of the American Oriental Society* 76 (1956): 214–27.

Lewis, Oscar (1914–70). "Further Observations on the Folk-Urban Continuum and Urbanization with Special Reference to Mexico City." In Philip M. Hauser and Leo F. Schnore, eds., *The Study of Urbanization*, 492–503. New York: Wiley, 1965.

Liao, W. K. (b. 1905), trans. *The Complete Works of Han Fei-tzu.* 2 vols. London: Arthur Probsthain, 1939, 1959.

Liebenthal, Walter (b. 1886). *The Book of Chao (Chao-lun).* Monumenta Serica, monograph 13. Peking: Catholic University, 1948.

Link, Arthur E. "Remarks on Shih Seng-yu's *Ch'u san-tsang chi-chi* as a Source for Hui-chiao's *Kao-seng chuan* as Evidenced in Two Versions of the Biography of Tao-an." *Oriens* 10 (1957): 292–95.

————. "Shyh Daw-an's Preface to Saṅgharakṣa's Yogācarabhūmi-sūtra and the Problem of Buddho-Taoist Terminology in Early Chinese Buddhism." *Journal of the American Oriental Society* 77 (1957): 1–14.

————. "Biography of Shih Tao-an." *T'oung pao* 46 (1958): 1–48.

MacMullen, Ramsey. *Constantine.* New York: Dial Press, 1969.

MacMunn, Sir George Fletcher (1869–1952). *The Underworld of India.* London: Jarrolds, 1933.

Maspero, Henri (1883–1945). "Communautés et moines bouddhistes chinoises aux IIe et IIIe siècles." *Bulletin de l'Ecole Française d'Extrême-Orient* 10 (1910): 222–32.

————. "Le songe et l'ambassade de l'Empereur Ming, étude critique des sources." *Bulletin de l'Ecole Française d'Extrême-Orient* 10 (1910): 95–130.

————. "Les origines de la communauté bouddhiste de Lo-yang." *Journal Asiatique*, no. 225 (1934): 87–107.

Mather, Richard, trans. *Shih-shuo hsin-yü: A New Account of Tales of the World, by Liu I-ch'ing (403–44).* Minneapolis: University of Minnesota Press, 1976.

Munkácsi, Bernát (1860–1937). Review of K. Shiratori, *Über die Sprache des Hiung-nu Stammes und der Tung-hu-stämme. Keleti Szemle-Revue orientale* 4 (1903): 240–53.

Nivison, David S. "Communist Ethics and Chinese Tradition." *Journal of Asian Studies* 16 (1956): 51–75.

Nobel, Johannes (b. 1887). "Kumārajīva." *Sitzungsberichte der Preussischen Akademie der Wissenschaften. Philosophisch-historische Klasse*, no. 20 (June 23), 206–33. Berlin: Akademie der Wissenschaften, 1927.

Overmyer, Daniel L. *Folk Buddhist Religion: Dissenting Sects in Late Imperial China.* Cambridge: Harvard University Press, 1976.

Pelliot, Paul (1878–1945). Review of E. H. Parker, *China, the Avars and the Franks, The Ephthalite Turks,* and *Chinese Knowledge of Early Persia. Bulletin de l'Ecole Française d'Extrême-Orient* 3 (1903): 99–101.

————. "Les kuo-che 國師 ou 'maitres du royaume' dans le Bouddhisme chinois." *T'oung pao* 12 (1911): 671–76.

————. "Autour d'une traduction sanscrite du Tao tö king." *T'oung pao* 13 (1912): 351–430.

————. "L'origine du nom de Chine." *T'oung pao* 13 (1912): 727–42.

————. "Meou-tseu ou les doutes levés." *T'oung pao* 19 (1920): 255–433.

————. "Notes sur l'histoire de la céramique chinoise." *T'oung pao* 22 (1923): 1–62.

————. "Notes sur quelques artistes des six dynasties et des T'ang." *T'oung pao* 22 (1923): 215–91.

Průšek, Jaroslav. "Narrators of Buddhist Scriptures and Religious Tales in the Sung Period." *Archiv Orientalni* 10 (1938): 375–89.

Ramstedt, Gustaf J. (1873–1950). "Zur frage nach der stellung des tschuwassischen." *Journal de la Société finno-ougrienne* 38 (Helsinki, 1922): 1–34.

Redfield, Robert (1897–1958) *Peasant Society and Culture*. Chicago: University of Chicago Press, 1956.

Reischauer, Edwin O. *Ennin's Travels in T'ang China*. New York: Ronald Press, 1955.

Rémusat, Jean Pierre Abel (1788–1832). *Nouveaux mélanges asiatiques, ou Recueil de morceaux de critique et de mémoires, relatifs aux religions, aux sciences, aux coutumes, à l'histoire et à la geographique de nations orientales*. 2 vols. Paris: Schubart et Heideloff, 1829.

Rogers, Michael. *The Chronicle of Fu Chien: A Case of Exemplar History*. Chinese Dynastic Histories Translations, no. 10. Berkeley: University of California Press, 1968.

Rotours, Robert des (b. 1891). *Le traité des examens*. Paris: Ernest Leroux, 1932.

————. *Traité des fonctionnaires et traité de l'armée*. 2 vols. Leiden: E. J. Brill, 1947–48.

Sargent, Galen Eugene. "Tchou Hi contre le Bouddhisme." In *Mélanges*, published by l'Institut des Hautes Etudes Chinoises. Tome Ier. Bibliothèque de l'Institut des Hautes Etudes Chinoises, 11: 1–157. Paris: Presses Universitaires de France, 1957.

Schafer, Edwin H. *The Divine Woman: Dragon Ladies and Rain Maidens in T'ang Literature*. Berkeley: University of California Press, 1973.

Seidel, Anna. "The Image of the Perfect Ruler in Early Taoist Messianism: Lao-tzu and Li Hung." *History of Religions* 9 (1969–70): 216–47.

Shiratori, Kurakichi (1865–1942). *Über die Sprache des Hiung-nu Stammes und der Tung-hu Stämme*. Tokyo: Kokubunsha, 1900.

Soper, Alexander (b. 1904). "Japanese Evidence for the History of the Architecture and Iconography of Chinese Buddhism." *Monumenta Serica* 4 (1939–40): 638–78.

Takakusu Junjirō (1866–1945). "The Life of Vasu-Bandhu by Parāmartha (A.D. 499–569)." *T'oung pao*, 2d ser., vol. 5 (1904): 269–96.

————, trans. *A Record of the Buddhist Religion as Practiced in India and the*

Malay Archipelago (A.D. *671–695*), *by I-tsing.* London: Clarendon Press, 1896. Reprint. Delhi: Munshiram Manoharlal, 1966.

Waley, Arthur (1889–1966). *The Analects of Confucius.* London: George Allen and Unwin, 1938.

———. *Three Ways of Thought in Ancient China.* New York: Macmillan, 1939.

———. *The Life and Times of Po Chü-i, 772–846 A.D.* London: George Allen and Unwin, 1949.

———. "The Fall of Loyang." *History Today,* no. 4 (April 1951): 7–10.

Ware, James. "Wei Shou on Buddhism." *T'oung pao* 30 (1933): 100–81.

Wassiljew, W. [Vasil'ev, Vasilii Pavlovich] (1818–1900). *Der buddhismus, seine dogmen, geschichte und literatur.* Trans. from Russian by Anton Schlefner. Saint Petersburg: Kaiserliche Akademie der wissenschaften, 1860.

Watson, Burton, trans. *The Complete Works of Chuang-tzu.* New York: Columbia University Press, 1968.

Watters, Thomas (1840–1901). *On Yüan Chwang's Travels in India, 629–645 A.D.* Edited by T. W. Rhys Davids and S. W. Bushnell. 2 vols. London: Royal Asiatic Society, 1904–05.

Wechsler, Howard J. *Mirror to the Son of Heaven: Wei Cheng at the Court of T'ang T'ai-tsung.* New Haven: Yale University Press, 1974.

———. "The Founding of the T'ang Dynasty: Kao-tsu (Reign 618–26)." In D. C. Twitchett, ed., *The Cambridge History of China, Vol. 3: Sui and T'ang China, 589–906, Part I,* 150–87. Cambridge: Cambridge University Press, 1979.

Welch, Holmes (1924–81). *The Practice of Chinese Buddhism, 1900–1950.* Cambridge: Harvard University Press, 1967.

———, and Anna Seidel, eds. *Facets of Taoism: Essays in Chinese Religion.* New Haven: Yale University Press, 1979.

Wieger, Léon (1856–1933). *Bouddhisme chinois: Extraits du Tripitaka, des commentaires, tracts, etc.* Vol. 1, *Monachisme*; vol. 2, *Les Vies Chinoises du Bouddha.* Sien-hsien (Hokienfu): Imprimerie de la Mission catholique, 1910–13. Reprinted in one vol., Peking: Henri Vetch, 1940.

Wilhelm, Richard (1873–1930). *Frühling und Herbst des Lü Bu Wei.* Jena: E. Diederichs, 1928.

Wright, Arthur F. (1913–76). "Fo-t'u-teng: A Biography." *Harvard Journal of Asiatic Studies* 11, nos. 3–4 (Dec. 1948): 321–71. Reprinted in this volume.

———. "Fu I and the Rejection of Buddhism." *Journal of the History of Ideas* 12, no. 1 (1951): 33–47. Reprinted in this volume.

———. "Biography of the Nun An-ling-shou 安令首." *Harvard Journal of*

Asiatic Studies 15, nos. 1–2 (June 1952): 193–96. Reprinted in this volume.

———. "Biography and Hagiography: Hui-chiao's *Lives of Eminent Monks.*" *Silver Jubilee Volume of the Jimbun-Kagaku-Kenkyūsyo,* 383–432. Kyoto: Kyoto University, 1954. Reprinted in this volume.

———. "Buddhism and Chinese Culture: Phases of Interaction." *Journal of Asian Studies* 17, no. 1 (Nov. 1957): 17–42. Reprinted in this volume.

———. "The Formation of Sui Ideology, 581–604." In John K. Fairbank, ed., *Chinese Thought and Institutions,* 71–104. Chicago: University of Chicago Press, 1957.

———. "The Economic Role of Buddhism in China." Review of Jacques Gernet, *Les aspects économiques du Bouddhisme dans la société chinoise du Ve au Xe siècle. Journal of Asian Studies* 16, no. 3 (May 1957): 408–14.

———. "T'ang T'ai-tsung and Buddhism." In Arthur F. Wright and Denis C. Twitchett, eds., *Perspectives on the T'ang,* 239–63. New Haven: Yale University Press, 1973.

Wylie, Alexander (1815–87). *Notes on Chinese Literature.* Shanghai: American Presbyterian Mission Press, 1867.

Yang Lien-sheng. "Notes on the Economic History of the Chin Dynasty." In idem, *Studies in Chinese Institutional History,* 119–97. Originally published in *Harvard Journal of Asiatic Studies* 9 (1946): 107–85.

———. *Studies in Chinese Institutional History.* Harvard-Yenching Institute Studies, vol. 20. Cambridge: Harvard University Press, 1963.

Zürcher, E. *The Buddhist Conquest of China: The Spread and Adaptation of Buddhism in Early Medieval China.* 2 vols. Leiden: E. J. Brill, 1959.

INDEX